D1121970

ALBERTO MORAVIA

Jane E. Cottrell

Frederick Ungar Publishing Co.
New York

R01 0198 3942

75-037053-8

HOUSTON PUBLIC LIBRARY

To Robert

Copyright © 1974 by Frederick Ungar Publishing Co., Inc.
Printed in the United States of America
Library of Congress Catalog Card Number: 73-84599
Designed by Anita Duncan
ISBN: 0-8044-2131-5 (cloth)

Contents

Chronology

1907: Alberto Pincherle Moravia born on November 28 in Rome.

1916: Contracts tuberculosis of the bone; constantly ill and bedridden for long periods during the next nine years.

1925: Begins writing first novel, *Gli indifferenti*, completed three years later.

1927: "Cortigiana stanca" and "Delitto al circolo di tennis."

1929: *Gli indifferenti.*

1930: Begins traveling extensively for ten years; spends long periods in Paris and London, and also visits the U.S., Mexico, Greece and China as foreign correspondent for *La Stampa* and *Gazzetta del Popolo.*

1935: *Le ambizioni sbagliate.*

1941: *La mascherata*; marries novelist Elsa Morante from whom he is later divorced.

1943: Flees Rome and hides with wife in mountains south of the capital for nine months until Allies arrive.

1944: Film critic for *La Nuova Europa* until 1946.

1945: *Agostino*; awarded the Corriere Lombardo Prize.

1947:   *La romana.*

1948:   *La disubbidienza.*

1949:   *L'amore coniugale.*

1951:   *Il conformista.*

1952:   Chevalier de la Légion d'Honneur; Strega Literary Prize.

1953:   Co-editor with Alberto Carocci of bi-monthly magagine *Nuovi Argomenti.*

1954:   *Il disprezzo; Racconti romani* (originally published individually in *Corriere della Sera* to which Moravia had become a frequent contributor).

1955:   Film critic for *L'Espresso;* visits U.S. as guest of State Department.

1957:   *La ciociara.*

1958:   First of travel books to appear, *Un mese in U.R.S.S.,* a collection of articles originally published in *Corriere della Sera.* In the twelve years that follow Moravia travels extensively in the U.S., Turkey, India, Egypt, Greece, Japan, China, and Africa as well as in Europe, and publishes articles on his travels, some of which are later collected in books.

1959:   *Nuovi racconti romani.*

1960:   *La noia.*

1961:   Viareggio Prize (for *La noia*).

1963:   Marries novelist Dacia Maraini.

1964:   Lectures at Queens College, New York.

1965:   *L'attenzione.*

1968:   Lectures at various schools in the U.S.

1971:   *Io e lui.*

1

*The Man,
His Thought
and His World*

Moravia is probably Italy's most controversial contemporary writer. Indeed, he has continually aroused controversy throughout the forty-odd years he has been publishing books. Although he has had considerable commercial success in Italy, and is a well-known author in translation in many foreign countries, each book he has written has engendered both praise and sharp criticism, sometimes from the same reviewer.

Few readers, if any, would deny that Moravia is a skilled craftsman, that he can tell a story well, and that he is a master of description. The argument about his position in the literary pantheon arises because of (1) his ideas and world view, and (2) the repetitiveness of his themes, subjects and character types. His ideas are true to contemporary reality as he sees it, and he refuses to compromise by depicting the world as being better than it is. As for the repetitiveness in his fiction, Moravia does not deny the charge. In fact, he considers repetitiveness a virtue. "One good tune is enough," he stated in an interview published in *The New Yorker*. "Good writers are monotonous, like good composers."[1] Because truth is self-repeating, good authors, he believes, quite naturally keep rewriting the same book.

A precocious writer, Moravia was twenty-one years old when his first piece of fiction, the short story "Cortigiana stanca" ("Tired Courtesan"), was published in 1928. A year later his first novel appeared, *Gli indifferenti (The Time of Indifference)*,* and was an astounding success. Not that it was liked by all who read it; but it was widely read and discussed at length. More than anything it irritated its readers by its stark por-

* Published translations are distinguished from literal translations by the use of italics or quotes, depending on the genre.

trayal of the decadence and moral rot of the middle-class Italian society of its day. However, the decay of the middle class was only a secondary theme; its principal subject was the despair and alienation of people entrapped in what would later come to be known in literature as "the absurd." For in retrospect, *Gli indifferenti* can be seen as the first European existentialist novel, published some nine years before Sartre's *La Nausée* (*Nausea*), and thirteen years before Camus' *L'Étranger* (*The Stranger*). Since his first novel, Moravia has explored again and again in his fiction the same ideas and themes.

Novelist, short-story writer, essayist, critic, playwright, film script writer, travel writer, editor, and journalist (a regular contributor to Milan's *Corriere della Sera*), Moravia has over the years been intensely active in a variety of literary fields. However, it was not until the translation in 1949 of *La romana* (*Woman of Rome*) that his fame spread to English-speaking countries. Since then, a number of his short stories and novels have been made into movies. Unfortunately, not all of Moravia's prewar work has been translated into English; the earlier short stories especially have been neglected, and they include some of his best and most representative short fiction.

Little is known of Moravia's private life or family background, for he has been unusually reticent about publishing information concerning himself. There has been much confusion about his name; it has been widely believed that Moravia is a pseudonym, while Pincherle is his family name. In a letter to the critic Luciano Rebay, Moravia states that his name, as it appears on his birth certificate and passport is Alberto

Pincherle Moravia (Pincherle being in fact a middle
name and not his family name).[2]

He was born in Rome on November 28, 1907, of
well-to-do middle-class parents. His Venetian father,
an architect, was a Jewish agnostic; his mother, a
countess,. was a Roman Catholic, and Alberto, his
brother, and his two sisters were brought up in that
religion. Plagued by poor health most of his childhood, he was stricken with tuberculosis of the leg bone
at the age of nine. Moravia subsequently spent some
five years in bed and a good deal of time in sanatori-
ums. Until the age of twenty-five he suffered from the
effects of the disease.

When he was eighteen he began writing *Gli indifferenti*, which was published four years later. Pur-
suing his literary career, Moravia continued to live in
Rome, the city in which he has always made his home.
However, he traveled extensively throughout the
world, especially during the decade between Hitler's
rise to power in 1933, and the fall of fascism in 1943.
In 1935 he taught Italian for a time in New York City,
and in 1937 made his first trip to China. During this
same period he also traveled widely in Europe.

In 1941 he married novelist Elsa Morante, from
whom he was later divorced. That same year, the fascist censors forbade him to publish anything, or to
write for newspapers. However, he continued to write
under the pseudonym of "Pseudo." After the Nazi
occupation of Rome in 1943, Moravia was forced to
flee because of racial harassment and impending ar-
rest, and for several months he hid in the mountains
south of Rome. He returned to the capital in 1944
after the liberation and resumed his writing career.
His books on Russia (1958), India (1962), China
(1967), and Africa (1973) attest to his continued inter-

est in travel, as do his many newspaper articles on both those countries and on Japan, the United States, and Egypt. In 1963, Moravia married novelist Dacia Maraini.

Moravia has continually maintained that a literary work should exhaust its subject; indeed, there is very little left unexplained in his fiction, very little for the reader to discover for himself. In addition, Moravia has often been a primary interpreter of his own works, explaining their meaning in press interviews and in detailed essays on his literary, political, and social ideas.

Freud and Marx, he has declared, represent the two poles of his thought (although he disclaims any direct influence from the works of either). No reader could fail to notice Moravia's constant preoccupation with sex as the basic psychological principle and the most significant activity of life. Nor could he miss the emphasis on social and class issues, and the prominent position that money holds in his works. The synthesis of Freudianism and Marxism is effected in Moravia's fiction by means of the mysterious bond he sees operating between sexuality and money.

In an interview published in *The Guardian*, Moravia declared: "A writer has few themes if he is faithful to himself. He should not have much to say, but what he has to say he should give depth to and say in different ways. One's books are really variations on a theme."[3] And the theme for him, as he has said many times, is "the relationship between man and reality," "between man and what is outside him." Of course, the reality outside him can only be perceived subjectively.

The Italian title of a book by Moravia often reveals the particular variation of the basic theme that the author is dealing with in that work, and it includes words evoking indifference and ambition, disobedience and conformity, boredom and attentiveness, masks, and conjugal love. Moravia often explores an idea in one novel and then takes up its opposite in another. His best-known short stories deal with subjects like crime, sickness, the end of love affairs, dreams and social issues—all typically Moravian subjects.

Taken as a whole, his works also present a panorama of major twentieth-century literary preoccupations. In addition to Freudianism, Marxism and existentialism, there are reflections of phenomenology (in the form of problems concerning the nature of reality), of the process of artistic creation, and of neorealism. From the 1960s on, Moravia began exploring in greater depth two currents that had become fashionable: the dehumanizing quality of modern life which tends to make things, or automatons, out of us; and the crisis of the breakdown of language as a part of the syndrome of solitude, alienation and noncommunication.

It has often been noted that Moravia's fiction is lacking in any metaphysical dimension, that it is firmly rooted in the physical world. Surrealism and dream sequences, where they occur, are used only as illustrations of psychological or social ideas. Nor is there any clearly defined notion of good or evil in this fictional world, for it is singularly amoral. The touches of evil and the diabolical which are present in some of the early works are imitations of Dostoevsky; and it is clear that they are ornaments rather than expressions of a reality. Moravia's characters act in a moral vacuum, wanting but never finding their own salvation, so involved in their own problems that they are almost always incapable of understanding those of another person. In the final analysis, they seem to care about others only as instruments of their own pleasure.

If there is no metaphysical dimension, there is, however, a strong deterministic force running through Moravia's fictional world. No one is responsible for the way he is—or for the way things are. "We are all guilty, and we are none of us guilty" is a phrase that is used in several works. In his essay "L'uomo come fine," or "Man as an End," Moravia states that it is the condition of man as a means rather than an end which has made our condition what it is. "We have horizontal truths according to class, vertical truths according to nations, state truths, race truths, party truths, sect truths and group truths . . . Since Christianity has evaporated and man is no longer the end but the means, the modern world is like a perfectly organized, very efficient nightmare."[4] Within the nightmare, there are sometimes hints of ideals or dreams of a paradise where innocence and purity reign. But these ideals and paradises remain vague, like remembered scraps of the past or of paradises which have been lost, never to be regained. Moravia's characters are trapped in their situation; they are anguished but impotent observers of the self. Despite their fervent desires for a new life, they are never able to break out of their old one.

Given the conditions of modern life, Moravia believes that "man is man because he suffers." Man's relationship with reality is therefore that of suffering. One may say then that the theme of Moravia's work is

actually the suffering of man, which in his fiction
nearly always culminates in self-degradation or acceptance.

In Moravia's fictional world, physicality is so continually emphasized that if there is any other dimension it is imperceptible to his characters. They seek a
"relationship with reality" and find it most often
through sexuality. For, in the author's own words, sex
is "a way of relating with reality. It is one of the main
ways of getting in touch with another person, one of
our best means of connection."[5] The novella, *La
disubbidienza* (*Luca* in *Two Adolescents*), provides
the clearest articulation of sex as the link with reality.
But a sexual relationship does not mean a love relationship. According to Moravia, sex is what has replaced love in the modern world. As he wrote in his
introduction to *La revoluzione culturale in Cina*
(*The Red Book and the Great Wall*): "Here and
now, in the world of today, love and the sexual relationship are foreign to each other. They are opposed
and inimical."[6] His focus, it may be noted, is on
heterosexual relationships; there is very little explicit
or implicit homosexuality in his works, the ambiguous
allusions in *Agostino* being the most notable exception.

It is thus not surprising that a character's body
and physical appearance are important in Moravia's
stories. Very often his characters are physically distorted, ill-favored, or at least unattractively past their
prime. The females tend to be of three distinct types:
earth-mother figures who are well-proportioned but
rather too ample and filled-out; those who have sensual but distorted bodies, with a head too large, legs

too short and stocky, bust too pendulous and hips too narrow or too large; and occasionally, in the later works, small-breasted women who have become asexual through adoption of middle-class values, or who have abnormal sexual tastes. As for the men, they are generally "not handsome," short, thick-bodied, bald or balding figures—the kind one would pass on the street without noticing. Physical beauty is not given to Moravia's characters, but their very unattractiveness is generally what they find attractive in each other. For the aging Moravian male, the young girls with a doll-like face on top of the body of a mature woman are an irresistible combination of innocence and corruption.

Refusing to compromise with the physical reality he perceives, Moravia fashions his people according to what their sexual urges make of them at a given stage of life and according to the crises they consequently undergo. The unhappiness, chaos, and turbulence of awakening sexuality in adolescence have been brilliantly and unforgettably described in such novels as *Agostino* and *La disubbidienza*. For mature men the crisis is linked to a spoiled sexual relationship with a mistress or wife after a brief period of "happiness." Usually one sexual partner is shown as having suddenly become disgusting to the other, thus ruining the life of the hero by turning it into a void. As Cora tells Francesco in *L'attenzione* (*The Lie*): "If there isn't that [sex] between a man and a woman, then there's nothing."[7] Without a satisfying sexual relationship, everything becomes meaningless and there is no way the hero can communicate with persons or things outside himself. Substitute activities are doomed to failure, as are the sexual relationships themselves. Thus, a Moravian hero is condemned to a continual search for happiness through sex, a search that can only lead to failure.

Moravia once told an interviewer: "In most of my novels, the hero is an intellectual. They are about middle-class people and the hero is most of the time an intellectual because I'm convinced that the only positive hero interested in the middle class is the intellectual—the kind who does not make compromises with reality."[8] And yet, Moravia was strongly attracted to the lower classes. Four of his books have lower-class heroes or heroines as narrators (*La romana, La ciociara* and the two volumes of *Racconti romani,* or *Roman Tales*). Even in the works that have a middle-class intellectual protagonist, the lower classes are often prominently represented. The intellectual hero—generally a would-be writer or artist, or an architect or engineer—is sexually attracted to a lower-class girl, and a physical relationship develops. Apparently a Moravian female need only exude sensuality; she may be only semi-literate, or even totally illiterate, but in no case does she have intellectual interests, nor is she portrayed as being a thinking being. She lives by animal-like instincts and for sensual pleasure. Only Adriana (*La romana*) and Cesira (*La ciociara*) are deeply troubled by periods of philosophical crises (although short-lived ones that are quickly resolved). It is for the Moravian male to suffer at length, and to prolong his suffering through conscious intellectualization of his problems. Moravia's one-sided, mindless women characters are one of the least satisfying aspects of his writing.

The intellectual protagonists "fall in love" with these lower-class females ostensibly because of their irresistible sensuality. But there is another attraction:

the myth of the lower classes ("il mito del popolo"). Painfully aware of the hypocrisy and false values of middle-class society, the Moravian hero rejects his own class and turns to the lower classes which he sees as more "authentic"—because they are relatively uncorrupted by money—and somehow earthier. He may seek out squalor, ugliness, and women who give the impression of being corrupt or depraved—prostitutes especially, and better still, prostitutes who are also occasionally thieves. The combination of criminality and lower-class sensuality is for the hero a most powerful aphrodisiac; it is also a perfect challenge to false middle-class morality.

In Moravia's world men never seem to understand women. The female is always portrayed as more complicated than she at first appears, and she remains mysterious to her lover no matter how much he tries to probe her secrets and to possess her. A man sometimes has the illusion he can possess a woman through sex, which is precisely Dino's situation in *La noia* (*The Empty Canvas*) and that of the narrator of *L'amore coniugale* (*Conjugal Love*); but women remain elusive (*inafferrabile*). Indeed, it might be argued that Moravia himself does not understand women very well. His ideas about female sexuality appear ill-informed, or at best, not representative of the great majority of women. And his reasoning about why women become prostitutes is simplistic. Merely to affirm that it is in one's nature to become a prostitute (*La romana*) or to become sexually promiscuous once one is freed from inhibitions (*La ciociara*) provides little insight into feminine psychology; such "explanations" seem self-indulgent and wish-fulfilling.

It is of course not surprising that the relationship of the intellectual, cogitating male and the semi-literate, instinctual female is doomed to be short-lived. Nevertheless, the situation has provided Moravia with ample material for his fiction. The variations are seemingly endless: the woman who discovers one day that her husband does not correspond to her image of a man (*Il disprezzo,* or *A Ghost at Noon*); the man who becomes bored with a routine of daily sex without words (*La noia*); the man who sees his lower-class wife become bourgeoise after marriage and thus loses interest in her (*L'attenzione*). In addition, there is also the type of man who decides that he has to give up sexual relations with his wife in order to devote his libido to art—with disastrous consequences (*L'amore coniugale; Io e lui,* or *Two*). Regardless of the cause that precipitates the end of a relationship, the woman always seems to remain intact while the man crumbles —for the Moravian intellectual is portrayed as being spiritually impotent.

This impotent intellectual is very frequently paired with a virile (*prepotente*) nonintellectual who may be thoroughly odious, but who is masterful, sure of himself, and successful in precisely those areas in which the hero is a failure.[9] The Michele-Leo pair from *Gli indifferenti* is the first of this long fictional line. In *Io e lui* the "impotente-propotente" struggle is translated into Freudian terminology as a struggle of sublimation and desublimation, with the narrator Federico continually trying to come out "on top" in dealing with other persons but instead finding himself "underneath." Thus, after more than forty years, the basic problems of the Moravian intellectual remain the same.

In keeping with Moravia's insistence on the physical order, the setting functions as an integral part of a story. Just as a person's physical appearance may betray much about his character in Moravia's works, so his neighborhood, the kind of house or apartment he lives in, his furniture, and his personal belongings are shown as reflections of his nature. And as if in a primitive bond with the elements, a character's drama is played out under appropriate skies, in a suitable season.

The place is usually Rome, or one of the popular seaside resorts in the vicinity. But this is not the Rome most tourists would recognize. Moravia's Rome is plagued with leaden skies, swollen clouds, the heavy atmosphere of an imminent storm; or it is soaked with a despairing, steady rain. However, at the seaside resorts the sun shines hot and bright, and the warm, humid, immobile air (the *afa*) is oppressive. There the sea provides the only hope of escape from the heat and suffocation.

If the preferred seasons for the throes of inner conflict and struggle are autumn and winter, the oppressive heat of summer is a favorite setting for the end of a love relationship. The sea, with all its associations of sexual potency ironically looms behind the unhappy lovers as they swelter through their summer crises. Springtime is of course the season for short-lived hope and happiness. *La romana* illustrates how closely Moravia sometimes coordinates seasons and the events of his characters' lives. The novel begins in spring when Adriana is a young woman of eighteen who hopes to get married soon and start a family. That spring she meets a man who becomes her fiancé; it is not until late autumn that she learns he is already married and has never intended to marry her. She becomes a prostitute and her life is a merry-go-round of lovers until the winter of her twenty-first year,

when she goes through a crisis of consciousness and a
period of self-questioning and despair; she also discovers that she is attracted to violence and to a murderer. She falls in love with a student who goes
through a crisis in late February and subsequently
commits suicide just as Adriana is beginning to regain
hope for her life. The novel ends in late spring when
Adriana, who is pregnant with a murderer's child, has
once again accepted life as it is and has regained hope
through her unborn child. While not all Moravia's
fiction is so carefully coordinated with the cycle of
nature, in most works there are repeated references to
seasons or the weather, with clear parallels to a character's inner drama.

The expression "Moravia's Rome" began to be
used by Italian critics after the publication of the *Racconti romani*. This Rome is never described at length.
A few quick brush strokes serve to give the reader a
sense of being in the animated streets of the inner city,
or along the highway on Sunday when everyone is
going to the beach, or in the deserted streets across the
Tiber at night in winter. But "Moravia's Rome" is,
more than anything, a particular neighborhood in any
given story. There are the old neighborhoods—the
aristocratic ones that have large villas with enclosed
gardens, vast entry halls, and long dark corridors.
Here the wealthy middle class plays out the empty life
it had bought with money. And there are the old,
squalid slum areas of ugly tenement buildings with
their crumbling stairs and small crowded apartments
where the lower class lives its life of rationed plea-
sures, stultifying hard work, and misery. Between the
two extremes are the old Roman *pensioni* or boarding
houses, their labyrinthian corridors lined with rooms
where young protagonists (usually students) live tem-

porarily while on their way to something better. Inexperienced, naive, and ingenuous, they suffer the
pain of a brief but intense passion which ends unhap-
pily and from which they come away visibly scarred.
But most striking of all are the new neighborhoods
which many Moravian characters have recently moved
into, often taking apartments on the ground floor of
an unfinished building. These are the uprooted souls
who are still looking for something in life, although
they don't quite know what. Their lives are as unfinished as the buildings they live in, and, like the
buildings, will be completed with the same slabs of
inert, characterless materials that fashioned the existing part of the structure.

Furniture is often described in some detail, but
once again, there is just enough description to make
us feel that we have viewed the scene without having
surveyed it for an inventory. Furthermore, the objects
described serve to reveal some characteristic of the
person who owns or uses them. In *Gli indifferenti*, for
example, Lisa's furniture wears its owner's mask of
rosy youthfulness, but a closer look reveals that in
reality it, too, is old and worn. To Adriana of *La
romana*, the new furniture she buys for her room is a
symbol of the happy life she hopes to live with her
future husband, and as such it is modest, but clean
and sparkling. When she later becomes a prostitute,
and the furniture is not used by her husband but by
strangers, it takes on an impersonal appearance in her
eyes. Finally, when she falls in love again she sees her
furniture as sordid and impoverished, like the past life
of broken hopes and poor consolations which she has
abandoned. At the other extreme, the furniture of
Dino's mother in *La noia* was all chosen by that rich,
middle-class woman to reflect her standards and her

wealth. In her house vulgarity reigns, for all her furniture must be, or must appear to be expensive; she can
think only in financial terms.

"Moravia's Rome" is then a personal Rome. Not
the portrayal of a great city as it might be presented
by an impartial observer, it is a series of sketches that
reveal the intimate lives of the fictional characters
who reside there.

2

卍卍卍卍卍卍卍卍卍卍卍卍卍卍卍卍卍卍卍卍卍卍卍卍卍卍卍

Style, Form
and Imagery

A number of critics have said that reading Moravia's fiction is like reading a clinical psychology report. While Moravia's style is journalistic in its economy, it is artistic in its result; far from being disinterested or clinical, it surges with hidden passion and anguish conveyed by seemingly neutral words. Just as the eye is selective in examining a person or a place, so Moravia in his descriptive passages tells only what is necessary to give the reader a sense of being there, of seeing. Enough information is given to satisfy the mind so that the eye does not look elsewhere for more information. After reading one of Moravia's brief descriptions, a reader clearly has the impression of having seen what is described; and yet, if he looks back on it, he can only be surprised at how little information is actually provided.

The role of the artist, according to Moravia, is to express what everyone represses: "In a sense, art has the same function in social life that dreams have in physiological life."[1] He believes that the artist, contrary to the intellectual, does not seek to change the world but to reflect what it is. However, he admits to partaking of two opposing natures: "To my misfortune, besides being an artist I am also in part an intellectual. That is to say, I am sometimes torn between the instinct to portray the world as it is and the desire to change it." Indeed, the intellectual nature does at times displace that of the artist, and the result is didactics mixed with fiction.

Moravia has often stated that he is less of a realist than almost any other writer because it is not reality itself that interests him but the theme that can be found beneath the reality. He believes that there is always a theme there, and that the writer has only to find it, then study it in depth.[2] Whatever the theme,

Moravia presents and examines it in the form of dialogue (or monologue) combined with reported action, which is interspersed with the author's explanations and analyses of what has happened. In short, Moravia provides a running commentary on what his heroes experience. Once he identifies the theme of a book, Moravia then develops it in the manner of an essayist and moralist, although he may be writing within the framework of a novel or short story.

The novel, according to Moravia, is a kind of metaphor which is very far removed from life, which is indeed a substitute for life. More specifically, the novel for him is a kind of allegory.[3] Fiction is thus not conceived of as imitation, but rather as an incarnation of a subjective reality; furthermore, its aim is didactic. In his fiction, Moravia attempts to convince, teach or make us aware of hidden realities which he has identified and which he uses as "themes." Virtually each of his stories or novels published before the mid-fifties represents a complete study of a particular theme. Beginning with the *Racconti romani* (1954) and especially evident in the later collections of *L'automa* (*The Fetish and Other Stories*), *Una cosa è una cosa* (*Command and I Will Obey You*), and *Il paradiso* (*Paradise and Other Stories*), the stories become so brief, fragmentary and limited in scope that the theme comes through only as a cumulative effect of the whole volume. *Io e lui* (1971) bears witness to the same process of fragmentation in the novel. This, we may note in passing, parallels the evolution away from neorealism in the Italian film of the late fifties and the sixties: fragmented scenes, flashbacks, dream sequences, and imaginary happenings are presented to the eye of the spectator as if they were perceptions of objective realities, underscoring the artist's message—

that the "dolce vita" type of existence is merely empty spectacle.

Two major, closely related stylistic developments in Moravia's fiction have been widely discussed by both the author himself and his critics: the change from third- to first-person narrative, and the switch from middle-class to lower-class heroes. Apart from a few earlier scattered pages, *La romana* is the first work in which Moravia used first-person narrative, and also the first with a lower-class central character. In explaining the reasons for these changes,[4] Moravia relates that having been forced to flee Rome in 1943 when the fascists were temporarily returned to power by the Nazis, he took refuge in the mountains of the Abruzzi, in Ciociaria. The nine months he spent hiding there provided him with an experience unusual for intellectuals, he noted. Living with peasants, he developed a great interest in them and a sincere sympathy for their problems. This new interest is revealed most clearly in four books: two novels, *La romana* and *La ciociara*, and two volumes of *Racconti romani* (in all, 130 short stories). "The heroes of those books," he told *The Guardian* interviewer, "two simple women from the people who spoke in their simple way, and the short stories about workmen—they were a kind of relief for me as a writer . . . To make simple people talk, I had to create a style which was fresh . . ." He also explained that first-person narrative was better for him because third-person narration seemed too artificial, giving the impression that the writer is omniscient. (Curiously, Moravia seems not to have realized that French and English writers had a few decades before shown that the difference between first- and third-person narration is merely one of pronouns and grammar, and that third-person narration need be no more artificial than first-person). In any case, most of Moravia's fiction since 1947 has been first-person narration, with the notable exceptions of *La disubbidienza, Il conformista (The Conformist),* and *L'automa.*

The form of Moravia's novels—a form that could be defined as dialogue-action-commentary—is admirably suited to two modes of literature: the picaresque satire and the tragedy. Indeed, it is in these two modes that Moravia's work may be most easily classified.

The picaresque was a minor, although persistent aspect of Moravia's early fiction. Beginning with the *Racconti romani* in the fifties it became a far more important element until, by the time *Io e lui* was published, it was dominant. Moravia's debt to Belli[5] has been fully acknowledged by the author and widely noted by critics; however, Moravia's later collections of stories as well as *Io e lui* would appear to owe their inspiration more to Petronius. These later works are fragmentary and bitterly satirical; the reader has the impression of watching a freak show in which the mentally deranged or emotionally disturbed confess to the public. What was once a minor tendency—a few grotesques here and there in the literary gallery of Moravia's Romans—later became an obsession. It is interesting to note the corresponding developments in the Italian film industry: Federico Fellini, for example, was producing his film version of Petronius' *Satyricon* at the time that Moravia was writing his *Io e lui.*

Greek tragedy has greatly interested Moravia ever since he wrote his first novel, *Gli indifferenti.* In an essay dating from 1945, Moravia explained that he had wanted to write something that would follow the Aristotelian precepts of tragedy; with that first novel he came to the conclusion that it was impossible to write a tragedy in the modern world.[6] And yet, most of Moravia's novels may be seen as attempts to fuse the structure and major elements of Greek tragedy with the modern novel, as well as to include the theatrical techniques of various European playwrights.[7]

With the publication of *Il conformista* in 1952, a clear espousal of the form of Greek tragedy becomes evident. While Sophocles' *Oedipus Rex*, with its focus on sexuality and incest, is Moravia's avowed point of reference, his works as a whole are far more Euripidean than Sophoclean. The use of prologues, epilogues, references to a *deus ex machina*, bitter irony, emphasis on sexual conflict in its raw realities and interest in psychological probing—these are typical of Euripides, not Sophocles. *L'attenzione* (1965) represents the completed development of Euripidean tragedy in Moravia's novels, despite the many references to Sophocles. Even the plot reminds one of Euripides, in this case a modified version of the *Hippolytus*: a father in love with his stepdaughter, instead of a mother with her stepson (in neither case is the love consummated). Moravia has also used Greek tragedy in his theatre. *Il dio Kurt* (God Kurt) is a reworking of the Oedipus theme in a complicated play within a play dealing with an "experiment" in a Nazi concentration camp. Tragic blindness or willed ignorance are in fact central concepts in all of Moravia's fiction just as they are in Greek tragedy, for a Moravian hero remains blind to the very force that will prevent or ruin a relationship with a lover.

References to Greek myth and pagan religions also increase in the later works (for example, pagan goddesses, Zeus' famous loves such as Danae and Leda, Odysseus, Oedipus). But most striking of all is the role that Fate comes to play. As inescapable in Moravia's world as in that of Greek tragedy, Fate is that mysterious force which makes men what they are, and prevents them from being what they would like to be or from acting differently than they do. Adriana of *La romana* and Marcello of *Il conformista* are perhaps the characters most conscious of the Fate they embody. Adriana realizes that it is in her nature to be a prostitute, and Marcello knows after killing a cat as a child that he will kill a man; both learn that it is folly to try to fight against their destiny.

Despite the influence of Greek drama, however, Moravia's works are not tragedies. Whether or not it is true that tragedy is impossible in the modern world, Moravia has put his finger on one of the reasons he has not written tragedies: it does not seem possible to create tragedy around an anti-hero, in a world lacking moral values.[8] If, as the distinguished classicist Moses Hadas wrote, "In one sense all of tragedy may be defined as a demonstration that the hero is in fact heroic,"[9] then Moravia's works indeed do not qualify. His characters are impotent, or passive observers who submit rather than act. The problem is not that they are the "ordinary people" Moravia claims to write about; it is precisely that most of them are not ordinary enough when faced with ordinary problems. Thus, despite the fact that the form and content of a number of Moravia's works closely resemble Greek tragedy, his heroes are not tragic heroes. It is consequently easy to see how Moravia could have written *Io e lui* after *L'attenzione*: the Roman world of Petronius was not able to sustain tragedy either, and the *Satyricon* in its present incomplete form further underscores the fragmented quality of its narrator's life and his anti-heroic qualities. Satire was uniquely

Roman, and seems well-suited to decadent societies
past or present, and Moravia definitely sees his society
as decadent.

Sex, with its mysterious bond to money and its
natural tie to religion, is part of a composite symbol
in virtually all of Moravia's fiction. We have already
seen that Moravia believes that sex is a principal
means of contact with reality. Both his male and his
female characters are convinced of this. A surprising
number of Moravian women are either prostitutes or
are at least promiscuous, in order, we are told, to fulfill the urgings of their nature and to live as authentic
persons. Although more a masculine fantasy about the
nature of women than a well-founded analysis, this
concept permitted Moravia to extend his theory of sex
and reality to encompass all of humanity.

A woman, whether prostitute or mistress, is shown
as experiencing strong sensual pleasure upon being
handed money by her lover. Adriana, in *La romana*,
discovers this type of pleasure early in life. Celia, in
La noia, isn't given the opportunity to experience that
pleasure until rather late in her relationship with
Dino. She likes taking money from him—it doesn't
matter how much or how little, for the act of closing
her hand on the money Dino gives her is enough to
provide a type of sensual fulfillment. Money can also
sometimes substitute for sex. The unpleasantly rich
middle-class mothers who populate Moravia's fiction
have no need of fulfillment other than that provided
by wealth. In "L'avaro," or The Miser (*I racconti*), the
evolution of such a substitution is shown: Tullio finally rejects love when he realizes that living with a
woman he is attracted to would mean having to spend
some of his money to support her.

Although there is no place for a metaphysical

dimension in Moravia's fictional world of raw realities, some of his works are surrealistic, and in most of
the others religious allusions abound. Many of his
characters are depicted as unconscious worshipers of
pagan idols. The few who have any vestige of belief in
organized religion (Adriana in *La romana* or Rosetta
in *La ciociara*, both of whom, incidentally, are of the
lower class), are forced to abandon it as incompatible
with reality. The religious dimension in Moravia's
works is primitive and archetypal; it illustrates a psychological necessity, a way of viewing things, and a
type of behavior. The most obvious religious elements
in his fiction are the rites and rituals of sexual inter-
course, the woman being portrayed as fertility goddess
or earth mother, and the phallus as the object of
worship; initiation rites and images of resurrection or
rebirth are common. Money is shown as the object of
worship for the middle class, with banks and money
vaults described as religious temples.

In some of Moravia's works from the 1960s and
1970s—*L'automa, Una cosa è una cosa,* and *Il paradiso*—the atmosphere is more sterile in the sense that
sex often tends to be talked about or contemplated
rather than engaged in. In this atmosphere, the religious dimension has faded into its palest form, that of
the empty, repeated gestures of a meaningless existence. There is the woman whose life is reduced to a
series of empty gestures in a cult of the family imposed
on her by her husband ("Ah, la famiglia," or "Oh,
The Family," *Il paradiso*); or the engineer who, after
he and his wife have separated, spends his time com-
pulsively taking measurements of everything around
him ("Misure," or "Measurements," *L'automa*); or
the recent university graduate who, having made a
religion of his academic work and having seen his

professors as priests, feels lost and must now find a
new cult to follow in the business world ("Proto,"
Una cosa è una cosa).

The sea and the snake are often linked with sex
as symbols of death and life respectively. The sea is, of
course, a natural sex symbol, and many of Moravia's
stories that recount the "end of a relationship" are
played out at the seaside where the immense, rolling
sea contrasts ironically with a relationship that has
become sterile ("L'amante infelice," or "The Unfortunate Lover," *I racconti*, is a good example). But the
sea is also used as a symbol of return and of death.
Several instances of drowning or temptation of suicide
by drowning occur in Moravia's works, as for example
in the case of Molteni at Capri in *Il disprezzo*, and the
fascist government official in "Ritorno al mare," or
"Back to the Sea" (*I racconti*).

Moravia uses snakes as symbols of knowledge,
temptation and life. These three uses recall three
basic myths: the ancient earth goddess, Gaea who, in
the form of a snake, was the first oracle at Delphi; the
Judaic myth from *Genesis* of the Garden of Eden and
the fall of man; and Aesculapius, Greek god of medicine, whose attribute consisted of snakes wound on a
staff, for the snake was thought to be reborn each time
it shed its skin. In *Beatrice Cenci*, Olimpio tells
Marzio that life is like a serpent, ever young and ever
green, which changes its skin many times. In *Le ambizioni sbagliate*, the evening Andreina plans to commit murder, she hesitates a moment upon seeing a
snake on a tree in a pharmacy window as she is getting
into a taxi. And in "L'architetto," or The Architect *(I
racconti)*, the young Giacomo, invited for a ride in a
car by the girl who will soon seduce him, watches her
drive and is fascinated by her small foot which presses

on the accelerator as if it were the head of a serpent.

The entire world of a character may become sensualized. Dino in *La noia*, when frustrated one day in his attempt to make love to his mistress Celia, sees the landscape he is driving through as Celia's body. In his study of Moravia, the French critic Fernandez pointed out the large number of adjectives in Moravia's descriptions which denote overflowing, fullness, heaviness or swollenness, and he suggested that they are indicative of Moravia's visual emphasis on sexuality.[10]

Another cluster of symbols centers around the problem of self-knowledge: here light and darkness, mirrors, masks, and puppets are principal elements. All of Moravia's main characters are fascinated by the self they perceive, and it is the degree of consciousness of the self which determines the amount of suffering each endures. Images of light and darkness appear on almost every page of Moravia's prewar fiction. The quality of light is an integral part of the setting, and is noted with each change of scene by the author and his character. In the works of this period, the characters are often tormented souls forced to wander in darkness, seeking the light. However, when they find it, it blinds them, and pain impels them to return to darkness. Long, dark, serpentine corridors wind through a great number of the prewar works. The painful dramas in the lives of Moravia's people take form in these dark corridors, to be played out in the dim rooms they lead to or in the blindingly bright glare of the outside world. In one unforgettable story ("Intimità," or Intimacy, *L'epidemia*), two middle-class couples wander through the endless corridors of a mansion without ever finding the high-society party to which they were invited (after years of longing for an invitation to just such a party). They can hear the tantalizing sounds of the party somewhere in the house, but after hours of walking up and down the corridors looking for it they become weary and leave.

Mirrors and people who see themselves reflected in a looking-glass may often form a motif in a Moravian narrative. Characters catch an unexpected and revealing glimpse of themselves and are unpleasantly struck by what they see. Some scrutinize themselves carefully in an attempt to uncover their own secrets. Pietro in *Le ambizioni sbagliate* is disgusted when he catches a glimpse of his lipstick-smeared face in an elevator mirror. A few minutes later, dressing in front of a mirror in his room, he analyzes the reasons for his disgust and discovers that he is not the innocent man he thought he was, but really an ambitious person who has ulterior motives.

Narcissism is also a key element in this mirror imagery, for often Moravia's characters are infatuated, or at least fascinated, by their own image. In "L'Ufficiale inglesi," or "The English Officer" (*I racconti*), the young heroine examines herself in the mirror of a store window and, with a sudden command of her will, vows not to be led into the temptation of prostitution ever again. With a calmed spirit, she lingers in front of the mirror to scrutinize herself and to arrange her hair. As many scenes from Moravia's fiction show, nothing is more interesting to observe than the self, especially after one has had the existential experience of seeing oneself as another. All of Moravia's first-person narrators describe themselves unhesitatingly, like people thoroughly familiar with their subject from long observation. Cesira in *La ciociara* even describes with the same kind of absolute assurance her appearance as a young girl at the time of her marriage.

In the reflected image of the self, a Moravian character may unwittingly see the mask he wears (the situation of Pietro from *Le ambizioni sbagliate*, see above), or he may discover how much he resembles a puppet or mechanical doll. Masks naturally hide the self, and they are of prime importance in Moravia's early works. The title of one of his novels, *La mascherata* (literally, The Masked Ball), which Moravia later rewrote as a play, shows the considerable attention he has given to this theme. A mask is usually recognized for what it is by other people; thus it does not often succeed in hiding the self from others. Its function is to hide the self from the self. Hypocrisy is the companion to a mask, and is the predominant sin of the middle class for Moravia, who delights in unmasking the masked and exposing hypocrisy to his readers.

A mask may be consciously adopted by a Moravian character as a calculated method of getting along in life. Women's make-up is often described by the author as a mask that conceals the ravages of an aging face. Pretending and pretense (*fingere* and *finzione*) may also be consciously chosen as a way of life, for example by the characters of *Gli indifferenti* who can feel no true emotions, or by those of *Le ambizioni sbagliate* who must be hypocritical in order to achieve their goals of money and social position, or by those of *La mascherata* whose bit of social polish enables them to wallow in the corruption and vulgarity of a base society.

Dehumanization is the result, and many of Moravia's heroes come to the painful realization that they, and everyone around them, are mere puppets (*fan-tocci*). In "La solitudine," or Solitude (*I racconti*), Perrone sees that he and his friends do not act like people but rather like puppets who can only make one particular facial expression and repeat it tirelessly, who can only move in one particular manner; even when they touch each other, their wooden limbs remain inert and rigid. He sees people as being soulless and locked within their solitude and individuality, unable to communicate with each other, reduced to a few manias, a few mechanical stimuli of the instincts. Such puppets of Moravia's early works become the automata and the people-objects of his later works, those sad-looking beings who are no more significant than and not véry different from the machines and objects that surround them.

A final group of recurring images deals with problems of reality which, for Moravia, means of course reality perceived subjectively. As he said in an interview: "Nowadays we believe mostly in subjective reality. Everybody is his own reality, and your reality is not mine."[11] The implications of such an idea for personal relationships are devastating. Moravia explores the general problem of what is reality mainly through discussions of dreams and visions, words and language.

A hero's dreams or visions are as revealing in Moravia's works as in Freudian psychology, and are used by the author in much the same way—to uncover hidden reality. The narrator of "Il mostro," or The Monster (*Una cosa è una cosa*) has a dream in which he commits an unspecified crime. During his waking hours, he feels guilt and tries unsuccessfully to discover why. The story ends with an analysis of his situation: "Therefore a dream was needed to discover that the reality was there and that consciousness couldn't avoid being there." Many such dreams of anguish involving a reality not otherwise consciously acknowledged can be found in Moravia's works. In *La disubbidienza,* Luca's delirium and hallucinations when he is ill are an extreme example; all his confused emotions and his hatred of life come out in representative forms of grotesque little people and hideous animals. There are also the visions and dreams that compensate for unsatisfying reality. Agostino's vague, desperate desire to leave his old life behind him and follow the shoreline of the sea in hopes of finding a place to live where ugly things do not exist and where he could live according to his nature is of this type.

Many of Moravia's stories tell us that "life is a dream"; the tales in the collection *L'epidemia,* for example, involve some dream or vision representing a "truth." This thesis is also clearly illustrated in "L'orgia," or "The Orgy" (*Il paradiso*), in which a young wife and mother spends her days watching the orgy scenes that take place in the apartment across the way where a young, single woman lives. We discover at the end, however, that the apartment she has been watching all those days is empty; and as a final bit of irony, that apartment has just been rented to a couple with three children. The imaginary scenes, cinema-like sequences, were the principal reality of the narrator's life.

A number of Moravia's characters have difficulty distinguishing between a dream and reality; they are forced to try to find some principle by which to separate what is a dream from what is not. "Il sogno," or "The Dream" (*L'automa*), shows the processes a character may indulge in to try to differentiate dream from reality. A girl whom Silvio met at a party calls and invites him to lunch. He goes to the restaurant at the appointed time, but she does not appear, and he is greatly disappointed and perplexed. When he sees her sometime later, she is very distant with him; he begins to wonder about her behavior, and eventually comes to the conclusion that the phone call must have been a dream: "However the thing might have been, whether he had dreamt it or whether it had really happened, it was nevertheless a dream because it was not to be explained in a rational manner."

For some characters, life is a bad dream. In an earlier story, "Fine di una relazione," or "End of a Relationship" (*I racconti*), Renzo, a rich, empty young man finds that for inexplicable reasons life has become a torment to him. After breaking with his mistress, he is so unhappy that he becomes convinced he is dreaming. "One day I'll awaken and recognize the world again," he says to himself. Meanwhile, however, the cold of the night slowly penetrates him as it moves into the room through the open window.

Following a general mid-twentieth-century liter-ary trend, Moravia became more interested in words and language in the 1960s, particularly in the implica-tions of the investigations of Wittgenstein,[12] and of the phenomenologists concerning the subjective na-ture of our perceptions of reality and the highly indi-vidual manner in which we use words. For Moravia, the problem of language is twofold: (1) whether words create what is or whether they reflect realities; (2) whether words permit or prevent communication among human beings. One of the stories from *Una cosa è una cosa* ("I fumetti," or The Comics) treats the matter concisely: we become what we say, and words make us what we appear; what we really are, no one knows. In the same volume, "L'intimità," or Intimacy, has a narrator who is unable to communicate with his wife, and who gradually encloses himself within an impenetrable personal world. Since he wishes to communicate only with himself, he invents a special language, made up of nonsense words which economically express his thoughts and emotions. When a man in the park tries to make conversation with him, the narrator says that he doesn't understand Italian; he admits he can speak it but denies being able to understand it. In an ironic ending, the narrator's wife leaves him, and he does not understand her good-bye letter. But once he realizes that he is completely alone, he can only weep.

Il mondo è quello che è (The World Is What It Is), a satirical two-act play, explores some of the farcical aspects of the language-reality question. The ultimate goal of the language experiment presented in the play is to create for the masses a therapy which will teach them to speak without saying anything. People will thereby be led to the point of being better able to fulfill their historical function of producing for consumption and consuming for production.

Thus, it is clear that for Moravia the problem of words has special significance. It is linked to his humanistic premise that man should be an end, not a means, and at the same time it points to the gradual dehumanization of man in the modern world.

3

*The Early
Novels*

"My critics say I go on writing my first book. There is some truth in this. My first book was very intense and sowed the seeds of everything I was to write afterwards."[1] It is indeed easy to find in that first book the seeds of many of the themes that would reappear in subsequent works. *Gli indifferenti* (*The Time of Indifference*), published in 1929, is a novel about middle-class life. The preoccupation with sex and money is obvious, and the impotent intellectual hero is pitted against a virile, overbearing rival. Masks, hypocrisy, puppets, automata, mirrors, dreams, and the anguish of aging are key elements that function as motifs; the drama is played out against a background of wintry gray skies, on a stage of continually shifting patches of light and darkness.

The "indifferent ones" (*gli indifferenti*) could also well be called the "bored ones" (*gli annoiati*), since boredom is at the root of their problems, their desires, and their inability to do anything about their situation. The action of the novel covers a period of two days and three nights in the lives of five persons. The setting is the wealthiest area of Rome; it is winter.

Carla, who is twenty-four, and her younger brother, Michele, are both profoundly dissatisfied with life and with themselves. Carla has reached a point where she feels she cannot go on; alternately she wants to leave home and start a "new life," or to "end it all" and "ruin everything." (Dante's *Vita Nuova*, or *New Life*, echoes ironically throughout the novel.) Michele, the more intellectual of the two, suffers continually from his feelings of indifference toward everything, from the pain of seeing the hypocrisy and falseness of the people around him, and from seeing himself as he is—impotent and unable to do anything.

He wants to find his "concrete reality" and then begin a "new life," which he thinks might be possible if only he could manage to have one sincere emotion or to perform one sincere act. Both he and his sister are too weak, too inert to do anything to change their lives; besides, neither knows exactly what he wants out of life. They vacillate between romantic dreams of fulfillment and the desire for self-destruction.

Their mother, Mariagrazia, a middle-aged widow, would like to be younger and once again loved by Leo Mermucci, whose infidelity and indifference to her have increased with the years. Her pathetic and ridiculous attempts to be beautiful and seductive annoy everyone, as do her whininess and emotionalism. She is most often referred to as "la madre," an ironic reminder of fascism's fanatic adulation of motherhood. Mariagrazia is as far from an ideal of motherhood as can be imagined, and the few times she theatrically assumes the role of mother she appears nothing less than disgusting. Although Leo no longer has any interest in Mariagrazia, he continues to frequent the house because he wants to get her property away from her through a complicated scheme he has devised. He also has become interested in Carla and hopes to be able to seduce her despite his age. So, the glint of money and the lure of a fresh young thing to deflower keep him in a constant state of excitement. The last member of the cast is Lisa, an old friend of Mariagrazia's and a former mistress of Leo's. She is fat and flourishing, but she too feels the anguish of creeping age and believes that a pure, young love could renew her: "a bit of innocence can do you good," she tells herself.[2] She therefore sets out to seduce Michele.

Leo, the forceful non-intellectual male (the *prepotente*) in the novel, is a cynic about everything with

no illusions about anything; he is also the only one
who can act. After several grotesque and unsuccessful
attempts to seduce Carla he finally gets her into bed
with him. He then decides that marrying her would
be the best thing because it would further his two
main interests—sex and money. Carla will accept his
offer of marriage, because there is nothing better for
her to do. Lisa may get Michele, if only he can muster
up enough energy to become her lover. As for Mariagrazia, she knows nothing of either of the above in-
trigues, and ironically, on the last page of the novel,
has come to believe that Leo isn't unfaithful to her
after all and begins to look forward to happy times
with him once again.

Because Mariagrazia has been living beyond her
means for years, and because Leo has been there to
take advantage of her, she is, at the beginning of the
novel, about to be forced to give up her house and
property to Leo. She cannot bear the thought of being
poor, has never even been able to bear the sight of
poor people, and so would do anything to avoid falling into poverty. She is saved when Leo modifies his
mercenary intentions in order to get Carla to agree to
marry him. In exchange for Carla, he will allow the
family to remain in the house and will support them
all. Everyone appears to have his price: Leo will get
Carla; Mariagrazia "won't be a problem" as Carla
puts it, for she will quickly see that Carla's marriage
will enable her to ward off poverty and to continue
her social life among those who are richer than she;
Carla is bought by the prospect of becoming the rich
and elegant Signora Mermucci; and Michele can be
bought by the promise of a job and the possibility of
getting rich.

From the first page of the novel one is struck by

its theatrical quality. It has the atmosphere of a stage drama, but the techniques are those of the cinema, as if we were watching a filmed version of a dramatic performance. The stage is there, but so is the movie camera, ready to focus now on one character, now on another. The bulk of the work consists of dialogue and monologue, and expressions of thoughts and feelings, with descriptions that look like nothing so much as stage directions. The stark, compact style mirrors the repetitiveness and monotony, tension and indifference of the lives of the characters. The lighting effects are those of the stage: lamps radiate a circle of light in which a character is illuminated as if by a spotlight in an otherwise darkened room; or a patch of sunlight from a window forms a square in which a character stands.

It becomes clear in the course of the novel that the above mentioned aspects are not merely ornamental. The focusing on one character at a time reflects Moravia's primary interest in character. Reacting against nineteenth-century naturalism, he has stated that for him, a novel is character, and that by character he means a fragment of the author himself and not a creature formed from scientific observations.[3] Once a character is in focus, he is seen briefly from the outside; then the camera moves inside and begins to focus outward through his eyes.

Far more important than dialogue in this novel are monologue and dreams. Communication with another person seems almost impossible, and the characters are condemned to speaking hypocrisies or conventionalities. When, for example, Michele tries to talk about himself to Lisa, he sees that she cannot understand him, and indeed is not interested in the real Michele but wants only *her* Michele, a Michele who

makes certain gestures and movements. The interior
monologue which a character indulges in is a substitute
for the dialogue with others that he finds impossible.
Much of it consists of what he would have liked to say
or what he really thought while pronouncing some
false or meaningless phrase. Although very little satis-
faction is gained from this monologue, it is the only
kind of communication that is possible.

Everyone in the novel except Leo suffers from the
existential crisis of the consciousness helplessly observ-
ing the self, and the painful awareness of the self as an
object, a puppet or an automaton. Mirrors are the
favorite medium of these self-revelations. The women
frequently scrutinize their made-up faces, which are
described as painted masks; they examine their nude
or clothed bodies in order to determine their seductiveness as sex objects. There are also the cruel, unexpected reflections, such as Michele's when he sees
himself in a store window mirror, then notices a dis-
play dummy shaving his face next to the mirror and
recognizes himself in the mindless, single repeated action of that puppet.

A character may even see himself reflected in the
faces or the words of other characters and thus become
still more keenly aware of his status as an object to
them. Carla, for example, becomes aware at one point
that Leo is not talking to her but rather to her lower
abdomen, and indeed seems unable even to lift his
eyes to her face. She had previously seen Leo as a
robot, and later had felt like a puppet while riding
beside him in his car. But it is not until the end of the
novel, when Michele confesses that he had thought of
her as a piece of merchandise to be sold to Leo, that
Carla consciously accepts being an object to others:
"Everyone and no one was guilty, but she was tired of

studying herself and others; she did not want to forgive, she did not want to condemn; life was what it was; it was better to accept it than to pass judgment on it; anything to be left in peace."[4] She assures Michele that there is no need for him to ask for forgiveness because he has done nothing. In that statement Michele sees an important reflection of himself and his impotence: " 'I've done nothing,' he repeated to himself with amazement . . . 'it's true . . . I've done nothing . . . nothing but think . . . I didn't make love to Lisa . . . I didn't kill Leo . . . I did nothing but think . . . that's my mistake.' "[5]

Carla's consciousness leads to weariness and acceptance. However, it is clear that what she accepts is not the distasteful life with Leo she had originally imagined, but a kind of dream life. Her decision to accept Leo's offer is accompanied by a daydream of the future seen in terms of her life in the whirl of high society, in terms of her elegance and seductiveness; the liberating affair with a lover that will permit her to be pure again. Her last thoughts in the novel are that "everything is so easy." She must, she feels, tell Michele how easy it all is. Dressed for the masked ball she and her mother are going to, she feels like another person. Of course, we see that she has merely changed her mask.

Michele, too, has dreams—of riches, women, travel, hotels, of an intense life divided between successful business activities and engrossing amusements. These dreams pass before his eyes like a movie on a screen, and he only wishes they were a reality. More than anything he wants to escape from boredom.

Mariagrazia and Lisa also suffer to some degree, but the camera focuses less frequently on them, and their pains do not draw much sympathy from the

reader. Thoroughly middle-class in their thoughts, desires, and actions, they are perfect representatives of
the society that Carla and Michele were born into.
Their middle-class life remains inexorably gray. Leo is
the only character in the novel who is unabashedly
satisfied with himself. The last we see of him he is
standing in front of his bedroom mirror congratulat-
ing himself on being such a successful man.

The five characters are all concerned with satisfying their appetites, and since the only dimension of
their lives is the physical and material, sex and money
constitute the only realities of their world.

Throughout the novel, the intricate play of darkness and light underscores what is occurring in the
lives of the characters. In fact, darkness and light are
an integral part of a character's drama, something
akin to physical forces which act on him and on his
situation. This is most evident in the scene of the
storm in which the electricity goes out in Mariagrazia's house. In this scene, shadows and flickering
candles with their serpentine wisps of twisting smoke
are the silent actors who lead the action toward a
climax: Michele begins a relationship with Lisa, and
Leo embraces Carla for the first time.

It has been clear all along that the five characters
are all creatures of the night who are blinded by the
light of day. Michele, accosted by Lisa for the first
time, finds that his eyes are full of darkness and he can
no longer remember ever having seen the light. Later,
Lisa leads him down the dark corridor of her house to
her boudoir, which at first is filled with blinding light
and then darkens when Michele kisses her. Mariagrazia's painted mask fails her in the light of day, for
the light reveals her wrinkled face. When she walks
down the street, we see her lose color as she passes

through patches of sunlight until she finally melts into the shadows and becomes a black spot at the end of the street. Carla, once she is in Leo's bed, has an avid thirst for darkness and wonders if this thirst is not part of her program to abase herself completely by plunging into the "shadows of the promiscuity of the night."[6]

Michele's last thoughts in the novel are of darkness: " 'It's impossible to go on like this.' He felt like crying; life's forest surrounded him on all sides, labyrinthian and blind; no light shone in the distance: 'impossible'."[7] But he had already summed up his situation earlier when he realized that "there's only darkness . . . nothing but darkness."[8] Andreina, the heroine of *Le ambizioni sbagliate*, will learn the same harsh truth about herself and her situation.

In his essay on *Gli indifferenti*, Moravia reconstructed his ideas and state of mind at the time he was writing this first novel. Admittedly he knew almost nothing of life at age eighteen, having spent most of his adolescence in bed, paralyzed by a diseased leg bone. He began to write, he tells us, without a plan in mind: "Over a period of many years I had read innumerable plays and novels. I had become convinced that the summit of art lay in tragedy, while on the other hand I felt more drawn to writing novels than writing for theater. So I got the idea of writing a novel that combined the qualities of narrative and drama, a novel with few characters, very few changes of scene, with a plot that unfolded in a short span of time, a novel in which there was only dialogue and background."[9]

However, as he wrote, he began to see that his idea could not be carried out: "I began to see the impossibility of tragedy in a world in which nonmaterialist values seemingly lacked any right to exist, and where moral conscience had become so hardened that people acted from appetite only and were more and more like automata."[10]

Many readers immediately saw the book as an attack on the middle class. Moravia, however, denies having been politically or socially motivated. He was, he says, merely reflecting the only reality he knew: "The fault or merit . . . belongs to the middle classes, especially in Italy where they have hardly any qualities capable of inspiring (let us not mention admiration) even the remotest sympathy."[11]

Some critics have gone so far as to call *Gli indifferenti* Moravia's finest book. It is a young man's work, an intense groping toward understanding rather than a mature statement on life. Though it does have the ring of the sincerely believed, at times its romanticism seems somewhat heavy.

After *Gli indifferenti* Moravia made another attempt at tragedy in the novel before trying his hand at comic satire. Neither of these next two novels can be considered wholly successful.

Le ambizioni sbagliate (*Mistaken Ambitions*), 1935, is a Dostoevskian novel (Dostoevsky had an admittedly strong influence on Moravia) which contains many of the theatrical elements of *Gli indifferenti*. It also exaggerates many of the less felicitous aspects of that first novel—the heavy romanticism, complicated and sordid love affairs, and one-dimensional characters.

A long novel of some 460 dense pages, it has an extraordinarily complicated plot. Here is a bare outline of the most important parts: Maria Luisa, a society woman who gained her wealth through her first marriage, has discovered that her present husband, Matteo, is having an affair with a young woman named Andreina. She moves out of her house in a huff and cuts off all funds to Matteo, leaving him virtually penniless (he is of a noble but impoverished family). Matteo's sister, Sophia, tries unsuccessfully to effect a reconciliation; she, too, depends on Maria Luisa's money to maintain her social position. Sophia's fiancé, a journalist named Pietro, also becomes involved in the reconciliation attempts. He subsequently falls under the spell of Andreina, becomes her lover, and eventually breaks off his engagement with Sophia. Pietro is not, however, as completely under Andreina's control as she had hoped, for he refuses to take part in her plot to kill Maria Luisa. Andreina's motives remain somewhat mysterious; hers is an act of revenge, although she also claims to want a share of Maria Luisa's fortune. In the end, Andreina is driven by the forces of evil within her; she commits the crime herself and then disappears into the night.

Such is the main thrust of the action, but, as in a long Dostoevskian novel, there are many more characters involved, and a number of subplots weave through the main action. In *Le ambizioni sbagliate*, however, the events are improbable and contrived, for Moravia has packed this work with an amazing number of extraordinary coincidences and bizarre interconnections.

The novel is divided into three parts and deals with three days (from morning to night) separated from one another by one month intervals. Thus the action is spread out over a period of approximately three winter months. Once again Moravia carefully structured the time element. The action itself consists principally of dialogue (either conversations or dialogues with self) which takes place in enclosed rooms, with the characters coming and going between the rooms. Entrances and exits tend to be dramatic, and the episodic structure again resembles scenes within a dramatic work. Furthermore, the influence of the cinema is even more pronounced in the novel's shifting camera technique, its use of the play of darkness and light, and its descriptions of scenery, houses and rooms that seem like scenes from a mystery film.

The title bears witness to the author's intent. If in his first novel Moravia's criticism of the middle class was unconscious, as he claims, here it is deliberate. A statement, presumably written by Moravia himself, found on the novel's inside cover explains that the author is here studying the opposite of indifference (that is, ambition), and further discusses the meaning of the work:

This novel can be defined as a description of the passion that guides and dominates the relationships of individuals with the world—ambition. Here ambition is judged severely as one of the many aspects, perhaps the most destructive, of human egoism. In *Le ambizioni sbagliate*, therefore, the reader will find not apathetic or irresolute characters, but rather obsessed and avid ones; not the static atmosphere of the absence of passions, but rather the turbulence of numerous, unchecked passions.

Moralizing is not confined to the inside cover; the novel itself abounds with judgments by the author, not only on the characters, their actions and their milieu, but also on man in general, human nature and human society.

Andreina and Pietro gradually come to occupy the center of the stage, forming the same kind of axis as that of Carla and Michele in *Gli indifferenti*.

Andreina, like Carla, reaches a point of desperation and wills her own ruin, rushing down the road she knows will lead her to it. In two interesting respects she is also a prototype of the lower-class female of Moravia's later novels. She has tendencies that have led her to prostitution, and she also has tendencies that lead her to thievery (we learn that she is responsible for the theft of Maria Luisa's jewels, although her motive is very vague). As for Pietro, he is as powerless and incapable of acting as Michele. And like Michele, he longs for innocence and purity, but is forced, under Andreina's prodding, to see himself as he is—base and self-seeking.

Throughout the story an ill-defined force of evil slowly tightens its grip on the souls of the characters. It exudes from the bleak wintry landscape, the dark streets, the night, the wind, the cold and the rain. It is this evil force which leads Andreina to crime and ruin; it took hold of her ten years before when she was seduced by Stefano, Maria Luisa's brother. She had vainly tried to struggle against it, but it had the power of Fate. Her killing of Maria Luisa is, we learn, an act of revenge for her lost innocence and purity (the paradise lost motif becomes more and more prominent in Moravia's subsequent works).

In the final analysis, Andreina is a possessed creature of the Dostoevskian mold. She is, we are told, a child of darkness: "Now she cursed herself and her ambition; she was born for this darkness; why had she tried to break out of it?"[12] She is most frequently seen in a dark setting, and often there is a diabolical quality associated with her presence. We wonder, as she does herself, if it is the devil who chauffeurs the taxi that seems to be waiting for her, not once but twice, on the night she kills Maria Luisa. After strangling

Maria Luisa, Andreina feels as if all her ties with the world have been severed: " 'Here I am beyond the bounds of reason,' she thought, 'beyond the bounds of love, of any human intervention, in the realm of chaos and of the night.' "[13] With a storm beginning to rage outside, she rushes from her house and melts into the night, leaving Pietro behind to search vainly for her in the "dark, narrow garden" where the trees were creaking and groaning as "their nude branches unknotted like serpents awakening from their lethargy."[14] He then rushes into the street where lightning begins to flash all around him; the first drops of rain are beginning to swirl through the air, "mixed with the disordered gusts of the wind." But Andreina has disappeared into the chaos.

Moral disorder and chaos are also the subject of Moravia's next novel, *La mascherata* (*The Fancy Dress Party*), 1941, his most Stendhalian novel. While much shorter than *Le ambizioni sbagliate*, it is hardly less complicated, and the moral intent, if not as explicitly stated, is nevertheless just as evident. Published during the height of the fascist period in Italy, it is a political satire which uses the stock farcical elements of eighteenth-century social comedy. Moravia later adapted it for the stage with very few changes, and in 1958 he published it under the same title as a three-act play.

Before writing this novel, Moravia had already fallen out of favor with the fascist government. By order of the censors, his second novel had gone unreviewed. Apparently the satire in *La mascherata* was oblique enough to get past the censors, at least for a while; however, when the novel was in its second edition the government finally ordered it removed from circulation.

The story, in skeleton form, is as follows. After ten years of civil war, an imaginary (probably South American) country had fallen under the military dictatorship of a general named Tereso Arango. A shrewd, cruel man, his tastes are simple and austere, but he has one weakness—women. A certain rich society woman, Duchess Gorina, has finally managed to lure Tereso to one of her parties by using as bait the beautiful Marchioness Fausta Sanchez, to whom Tereso has been attracted for some time. The duchess organizes a masked ball to show off her prized guest and to provide an appropriate meeting ground for Fausta and Tereso. Fausta is willing to add Tereso to her string of lovers on the condition that she gain certain favors from him, including benefits for her brother. Unfortunately, in order to accommodate Tereso, one of her present lovers, Sebastiano, will have to be let go.

Meanwhile, an assassination plot has been formed by a group of communist style revolutionaries who plan to kill Tereso at the masked ball. In actual fact, all members of the group except one are secret police agents who have concocted the plot so that at the proper moment they can uncover and foil it, thereby showing Tereso how necessary and efficient they are. The one sincere revolutionary is a poor buffoon named Severo, who is the half-brother of Sebastiano. Sebastiano himself gets mixed up in the assassination plot in order to be near Fausta, for he refuses to give her up.

Thus the masked ball becomes a "crossroads of interests," as Moravia himself states in the text.[15] In

the end, Tereso discovers that Fausta is merely playing with him. However, before he can avenge himself
on her she is accidentally killed by Severo in the
phoney assassination plot, just prior to the beginning
of the ball. Her funeral takes place in the small chapel
next to the ballroom where the masked guests are as-
sembled for the ball. Severo is shot on the way to
prison by the very men he believed to be his friends
and fellow revolutionaries. All these complicated
events are packed into a two-day period.

The masked ball is a particularly good vehicle for
Moravia's intended satire. Pretending and pretense
are a way of life for the members of this society. Everything connected with them is pretense, illusion, pho-
niness and trickery—even the decor they live in (the
duchess' palace park is filled with artificial scenery
such as fake chalets and grottos). Many of the guests
invited to the ball come dressed as animals, devils and
lower-class characters. Ironically, the mask each dons
for the ball is a true-to-life representation of the self
hidden under its usual society mask. The beautiful
Fausta, for example, dresses as a lowly, besmudged
chimney sweep; and the duchess, whose sexual appetite for young male flesh is never satiated, masks as a
whorish bar girl.

As a study of egoism and self-interest, *La mascherata* is even more damning than *Le ambizioni
sbagliate*. It may be considered political satire because
it is a thinly veiled representation of Mussolini and
the people who supported him. However, it is pri-
marily social satire, for Moravia's main interest is to
portray the decadence and moral bankruptcy of Italian society as he saw it.

In the fascist society Moravia depicts, love,
friendship, trust, and honesty cannot exist; the only

possible social bonds are complicated webs of self-interest. In such a world everyone must be a trickster in order to survive; and the corollary is that everyone is also tricked. But the sincere revolutionary is not spared either. Moravia chose to depict him as a simpleton, unable to be anything but a tool of the secret police.

Only one of the characters escapes being completely discredited—Sebastiano, who is a thoroughly Stendhalian character. In order to escape the boredom that plagues him, he consciously creates romantic illusions by which to live. The origin of this boredom is in his skepticism about the destiny of his country and of mankind. His generation, we are told, "didn't believe in anything, not in the state, not in revolution, not in liberty, not in authority." The result is that it was led "to dreams, to boredom, to inertia and to dilettantism."[16] That generation was Moravia's, and Sebastiano is obviously a fragment of an autoportrait.

This work is neither the comic satire nor the social tragedy it could have been, but a strange hybrid of the two which leaves the reader uncertain of its artistic aim. Although riddled by the author with annoying intrusions and continual judgments on the characters and their actions, *La mascherata* can be admired for its skillfully handled plot, its many artfully constructed scenes, and its portrayal of the complicated emotions and reactions of the main characters.

4

*Agostino
and Luca*

*A*gostino, 1944, and *La Disubbidienza (Luca)*, 1948, (translated into English and published together under the title of *Two Adolescents*), have been called by many critics two of Moravia's finest works. As has been frequently noted, the story of Luca in *La Disubbidienza* completes that of Agostino, for *La Disubbidienza* begins at the point where *Agostino* ends. Both novels are stories of anguish; in each, the young protagonist experiences a sense of lost purity and innocence, suffering intensely when confronted with the reality of a world so different from that of his desires, dreams, and ideals. In a word, Moravia has given us two intimate studies of a time of crisis during the painful period of growing up. Each focuses almost exclusively on the boy-hero, has a simple story line, and is brief enough to be called a novella.

Although Moravia did not entirely abandon the moralizing so evident in his earlier novels (indeed, his most recent books reveal the same tendency), in these two works he reduced its intrusiveness considerably. At the same time he began to probe more deeply than before into the psychology of his characters. The dominant tone of these two works is elegiac, the mood of much of Moravia's most successful fiction to come. It is also in these and other works of the 1940s that the religious theme becomes important—it was to be used and explored many times in future novels and stories.

Two distinct threads are woven into the fabric of *Agostino*. There is first of all the intimate drama of a thirteen-year-old boy's awakening to the realities of sexuality and of evil; but there is also the social-economic initiation of the rich, middle-class boy suddenly faced with the world of the lower class and its harsh values. It is in *Agostino* that the bond between sex and money, adumbrated in *Le ambizioni sbagliate* and in earlier short stories, is treated directly.

Agostino's story takes place in an Italian seaside resort (probably on the Mediterranean coast) where the boy and his mother are spending the summer. The action spans a short period during the peak of the summer season, and ends with the approach of autumn. Agostino's father is dead, and thus he has had his mother entirely to himself for some time. His love for her is described as adoration; he is proud and happy to be seen with her in public. One day, however, a young man named Renzo intrudes on Agostino's paradise and quickly becomes the companion of the boy's mother, thus spoiling the relationship between mother and son. Humiliated and jealous, Agostino feels he has become a mere object to his mother; in an attempt at self-protection, he vows to learn to love her less. This abrupt shattering of Agostino's relationship with his mother marks the beginning of the painful coming-of-age process, of which we see only the first unhappy stage in this novel.

At about the same time, Agostino attaches himself to a band of lower-class boys, mostly the sons of beach attendants. He is both attracted and repelled by the band, but eventually attraction proves to be the stronger force. In an obvious desire for self-debasement and for escape from his painful situation with his mother, Agostino tries to be more and more like the other boys, although he realizes he is too different from them to be accepted fully.

It is from the boys that he first learns about sex—both the heterosexual and the homosexual variety, for the band includes a mature man named Saro who has the distinction of having six fingers on each hand and

of being a homosexual, and a young black boy named
Homs who is Saro's special friend. What Agostino
learns about sex further degrades his mother in his
eyes, for he constantly tries to imagine what she and
Renzo must be doing together. From that time on, life
for Agostino means only suffering and anguish. He
longs for a world of innocence and purity, a paradise
where he could be happy; but that world is out of
reach. His next hope is to experience sex for himself
with a woman, but he is turned away from a house of
prostitution because of his age. The novel ends with
his return to life with his mother, his conflict unresolved.

A delicate and finely woven story, *Agostino* has
many admirable touches and few flaws. The sea and
the persistent summer heat provide the perfect background for this story of sexual awakening and suffering. Although it is a third-person narrative, most of
what occurs is seen through the eyes of Agostino. The
story begins with a description of how Agostino and
his mother have spent their mornings together, going
out on the sea in a rented boat. The mother (she is
never named) is said to be a "big, beautiful woman
still in the flower of youth."[1] Agostino feels as if the
beach were a kind of stage, as if the eyes of a vast
audience were upon him and his mother as they em-
bark on the boat; as a result, each morning his actions
and speech become theatrical as preparations for the
embarcation take place. As we see more of his mother
through Agostino's eyes, she takes on the qualities of a
primitive sea goddess whom Agostino worships with
fixed rituals: there are the seabathing and sunbathing
rites, the managing of the small boat, and the many
little attentions he lavishes on her. Agostino worships
with a love that is pre-sexual adoration. Later, after

Renzo appears, the mother takes on the distinct qualities of a fertility goddess; this sea change which the
mother undergoes in her son's eyes as she becomes
vulgar and awkward is superbly recorded by Moravia.
No less admirable is the portrayal of the beginning of
a summer romance between a handsome young man
and a beautiful woman.

But best of all is the study of humiliation, from
its inception to its point of intolerability. Agostino is
forced to accompany his mother and Renzo on morning boat rides; thus the scene of his former bliss becomes that of present torment, further increasing his
suffering. He is now a mere object to his mother, who
is completely caught up in her desire. Just as he was
formerly given happiness by his mother in many little
ways, so is he now hurt by her in many little ways.
Because he is hurt by her, he tries to hurt her in
return, and one day she slaps him, definitively ending
their old happy life together. Agostino has intuited
sexuality before fully understanding what it is, and a
link between sexuality and cruelty has been forged in
his mind before he is capable of formulating thoughts
to express what he has experienced.

Immediately after his mother slapped him and
irremediably ended his happiness, Agostino encoun-
ters evil for the first time at the hands of Berto, one
of the boys from the band. Berto induces Agostino to
smoke, then maliciously burns him on the hand with a
cigarette, punches him in the stomach, and starts to
beat him savagely. Agostino's reaction is one of stupe-
faction: "It seemed incredible that he, Agostino, with
whom everyone had always been affectionate, was now
the object of such deliberate and pitiless cruelty."[2]
But that is just the beginning; because he is rich he is
tormented by all the boys in various ways. Later, he

learns an even more bitter lesson in injustice when he
is wrongly accused of homosexuality after going out in
a boat with Saro. In the marvelous scene that follows
that accusation, the boys rush off to go swimming in a
nearby river, away from the crowds at the seashore.
They strip off their clothes, each loudly proclaiming
his virility, and then with shouts and laughter they
jump joyfully into the water one after the other like
frogs frightened from the edge of a pond. In poignant
contrast to them, Agostino swims a short distance
away, alone and suffering, dreaming of leaving behind
his old life and following the river to a new country
"where all these ugly things did not exist . . . and
where he could forget everything he had learned, in
order to relearn it without shame or outrage, in the
gentle and natural way that must be possible and that
instinctively he felt had to exist."[3]

Thus, like Moravia's "indifferent ones," Agostino
wants a new life, one of innocence and purity. In any
case, he must escape from suffering, and finally decides
that this can only be done by freeing himself from his
mother, by being able to look at her as "nothing but a
woman." To this end he begins to spy on her, hoping
to see her nude and thus convince himself that she is
just another woman. And he tries to draw closer to the
band of boys, dressing like them, pretending to strangers that he is a beach attendant's son. It is only after
all these attempts fail that he becomes desperate and
resolves to sever the tie with his mother by experiencing sex with a woman himself. He has been shown a
house of prostitution and has been told that one must
pay for a woman in such a house, but he cannot understand how money, which usually buys objects, can
also buy the caresses and flesh of a woman. This ques-

tion will not be explored until Moravia writes *La romana*.

The afternoon that Agostino returns home to get some money in order to buy a sexual experience, he finds his mother playing the piano, with Renzo beside her. In a beautifully executed scene, Moravia describes Agostino hiding in the dark corridor of the house to listen to the impudent music his mother is playing—music which sounds "vivacious, tumultuous, scintillating."[4] He also witnesses a kiss exchanged by the two lovers, and sees his mother's reaction to that kiss, her eyes burning, her hair disheveled with one strand hanging down her cheek and swaying like a serpent. Agostino realizes confusedly that her state of excitement matches what he himself is feeling at that moment.

But Agostino is to be thwarted also in this last attempt to end his suffering. Tricked by one of the boys who takes his money, he is refused entrance at the door of the brothel, and he is reduced to peeking in a window. All he sees is a vulgar, fertility goddess figure in a transparent gown like the ones his mother wears; she appears for a few moments, then quickly disappears from his view. And that, we are told, is all he will be able to know for years. His mother has retained her former image of majesty in his eyes, but superimposed on that old image is the new one of sexuality and vulgarity. And the conflict of the two images remains unresolved for Agostino. Thus he, like Michele in *Gli indifferenti* is in the painful position of being only an observer, impotent and incapable of acting, unable to end his suffering.

The story of Luca in *La disubbidienza* is more flawed than that of Agostino. Moravia has crammed it with heavy symbols, obvious psychological images, and obtrusive explanations of Luca's behavior. At times, the novel reads more like a treatise on adolescent psychopathology or an analysis of the evolution of existential nausea than a piece of fiction. And yet, there are many fine scenes and pages, and Moravia excels in painting the portrait of an unhappy adolescent who literally makes himself sick.

La disubbidienza (literally, Disobedience) begins with a return from a summer at the sea, just at the point where *Agostino* ends. Luca is fifteen years old, and, we are told, has recently grown in a spurt to the height of a man. He is clumsy and feels as if his body were undermining him and as if the entire world were hostile to him. The novel is a study of this enmity that Luca feels between himself and reality—an antagonism which leads to his rebellion against individual things first, then against his family and his environment, and finally against himself. After carrying rebellion as far as it can go, there is nothing left for him to do but to die, like an animal unadapted to life, and he does indeed almost die during a serious illness. However, he is ritualistically resurrected by a nurse who carefully draws him back to life and then initiates him into the mysteries of sex. It is through this initiation, portrayed in religious symbols, that Luca is definitively reconciled to life and enters into a new relationship with reality. Henceforth, all things will have meaning for him.

The action of the story covers an approximately six-month period, beginning in early autumn with the return from vacation, lasting through the winter when Luca's illness occurs, and ending with his resurrection in early spring. At the beginning of the novel we are told that Luca has been subject to sudden rages for some time. One incident in particular has confirmed for him the clear enmity that had grown up between himself and reality: he got a severe shock one day while repairing a fuse and wept disconsolately in his mother's arms, feeling with bitterness that she could no longer protect him as she once had. An even more important incident is the train ride home from the sea resort and Luca's sudden rage when his parents decide, without asking him, to have sandwiches for lunch in their compartment instead of going to eat in the dining car. Disappointed, enraged, and feeling as though he were being treated like an object, Luca chokes down his lunch and then becomes nauseated. He feels for the first time that he is outside of everything, that he does not belong. When he and his parents get off the train, Luca vomits against the locomotive. With an explicitness that is unnecessary, that indeed lessens the dramatic impact of the scene, Moravia explains that Luca's vomiting is an act of revenge against the train for bringing him back to the city and to school.

Back at home, Luca's conscious rebellion begins slowly. First there is a state of torpor and a constant desire to sleep. Next he is shown as cutting himself off from the other boys, and becoming an observer of their activities as well as an observer of himself in his various daily situations. He then undertakes to rebel against everyone in his world: parents, teachers, and friends. The idea of disobedience pleases him, and it soon becomes a game to disobey methodically everyone and everything.

Luca had begun to cease loving his parents some time before, although he can't remember exactly when. There had been a time when he had felt for them "a kind of reverence that was almost religious, when they seemed to him to be almost perfect."[5] Then, as in the case of Agostino, there was a period of a fall from paradise, during which the image of his parents changed in Luca's eyes until he finally saw them as "degraded to an inferior level . . . With their degradation to the state of insignificant objects, the warmth that once infused his life had disappeared . . . Instinctively he felt that his revolt against the world must have begun at the time when that warmth started to diminish."[6]

The definitive rupture with his parents and with his old happy life occurs in an unforgettable scene when Luca affectionately but impetuously enters his parents' bedroom one night. The room is lighted, the bed with its covers turned back is empty, and Luca's father in pyjamas and his mother in a transparent nightgown are standing next to the bed. Unnoticed by them, Luca observes his parents placing bank notes and industrial bonds into a safe hidden behind a picture—a reproduction of a Madonna by Raphael, the very picture that Luca as a child was made to kneel in front of while saying his prayers to the Virgin. Troubled afterwards by the scene he has witnessed, by the idea of a safe hidden behind the picture and his seminude parents standing before it with their arms full of money, Luca mentally asks his parents this bitter question: "Why did you make me kneel down to pray in front of your money for all those years?"[7] Thus money and property are satirically linked by Moravia to the religion of the middle class; and sex forms part of that bond, although its role is still somewhat vague in this novel.

Luca's rupture with life begins soon after the above incident with his parents. First he gives away his "sacred" property, including his once dearly loved collections of puppets, stamps, sports equipment, and books, all of which have become symbols of ties to his old, hateful life. Finally he gets rid of all his money, also considered "sacred" in his milieu, by burying it in a hidden corner of a park where he once imagined a young murder victim to have been buried.

The slow decline toward death begins for Luca in December, just after the burial of the money. During this period, he experiences his first stirrings of sexual awakening with a governess who touches and kisses him; but he feels only disgust, especially at the kiss, for the governess' tongue seems to him to be a large snail entering his mouth (a variation of Moravia's frequent snake symbol). When he eventually decides to accept her invitation to visit her at home, she is too ill to receive him, and dies soon afterwards. Luca's own almost fatal illness ensues. He is sick for three months, wanting to die and certain that he is about to die. Chapter thirteen describes in detail his long period of delirium. An orgy of grotesque phallic animals and plants, interspersed with insects and strange little men who pop out of bottles, it is set against a background of female sexual images such as a pregnant abdomen, the governess' snail-like tongue, and a nude woman. One day Luca awakens to find before him a woman who is not an hallucination—the nurse who gently leads him back to life and to the desire to live. With his return to life, Luca begins to love the nurse and the world around him.

When he is well enough, the nurse initiates him into the sexual act in a simple, natural manner. Massively formed, she is a fertility goddess figure whose every gesture is majestic. At the moment of their sexual union Luca feels as if he is being led into a mysterious cave that is dedicated to a rite, and he wonders if the nurse might not be a goddess. Consummation is described as a series of tremors of veneration. The nurse, portrayed as a life-giving goddess, thus contrasts sharply with the death-giving governess, representing the two dimensions of sexual experience.

A train ride brings the action to a close, just as a train ride marked its beginning. It is now March, and Luca is being taken to a sanatorium in Switzerland where he will remain until his health is fully restored. Thinking back over his experiences, he remembers his moment of initiation when he had felt a strong desire to enter completely into the belly of the woman and to curl up there in the warm darkness. He recognizes that desire is the essence of life—to be buried in flesh and to feel the darkness. Although his first sight of the Alps from the train window is a disappointment, he is suddenly flooded with joy at the view of a snow-capped mountain peak illuminated by the early morning sunshine. The train passes through a misty area, and "then, with another whistle, it emerged into the light of day."[8] With those words, so laden with symbolic meaning, the novel ends.

Luca has gone through the long, unhappy time predicted for Agostino before an adolescent can understand love and become a man. Having learned about sex in the natural way that Agostino had so ardently desired in his dream of earthly paradise, Luca is fully reconciled with life as it is. Luca's nurse was described as being in her "autumn years," but Luca, in his springtime, doesn't mind at all that life has come to him in "autumn garb."[9] This felicitous image brings the novel full circle: the autumn that almost brought death to Luca now brings him life. For, of course, autumn paves the way to winter, but also to spring.

5

*Two
of Moravia's
Women*

As a result of his wartime experiences, Moravia focused his attention on the lower classes. His first book with a lower-class protagonist was *La romana* (*Woman of Rome*), published in 1948, which was also his first extended first-person narrative, and his first novel with a woman as a protagonist. *La ciociara* (*Two Women*), while not published until 1957, belongs to this period of inspiration, for it was conceived and begun in 1944, although abandoned after a few pages. Both of these novels won high critical acclaim, but as usual, the praise was tempered with reservations.

The heroine of each novel has distinct advantages over many of Moravia's characters: she engages the reader's sympathy immediately, is a multi-dimensional figure instead of a one-dimensional puppet, and gives the impression of being a living human being rather than a case history from some psychological or social treatise. Unfortunately, however, the same cannot be said of the characters who are part of her story.

In both *La romana* and *La ciociara* Moravia used the pattern of Greek tragedy—this time a tragedy with a happy ending—which he had been slowly developing since his first novel. A kind of prologue describes the happy times soon to be ended; a fall from happiness occurs, a crisis and conflict ensue, and a *deus ex machina* solution follows; both stories end with a final image of rebirth. These two works also bear witness to a clear development in Moravia's ideas; from the studies of indifference, ambition and social masquerade, he had proceeded to the portrayals of the adolescent's awakening to the world and his initiation into a sexual experience, to the experiences of a young woman and then an older woman who painfully arrive at an understanding of the meaning

of life. *La romana* and *La ciociara* also show the evolution of a soul, from its indifferent ego-centered state,
to a feeling of genuine compassion for other people.
And finally, with the introduction of lower-class figures as main characters, Moravia was able to develop a
panoramic portrayal of Italian society as he saw it.

La romana was the first novel to win international readership for Moravia. Translated into English in 1949, it no doubt benefited from GI nostalgia
for Italy and had popular appeal as a story about "a
prostitute with a heart of gold." It is of course much
more than that. For a serious reader it is the story of
the evolution of consciousness in a young woman who
slowly comes to terms with herself and with the reality
of her world. Adriana tells the story of her life, beginning at age sixteen, as a series of past events that for
the reader have all the immediacy of present occurrences.

One of Moravia's longer novels, *La romana* is divided into two approximately equal parts: the first
part concerns Adriana's life from age sixteen to
twenty-one, and the second covers a few months of her
life at age twenty-one. Because of her mother's ambitions for her, the beautiful Adriana became a painter's model at sixteen, although all she wanted to do
was to get married and have a family. Naive and unconsciously sensual, she was an easy prey for Gino, a
chauffeur who seduced her with promises of marriage.
Adriana discovers some time afterwards that he is already married and, since her hopes and dreams are
shattered, she decides to become a prostitute because
she "likes love and money and the things that money
can buy."[1] Her experiences as a streetwalker hasten
the development of her consciousness, and we see her

struggling to come to terms with herself at the end of part one.

In part two, Adriana shares the center of attention with Mino (Giacomo), a middle-class student she has fallen in love with, but who does not reciprocate her love. She feels shame at her way of life for the first time and tries to change in order to become worthy of Mino. This leads her to a crisis of authenticity which she eventually resolves. Mino, however, is not able to resolve his crisis of authenticity, for he is the typical existential man of "bad faith." An idealist who cannot fully believe in his ideals, he suffers from his awareness of his situation. After ignobly betraying his communist comrades to the police he can no longer live with himself and commits suicide.

Mino's death is the last episode in an orgy of destruction that occurs toward the end of the novel: two of Adriana's other lovers—the sadomasochist police official, Astarita, and the crazed murderer, Sonzogno—die violent deaths just before Mino does. Adriana herself had been tempted by suicide during her crisis (she had thought of drowning herself in the sea), but by the end of the novel, despite the tragedy of Mino's loss, she has great desire to live. At that point she is pregnant with the child of Sonzogno, a child, as she puts it, to be born of a murderer and a prostitute. However, she can see happiness in the future for herself and the child because hers is a happy temperament, and she understands that it is her destiny to be happy.

Although the meaning of *La romana* is clear enough (Moravia even gives a running commentary throughout the novel), the author succumbed to the temptation to act as his own critic and published an article in 1947 entitled "Perché ho scritto *La romana*"

(Why I Wrote *The Woman of Rome*). It is evident, however, without his explanations, that a key to the meaning of the novel is to be found at the end of part one, where Adriana's first existential crises are described. At moments when she is alone, she suddenly becomes aware of the absurdity of human life and sees herself as suspended in nothingness. After reaching a point of desperation, she drifts into a nonthinking state and eventually finds that she is the same Adriana as before. Because she understands that such a reduction of life to a point of anguish must happen to everyone at least once a day, she feels that "all people, without exception, are worthy of compassion if only because they are alive."[2]

Later, Adriana learns a corollary to that first discovery: "I knew deep down that no one was guilty and that everything was as it should be, even if everything was unbearable; and that if one really insisted on seeing guilt and innocence, then everyone was innocent and guilty at the same time."[3] And finally, when she gives up the struggle against what appears to be her destiny, Adriana comes to the understanding that one can only be happy when one accepts oneself, for she believes that a person's temperament is his destiny. Her own strength lies not in trying to be what she is not, but in accepting what she is—a prostitute.

Two poignant images representing the kind of happiness Adriana desired but never attained are the amusement park and the modest little house where one day she saw through a window a family sitting down to dinner. Adriana was never able to go to the nearby amusement park as a child or adolescent. For her it symbolized the happy world from which she was excluded: "That's probably why all my life I've had a kind of suspicion of being excluded from the joyful, sparkling world of happiness—a suspicion that I can't manage to free myself from even when I'm certain that I am happy."[4] On the night Adriana meets Mino, the two images of unattainable happiness are joined. She had not passed by the amusement park since she was a girl, when she and her mother peered through the gates to enjoy the lights and music. Now when she sees it with Mino, it is dreary and lifeless under the dim street lights and winter skies. Nearby is the little house she had so admired, but now it looks run down and uninhabited. Adriana is not destined for that kind of simple happiness, and it is her love for Mino which will prove it to her.

From the very beginning of the novel, Adriana is identified with the Greek demi-divinity Danae. The first painter for whom she poses shows her a reproduction of a painting of Danae and tells her that her beauty is of the same type. Danae is an appropriate image for Adriana when one remembers how the young girl was impregnated by Zeus (who came to her in the form of a golden rain), and bore an heroic son, Perseus, who would behead the Medusa. Adriana (who takes money for love) will also be possessed by an overwhelming force of nature. Once she knows she is pregnant, she feels sure that her child will be favored by fortune, and will be able to conquer the monster of sadness that so plagued her own life.

But Adriana also incarnates a kind of dualism: on the one hand, she is endowed with ample proportions and an earth-goddess appearance; on the other, she possesses a cogitating mind. Paradoxically, it is this mind-body dualism which permits her a kind of reliable happiness that she recognizes as part of her destiny. After learning of the false Gino's trickery and after wanting to die, she explains that she could not die because her body "continued to live its own life, without regard for her wishes."[5]

A number of themes and images from earlier works are given more explicit treatment in this novel.[6] The sensual pleasure Adriana experiences (1) from accepting money for sexual services, (2) from stealing, and (3) from giving money to Mino, is described many times, although never satisfactorily explained. Light and dark images are often used, but the explanation of these is given by Adriana herself. It is of course no surprise to the reader that light is identified with joy and happiness, and darkness with anguish and death. What is surprising is that Moravia felt the need to give us such superfluous explanations of common imagery, while leaving the meaning of his personal imagery somewhat vague.

Adriana's profession provides Moravia with an opportunity to create portraits of various social types who become her lovers: the petty trickster, the sado-masochistic police official who indulges in sexual perversions, the egotistical traveling businessman, the brutish lower-class muscleman and murderer, and the "impotent intellectual" student who is a would-be revolutionary. In addition to the portraits of lovers, two of the most interesting sketches of minor characters are those of Adriana's prostitute friend, Gisella, who likes to pretend she is a rich respectable lady, and Adriana's mother who, after a life of poverty and hard work, literally turns to fat in her leisure once Adriana starts bringing in money.

But the street scenes are perhaps the best feature of the novel. Adriana loves the crowded streets of Rome and takes us out with her into them. There is a memorable afternoon of window shopping when Adriana and her mother meticulously examine all the

store windows along the Via Nazionale. It is in those
passages in which Adriana is jostled by rush-hour
crowds that the novel comes fully alive.

La ciociara was translated into English as *Two
Women*, but the Italian title refers to a woman from
the region of Ciociaria, the mountainous area of the
Abruzzi just south of Rome. The novel is the story of
the experiences of a woman named Cesira who was
forced to take refuge during the war in the mountains
of her native region, Ciociaria. If it has all the ear-
marks of a lived experience, it is because like his protagonists Moravia himself lived for many months in
little animal huts on the mountain side, suffering as
they suffered. Driven from Rome by threats from the
fascist government, Moravia tried to reach the free
zone of Naples but was able to get no farther than the
mountains of the Abruzzi. Because the novel narrates
many of Moravia's own experiences, critics have the-
orized that he used a female narrator in order to be
able to express emotions which a male would be reticent to admit. But that, of course, remains pure specu-
lation; Moravia had, after all, already used a female
narrator in *La romana*.

Cesira begins her story by recounting how as a
young woman she had left Ciociaria and gone to
Rome to marry an older man who owned a grocery
store. All her pleasure in life at that time came from
keeping up her house and working in the store. When
her only child, Rosetta, was born, all her affection
centered on her daughter. Cesira was soon a widow
and continued happily to run the store, for her passion lay in making money. She noticed nothing about
the war or the political events of her troubled times;
even the fall of Mussolini in 1943 did not draw her

attention, for at that moment she was preoccupied with a prosciutto deal. However, the time comes when she is forced to take note of what is happening, for she is soon compelled to flee from war-stricken Rome with her daughter.

After many difficulties, Cesira and Rosetta manage to reach a small mountain village where several other refugees have taken shelter in animal huts. She and Rosetta rent one of the huts to live in while they wait for the war to end. They wait as the seasons change from autumn to winter to spring, and see life become progressively harder and food scarcer until the situation of peasants and refugees alike is desperate. One of the other refugees, a student named Michele, becomes a special friend of Cesira. Although Michele at age twenty-five has not yet "lived," this middle-class intellectual is not the typical Moravian impotent intellectual (and is very different from his namesake in *Gli indifferenti*). He is a strong personality who commands respect from everyone, who stands up for his beliefs and who is the only one with any understanding of what is going on in Italy and in the world. His friendship is Cesira's salvation. However, one day he is taken away by German soldiers to serve as their guide through the mountains, and is killed while trying to defend a peasant from the brutality of one of the soldiers.

Having suffered and endured a great deal, Cesira and Rosetta leave the mountains at the time of the liberation; but the worst for them is yet to come. Rosetta, described throughout the novel as a perfect angel, a girl of seventeen who is deeply religious, compassionate, and sensitive, is raped by liberating Moroccans in front of the statue of the Virgin in a small village church. Rosetta's character subsequently

changes completely, as Cesira puts it, "from white to
black." She turns into a kind of nymphomaniac who is
hardened against everything and interested only in
sensual pleasure. Her daughter now "dead" for her,
Cesira falls into despair, having lost everything that
was dear to her. She is about to commit suicide, but is
saved by a dream-vision and begins to be reconciled to
life once again. Rosetta, too, returns to life (after experiencing an emotional shock), and the novel concludes in early summer with the end of the war and
the resurrections of Cesira and Rosetta.

The central theme of *La ciociara* is the Biblical
story of Lazarus. Michele reads it one evening to the
peasants of the little mountain village, but they neither understand it nor have any interest in it. He
becomes disappointed with them and tells them:
"Each one of you is Lazarus . . . and in reading the
story of Lazarus I was referring to you, to all of you . . .
in fact, to all of us . . . You are all dead, we are dead
and believe that we are alive . . . only when we realize
that we are dead . . . only then will we begin little by
little to come alive."[7] And that is precisely what happens to Cesira.

Cesira's dream crisis is the point at which she
becomes aware of being dead, and it is an excellent
portrayal of the merging of dream, consciousness,
thought, and sensory perception. (Moravia uses a similar sequence as a *deus ex machina* in *Il disprezzo*.)
Cesira's desperation leads her to decide that she no
longer wishes to live in a world where good people are
beaten down and only the delinquents prosper. At the
very moment she is about to hang herself, Michele
appears in the doorway (Cesira had learned that very
day that he had been killed) and with a gesture dis-
suades her from her desperate attempt. He talks to

her, but she can't hear what he is saying, and in her struggle to understand him she awakens. She recognizes that what she experienced was a miracle, but a half miracle only, for she couldn't hear Michele when he tried to tell her why life was preferable to death. She will therefore continue to live, but believes she will never know why.

However, the other half of the miracle does occur shortly thereafter when Rosetta's lover, Rosario, is gunned down by highway robbers as he is driving the two women back to Rome. The robbers are forced to flee when another car approaches, and all Cesira can think of is getting the money Rosario had in his pocket. Once she has the money in hand, she is afraid that Rosario might not be dead after all. Rosetta, meanwhile, expresses no emotion whatsoever. As mother and daughter ride back to Rome with a truck driver (who stopped for them only because Rosario's body was blocking the road), Cesira comes to the horrible realization that they have all been acting inhumanly: "So, there was no pity, no feeling, no human sympathy; a man died, and other people remained indifferent, each for his own reasons."[8] That kind of inhumanness might well continue long after the war, she feels.

But suddenly Rosetta, who has shown no emotion at all up to this point, begins to sing, and while she sings, tears run down her cheeks. Cesira vows to give the money she stole from Rosario's body to his mother, and realizes that she and Rosetta are saved, remarking that without Rosetta's grief, a thief and a prostitute would have returned to Rome. She now fully understands the meaning of the Lazarus story and why Michele said that it applied to all of them, and she gives us a complete explanation: "For some time Rosetta and I had also been dead—dead to the pity that we owe to others and to ourselves. But grief had saved us at the last moment . . . Because of grief we had finally emerged from the war which had entombed us in indifference and in evil, and had now begun to take up our life again."⁹

A sizeable portion of the novel is devoted to reflections on the social conditions in Italy at that time. Moravia continually points to the class system as the root of Italy's social ills, and he presents the bourgeoisie as oppressors of their country. Ironically, his most biting criticism of Italy is put in the mouth of a German lieutenant, who points out that his people would be ashamed to see their peasants live as miserably as the Italian peasants. An Italian lawyer answers him: "It is they who want to live like that. You don't know them."¹⁰ The German replies that it is not the peasants who want to live like that, but the middle-class property owners who force them to.

Some of the finest pages of *La ciociara* are those devoted to descriptions of the living conditions of the peasants and refugees in impoverished mountain villages. There are also excellent portrayals of German and Italian soldiers, and there is an unforgettable description of the American liberation army that rolls toward Rome with its gum-chewing soldiers lounging in bored indifference on tanks and trucks. In a magnificent scene, a huge, imposing cannon is pictured shaking the earth with its thunder, while one of those bored, gum-chewing soldiers casually shoves shells into it. There are also the wonderfully perceptive passages in which Moravia describes American soldiers throwing candy and cigarettes to scrambling Italians. The soldiers only do it because they think the Italians expect it, and the Italians only pretend to want what the soldiers throw because they think the Americans expect it. And there are the Italian-American soldiers, more cruel than the others, because they must try to pretend to stature before the war-battered Italians, to hide the fact that they who left Italy as nothing are nothing in America.

In many respects *La ciociara* is a very good book; many passages vividly convey the ring of true experience. However, it suffers from some of the same imperfections that mar *La romana*. Moravia too often assumes the task of critic of his own work within the work itself. The authenticity of the narrators—both seem far too sophisticated and analytical to be the lower-class personages they represent—has been questioned by many readers. Furthermore, Moravia's simplistic ideas about women detract from the credibility of his stories. Rosetta's transformation into a nymphomaniac after she is raped is scarcely believable as Moravia presents it. The portrayal of Cesira as being uninterested in sex because her passions go into making money is unconvincing. And Adriana, who becomes a happy prostitute because it is in her nature to be a prostitute and to be happy, because she "likes love and money and the things that money can buy," is certainly nothing but a male author's dream projection. But even these faults can be overlooked far more easily than the continual intrusions of explanations which often destroy the atmosphere and perhaps cause many of the ideas of both novels to appear more simplistic than they are.

6

*Three Postwar
Novels*

L'amore coniugale (Conjugal Love) marked a new direction in Moravia's novels, one that was to dominate his fiction. With this brief novel Moravia began using the artist as his main character, and, as subject matter, the double theme of artistic creation and the relationship of a couple. Sexuality is the dark force that binds together the elements of *L'amore coniugale* and most of the novels that follow it. With the exception of *La ciociara* in 1957, the protagonists of these later novels are male, middle-class artist-lovers who, for one reason or another, are unable to create as they had hoped. At the same time, they are caught up in insoluble difficulties with a woman, and this destroys "the contact with reality" they had previously established through sexuality. An existential crisis follows, and then a new contact is established with the world.

Although *Il conformista* falls outside the direct line of novelistic development involving the first-person artist-narrator, the story itself emphasizes the same kind of existential crisis of authenticity which is linked to a crisis of sexuality. And the general form of that novel is the same as that of *L'amore coniugale* and *Il disprezzo*: prologue, action leading to an inescapable conflict, a *deus ex machina* solution, and an epilogue.

L'amore coniugale was first published in 1949 in a volume with seven short stories that include some of Moravia's finest. This bitter-sweet novella tells the story of a man named Silvio Baldeschi who writes a novella entitled *L'amore coniugale*. Silvio's prologue is a description of his wife, Leda, and of his love for her. She is of a statuesque beauty, like that of a classic goddess, with blond hair, blue eyes and a noble nose. To Silvio this beauty is mysterious and elusive *(in-afferrabile)* and he emphasizes that he feels he can never fully possess Leda. One particularly mysterious aspect of her beauty is the manner in which it is sometimes transformed into ugliness. Silvio notes that whenever Leda's face is contorted in a particular grimace, her whole appearance changes from classic purity to sensuality and obscenity. But it is not until the end of the story that Silvio gains some insight into the mystery of Leda's grimace, which expresses fear, anguish, repulsion, and at the same time, desire.

The narration begins shortly after their marriage, when Silvio and Leda go to their country villa in Tuscany for the summer. There Silvio hopes that Leda will function as his Muse, for he wants to use their own story as the basis for a book about marriage. Unable to write as he had hoped, Silvio comes to the singular conclusion that his inspiration is inhibited by his indulgence in sexual relations with his wife, and that his vital force and creative energy are being drained away in their nights of love. Therefore he decides that he must abstain from sex until his book is finished.[1] Suddenly able to write with ease and rapidity, Silvio reaches the pinnacle of happiness and feels sure that he is producing a chef d'oeuvre.

So enamoured of his work is he that he loses interest in everything else, including his wife. However, someone else develops a keen interest in her—Silvio's Sicilian barber, Antonio, who comes to shave him every day. Silvio is blind to Antonio's intentions and to his wife's struggle with her own instincts. He even selfishly refuses to dismiss the barber when Leda begs him to do so.

After finishing his book, Silvio rereads it and discovers that it is a failure because it is totally false. Extremely disappointed in himself, he writes a critique of the book, then looks for Leda to comfort him.

She, however, is not in bed asleep as he had thought, and when he goes outside to search for her, he is just in time to witness a moonlight romp of Antonio and Leda around the haystacks, and to catch a glimpse of Leda's grimace when she finally submits to the barber.

Silvio considers suicide, but then comes to a kind of peace with himself when he realizes that the scene he witnessed had nothing to do with the love between Leda and himself, and that Leda's actions merely represented a fall into temptation. And so, at the end, he and Leda resume a normal conjugal relationship. Silvio has come to a greater understanding of himself through his experiences, although he realizes he still has much to learn. Leda suggests that he take up the novel again sometime in the future when he has learned more about both of them, for she feels that Silvio's book is a failure because he didn't know either of them well enough. The novel we have is apparently Silvio's rewritten version.

The mythological-religious apparatus of this story provides the major symbolism found within it; and as usual the meanings are perfectly transparent because of their explicit presentation. Leda's name is appropriate when one remembers the beauty and sensuality of the mythological Leda who was seduced by Zeus in the form of a swan. Antonio is no god, but his amorous exploits are notorious in the village. The fact that he is a barber (the cutting of hair often symbolizes deprivation of strength and virility, as in the case of Samson) makes him an appropriate rival for Silvio. It is in the pagan fertility dance of Antonio and Leda, observed by Silvio, that all the symbolic elements come together. The haystacks which had reminded Silvio of dolmens and the pagan rites of the Druids when he walked near them with Leda the night before are now ironically the site of his wife's infidelity. Silvio understands the meaning of Leda's grimace for the first time when he sees it on her face as she is embraced by Antonio. He will see it again the following day on a stone carved face of a sinner tempted by the devil in an ancient country church.

If Leda in her child-adult lasciviousness is the prototype of a Moravian female, Silvio is the prototype of the middle-class intellectual hero who can comprehend but not act, and who is forced to yield to a virile, strong-arm character. But unlike many of Moravia's intellectuals, Silvio is able to come to terms with his situation and thus avoids self-destruction and saves his relationship with his wife.

In the many echoes of other authors in *L'amore coniugale* (especially Proust, Pirandello, and Svevo), we can see Moravia, the man of letters, playing the role of a man of letters. And in the critique of his own novella by Silvio, we can see Moravia, the critic, gently mocking Moravia, the writer. *L'amore coniugale* is a playful treatment of the serious twentieth-century themes of the artist struggling to create and of the existential consciousness of absurdity. It is also a light-hearted treatment of the usually bleak Moravian theme of a moment of crisis in the relationship of a couple.

Il disprezzo (*A Ghost at Noon*), 1954, is as serious in tone as *L'amore coniugale* is playful, although in many other respects the two works are remarkably similar. Like Silvio, the narrator of *Il disprezzo*, Molteni, is an *artiste manqué* who also fails to understand his wife and what she expects of him until it is too late. And like Leda, Emilia is described as being graceful, majestic, and mysterious. But Molteni's mis-

understanding of his wife is more serious than that of
Silvio. Emilia is not only tempted into another man's
arms, she is thrust into them by her husband—or so it
seems to her.

In a brief prologue, Molteni, who works as a
movie script writer, tells us about his two years of
marital bliss with Emilia which came to an abrupt
end when she suddenly ceased loving him for no apparent reason. The story itself begins with a flashback
to the incident which revealed a perceptible change in
Emilia's behavior—the first time she is forced to be
alone with Molteni's boss, Battista, the movie producer.

The body of the novel concerns Molteni's attempts to discover why his wife no longer loves him as
she once did. Molteni's drama of anguish develops
slowly, first in Rome, in the new apartment which he
buys to please Emilia and which is located on a new
street in a new neighborhood, and later in Battista's
seaside house in Capri under the hot June sun. The
action consists of a series of dialogues during which
Molteni tries first of all to win back Emilia, and then
merely to find out from her why she no longer loves
him.

At first Molteni feels only an obscure sense of
anguish at the loss of Emilia's love. He is temporarily
sidetracked when he discovers a new sensuality in her
after she demands that he make love to her on the
bare floor of their new apartment (Moravia presents
Emilia's action as something akin to an animal's de-
fining of its territory). However, Emilia soon thereafter refuses to sleep with him, then to make love with
him, and finally she does everything possible to avoid
being in his presence.

After many long talks, Emilia concedes that she

no longer loves Molteni, although she refuses to say why. Finally, exasperated by his questioning, she admits: "I despise you, and you make me sick every time you touch me."[2] Molteni's suffering, his constant searching for light (he uses the word continually to describe his quest for understanding) and his desire to be able to see are motifs of a tragic hero who struggles in an inescapable conflict, blind to his grave error. What makes him suffer most is that he can find no reason for Emilia's contempt. It is not until his last talk with her that Molteni is able to obtain even a partial explanation from her. She tells him flatly: "You're not a man and you don't act like a man."[3] He doesn't understand immediately, but begins to later when he realizes that for her Battista is apparently the image of a man. Molteni had often been struck by her look of repugnance and perplexity when she was forced to confront Battista, but during their stay in Capri her eyes had also betrayed a look of admiration for the movie producer.

Battista is one of Moravia's ugly, strong and virile characters. Short-legged and monkey-faced, he is the vulgar film magnate who controls Molteni's economic life and who presses his attentions on Emilia until she finally yields to him. Molteni not only fails to recognize Battista's intentions, but he even fails to respond to Emilia's protestations whenever she is forced into Battista's presence. After her last talk with Molteni, Emilia agrees to return to Rome with Battista, despite her dislike of him; she apparently does so to escape from Molteni. But she is never to reach Rome alive. Battista, true to form, is speeding along the highway when he is forced to stop suddenly; Emilia dies of a broken neck.

At the moment of Emilia's strange death, she appears to Molteni on the beach at Capri and declares her love to him. The time is noon, whence the very un-Moravian, sensationalistic English title of the novel, *A Ghost at Noon* (a literal translation of *Il disprezzo* would be Contempt). But Molteni cannot be sure if it was Emilia's ghost he saw, or if it was merely an hallucination born of wishful thinking. Thus nothing is solved for him by her death because her feelings about him remain as mysterious as before.

A secondary theme in the novel concerns Molteni's desire to be a playwright and his frustrating, unsatisfying work as a movie script writer. Desperately in need of money to meet the payments on the new apartment, the twenty-seven-year-old Molteni has sacrificed his talents to the movie industry. In the course of the novel, he agrees reluctantly to work on a screen adaptation of Homer's *Odyssey*. The movie is to be directed by a German named Rheingold, whose Freudian interpretation of the relationship between Odysseus and Penelope is so outrageous that Molteni, despite his financial straits, finally refuses to work on the script.

Rheingold's interpretation, however, is quite useful when applied to Molteni and Emilia; furthermore it serves to elevate the novel's theme of an unfortunate misunderstanding between man and wife to the more universal plane of tragic misunderstanding between male and female, civilized man and primitive woman. Molteni himself recognizes its plausibility when applied to his own situation. He is the civilized man who is seen as despicable by the primitive woman, Emilia, because he doesn't react as she expects him to. He remains impassive in front of Battista who appears to be courting his wife, and although Emilia remains faithful to him (as did Penelope to Odysseus), she can no longer respect him. The problem is that Molteni cannot fully accept this as an explanation of what has happened in his situation because he cannot know whether or not it is the true one. Emilia will not, or perhaps cannot, express what she feels about him.

In Capri, as Molteni sees his relationship deteriorate irremediably, he is strongly tempted to commit suicide. This temptation is, by his own admission, a desire to reacquire purity through drowning in the sea,[4] and to win back Emilia by regaining the paradise lost where happiness had been possible. Ironically, it is Emilia who dies, thus liberating herself from the unhappy situation, and Molteni who lives to suffer because he cannot be sure whether Emilia loved him at the end, as his vision implied. He is thus condemned to continue his search for assurance that Emilia loved and understood him at the end of her life and did not really feel the contempt for him that she seemed to show. But his future is poisoned by the same ambiguities, doubts and anxieties that had ruined his past. Molteni's image of himself will always be tied to Emilia.

The novel we have is the story Molteni wrote in hopes of liberating himself and of finding Emilia once again. We see that this attempt, like his others, is doomed to failure. Just as the *deus ex machina* of Emilia's death and appearance to him in a vision solved nothing and untied no tragic knots, Molteni has not regained Emilia through his book, for in it he can only recount his loss. Paradise is thus not regained, but hell is rendered more painful.

Il conformista (*The Conformist*), 1951, was written and published between *L'amore coniugale* and *Il disprezzo*. It concerns the problems of an individual in his society rather than the difficulties in the relationship of a couple. For many readers, *Il conformista* is Moravia's least successful novel. It certainly is his least convincing story, and Marcello, the protagonist, is the most unbelievable and distasteful character he has created: The novel, which has heavy Manichean overtones, also has the disadvantage of serving as a vehicle for political and social criticism, and as such is often unpleasantly moralistic in tone. Through the study of the psychopathological perversion of the individual who is seen as corrupt early in his childhood, Moravia exposes the perversions of a society corrupted by fascism. Marcello inherited the seeds of corruption from his psychotic father and was permitted to indulge his worst instincts; similarly, Italian society had deep within it the seeds of fascism and permitted its own worst instincts to develop. At the end of the novel, Marcello and fascism die together, destroyed by the avenging forces of the Allies.

A long novel which spans a period of some twenty-five to thirty years, it is divided into four main sections: a prologue of some eighty pages, parts one and two of about 270 pages forming the body of the novel, and a fifty-page epilogue. The prologue concerns Marcello's life as a child up to age thirteen. From his earliest childhood he had had a taste for death and destruction, although at the same time he strongly desired order and normalcy. Three important incidents during this period marked him for the rest of his life: his killing of a cat, his father's voodoo act against Marcello and his mother, and Marcello's shooting of a man.

With his taste for death and destruction, Marcello amused himself as a child by slashing off the heads of flowers and lizards. One day he pretends to be killing his playmate, Robert, and shoots a stone from his slingshot into the bushes, inadvertently killing a cat. He tells the servants that it was his father who killed the cat, whereupon one of them predicts that a person starts by killing a cat, and ends up by killing a man. Marcello thereafter lives with the burden of impending tragedy, constantly trying to keep his frightening instincts in check. His father's act of madness in punching out the eyes in a photograph of Marcello and his mother also disturbs the young boy. Moravia, never content to be only suggestive, gives us a full explanation of the meaning of this for Marcello; it is a curse that reaffirms the fate he is trying to escape. Both the prediction of the servant and the curse of the father are carried out when Marcello, as a thirteen-year-old, is lured into a relationship with Lino, a defrocked priest. Lino attempts to seduce Marcello, and the boy shoots him. The prologue ends with Marcello's flight from Lino's room.

It is seventeen years later and Marcello is thirty when the story begins again. Parts one and two recount Marcello's life as a secret agent for the fascist government, his courtship and marriage to a "normal" middle-class girl, and his constant struggle to seem normal and to be normal. To that end he consciously conforms to what he identifies as normalcy in his society, and has therefore thrown his lot in with fascism. On orders from the fascist government, Marcello is forced to kill again, this time one of his former professors. The murder intensifies the feeling of obscure impending tragedy which had begun early in his life. He realizes that if fascism fails, he will be nothing but a miserable assassin. Soon after this murder, Marcello learns that he has killed unnecessarily: an order

had been sent out cancelling the mission, but it
reached him too late.

In the epilogue we see Marcello with his wife and
six-year-old daughter living in a new apartment on a
new street (such a setting is always indicative of an
empty life in Moravia's works). Marcello's career has
been very successful, but on the day we meet him
again, the fascist government has just fallen, and Marcello realizes that he has bet on the wrong horse. He
cannot remedy the situation because his image of self
and of normalcy is bound to fascism: to change would
be to annihilate the self he has so painfully moulded
and cultivated. But a *deus ex machina* unties the
tragic knot for Marcello. That night he meets up with
Lino, the defrocked priest he thought he had killed.
When he accuses Lino of having ruined his life by
corrupting his innocence, Lino tells him that everyone
loses his innocence, that it is a normal event of life. In
a kind of epiphany, Marcello thus understands for the
first time what normalcy is—an attempt to mitigate
the loss of one's innocence. He also sees that he has
been on the wrong road for twenty years, and feels
that now he is free.

As Marcello is fleeing from Rome toward his new
life and new freedom, he and his wife and child are
killed when their car is strafed by aircraft fire. This
final scene resembles nothing so much as an act of
divine vengeance that is scourging Italy with fire in
order to destroy the evil which had tumefied within
her. Moravia shows us here that a man for whom
normalcy is conformity that hides perversion does not
deserve to live; similarly, fascism, which was the epi-
tome of perversion and conformity, did not deserve to
survive.

Il conformista goes even further into the psychopathological than did Moravia's *La disubbidienza*. Far from being an effective allegory of the evil of fascism, it appears to be a case study of a mentally disturbed individual so unbelievable that it reveals little about human tendencies or the human condition. The social criticism is thus lost, as is the tragic dimension.

7

*Two Novels
of the Sixties*

Moravia's two novels of the sixties both deal specifically—almost philosophically and scientifically—with the problem of reality and a man's relationship or nonrelationship with it.[1] While the problem in both novels is the same, each narrator states his case in slightly different terms: for Dino of *La noia* (*The Empty Canvas*), 1960, boredom is the manifestation of loss of contact with reality, whereas for Francesco of *L'attenzione* (*The Lie*), 1965, the unauthenticity inherent in his life becomes apparent and painful when he begins to pay close attention to what is going on around him. Thus the novels complement each other, the first exploring the problem of reality using the idea of *noia* (boredom) and the second using the opposite concept of *attenzione* (attention or attentiveness).

Dino and Francesco are both middle-aged, middleclass *artistes manqués* whose grave difficulties with women exacerbate their fundamental philosophical difficulties with life. Each revolts in some way against middle-class life, and seeks a more "authentic" life. But both are forced to realize that their revolt is itself unauthentic for they cannot escape from themselves—and what they are in part is middle-class. In both works, Moravia continued to use the theatrical form of Greek tragedy which he had been developing in his novels. The use of this form finally became such a conscious device that the narrator of *L'attenzione* comments on it throughout the novel.

La noia, a full-length novel, develops many of the themes of Moravia's previous works. The story line is extremely simple: Dino, a rich man of thirty-five, is plagued by boredom (*noia*). He rebelled against his mother's wealthy middle-class life some ten years before and rented a studio on the Via Margutta where

he lived and spent his time painting. As his art became more and more abstract, he began to feel that he
was losing contact with reality until even objects such
as a glass of water no longer had any concrete reality
for him.

One day he slashes to ribbons the painting he had
been working on for two months, and he places an
empty canvas on the easel (whence the title of the
English translation). Overcome by the feeling of *noia*,
he gives up art, which for him means the loss of contact with reality. The body of the novel deals with
Dino's attempts to re-establish contact with reality by
means of a sexual relationship with a girl named
Celia, the former mistress of an artist neighbor who
had recently died. However, Celia remains elusive,
and despite all his attempts, Dino cannot fully possess
her. When she leaves him, he falls into despair and
tries to commit suicide by driving his car into a tree.
Although the suicide attempt fails, the old Dino does
die in the crash; the Dino reborn in a sanatorium is a
calm, resigned man who is no longer interested in
trying to possess reality; he is now content with just
contemplating it. The action covers a period of several
months, from autumn when Dino slashes his painting,
to early summer when he tries to commit suicide and
is reborn.

Dino is of the long line of Moravian impotent
intellectuals which began with Michele of *Gli indifferenti*; but more than any of the others he seems to
incarnate all the characteristics of the middle-class
male that Moravia has portrayed in his various novels.
Like Michele, Dino is plagued by existential consciousness coupled with the inability to act in a meaningful manner. Similarly, Celia is a typical Moravian
lower-class female. Half child and half mature woman,

she has an innocent face, a thin torso but a full bust, and is heavy hipped. As Dino puts it, "adolescent from the waist up, woman from the waist down."[2] Animalistic in her femaleness, she has a prodigious sexual appetite; sex for her is a kind of religion, which is described by Dino as involving instinctual ritualistic acts and gestures. She never indulges in intellectual activities such as thinking, and she even avoids talking as much as possible.

In the prologue, Dino gives us a history of the development of his *noia*. He discusses at some length what *noia* means to him, giving us definitions and examples.[3] First of all, it is insufficiency, inadequacy, or scarcity of reality. His examples illustrate what he means: it is like a blanket in winter that is too short, or like an electric current that is interrupted mysteriously, or like a sickness of objects, such as a flower that wilts and turns to dust. Finally, he ends up by saying that *noia* is incommunicability and the incapacity to extricate oneself. It is of course significant that Dino's art is abstract, that for years he had not painted human figures or recognizable objects, and that he finally gave up painting entirely because, as he puts it: "I have nothing to paint, or rather I have no relationship with anything real."[4] The only canvas he can now sign is the empty canvas on his easel. Moravia has no love for abstract art, and sees in it a kind of manifestation of madness. As he wrote in a newspaper article in 1959: "It [abstract art] corresponds to an historical moment in which a collapse of culture takes place, a rejection of the processes of the past, a rupture of traditional relations with reality."[5] Dino is, of course, the incarnation of this idea.

There is much in this novel that may be identified as an attack against the middle class as viewed by

Moravia: its total orientation toward money, its phoney values, and its vulgarity. Dino's mother, whom we meet in the first chapter, is like Moravia's other middle-class mothers and is the perfect representative of her class. Small, flat-chested (always a sign of sexlessness or of abnormal sexuality in Moravia's world), she wears a mask of make-up and big gaudy jewels, and spends her life managing her money, giving orders to her gardeners, and socializing with other rich, vulgar people. Money is her only link with reality, but it is a strong one, for it takes the place of sex and religion in her life, having assumed the ritualistic aspects of each. Her study is described as a "temple for a religion";[6] her safe is located in the bathroom (reminiscent of Luca's parents' safe in their bedroom), and opening its combination lock is likened to a religious ceremony. Above her bed is a picture of Danae reclining nude on a bed, watching with pleasure the rain of golden coins fall into her lap. (Moravia had used the Danae motif earlier in *La romana*.)

Dino's present crisis came about as a result of the consciousness that he is only playing a role—that of an impoverished painter. The origin of his *noia* was wealth, he tells us. For a while he was able to delude himself into believing that he could escape from his wealth by rejecting it and by becoming an artist. But he comes to realize that he cannot escape from himself, and that he cannot renounce his wealth because it is a part of him even if he refuses to spend it. However, he cannot accept his mother's reality either, and while searching for his own, he comes face to face with the example of a man who found his reality through art and sex: a sixty-five-year-old painter, Balestrieri, who has died of the sexual excesses he indulged in with his mistress—Celia.

Although Dino judges him a very bad painter, he cannot help being envious of Balestrieri for having been so completely obsessed with his mistress and with his pornographic vision of reality. Dino begins, unconsciously at first, to follow in the older painter's footsteps, although he has never been much interested in women. In fact, at the beginning of the novel he cannot conjure up enough interest to make love to his mother's maid when she offers herself to him. However, he now devotes all his energies to a woman in his attempt to grasp the reality of Balestrieri's Celia and make it his own, first of all by possessing her sexually, then through complete knowledge of her and of her life. When he sees that Celia remains elusive and mysterious, he attempts to create a relationship with her through cruelty. But she soon slips away from him even in a physical sense for she takes up with another lover, causing Dino still greater torment. Once Dino is consumed with jealousy, he does begin to experience a kind of reality of Celia; but it is a reality of absence, and it is so painful that his only desire is to rid himself of it and to return to his old *noia*. He finally resorts to trying to buy her with his mother's much-despised money. His action is particularly ironic because he now places himself in the position of his mother who had, earlier in the novel, tried to buy him at the price of a new sports car. It did not work for her and does not for Dino either. In a manner reminiscent of Adriana in *La romana*, Celia accepts money from him with pleasure, but she is not, he discovers, mercenary, and so she eludes him here too.

The final stage of Dino's crisis of desperation unfolds before us in some of Moravia's finest pages, beginning with a drive Dino takes in the country with Celia. After Dino is frustrated in his desire to make

love to her that day, the countryside becomes sex-
ualized in his vision. He furiously drives his car into
the hills and valleys that now represent Celia's body for
him, but the mound of flesh disappears as he is about
to penetrate it, and he is led to try to reach another
mirage of Celia's pelvis just ahead. Finally, in order to
break out of his "delirium of obtuse fury and impotence,"[7] he stops the car and proposes marriage to
Celia. This is his last attempt to possess her fully, for
if she marries him, she will become middle-class, artificial and corrupted, and she will lose her lower-class
mystery and naturalness (which is precisely what happens in *L'attenzione*). The cocktail party he finds in
progress when he rushes Celia over to meet his mother,
affords Moravia the opportunity of commenting on
the dehumanized, vulgar rich who are all gathered
together in the house on the Via Appia. Once again
Dino discovers to his dismay that he is one of them,
and that his attempts to renounce his wealth only
make him a rich man trying to renounce his wealth.

When Celia refuses the marriage proposal, Dino's
last desperate effort to entrap her is to cover her nude
body with bank notes from the bathroom safe, while
she lies on his mother's bed under the Danae painting.
She exhibits the pleasure and excitement he imagines
Danae to have felt, but once again she slips out of his
grasp, for she cannot be bought or fully possessed in
any way. In fact, it is she who appears to be the posses-
sor, for after she has made love with him, Dino notes
how much she looks like a snake who has just swal-
lowed an animal.[8]

Dino's epilogue is written from the sanatorium
where he is recovering from the accident in which he
tried to commit suicide by running his car into a
plane tree. We are reminded at this point that

Balestrieri did kill himself because of his passion for Celia, but even in this Dino has failed to attain the reality in which Balestrieri lived and died. Dino is now devoid of all desire to possess Celia, or anything else, and he spends all his time contemplating a tree outside the window—this one a Cedar of Lebanon. Reborn without active desires, resigned to and content with the role of passive observer, Dino tells us that he will love Celia in a new way in the future; perhaps he will even take up painting again.

There are many parallels between Dino's story and that of Luca in *La Disubbidienza*. For both characters the process of rebirth following a period of illness is filled with religious symbolism. The mystical overtones of Dino's contemplative life in the sanatorium are obvious. Furthermore, the Cedar of Lebanon is an excellent choice as the object of contemplation. It is mentioned several times in Psalms, and in Ezekiel 31:8–9 we are told: "Not a tree in God's garden / could rival its beauty./ I, the Lord gave it beauty / with its mass of spreading boughs, / the envy of all the trees in Eden, / the garden of God" (*New English Bible* version).

If in *Agostino* the young protagonist had dreamed of finding a kind of paradise, an Eden of innocence and purity where he could be happy, Dino shows us that such a paradise, once lost, can be regained only through contemplation and dreams.

Moravia's book on boredom has bored some readers with its minute descriptions of love-making, its long interviews with the inarticulate Celia who has nothing to say about herself, and its many details about the life of Balestrieri. However, other readers have seen these as features that faithfully reflect the boredom Moravia is writing about. Once again the

author has used his novel as a forum for criticism of
the rich middle class and has, in effect, written an
essay in the form of a novel.

In *L'attenzione,* Moravia turns his attention
more fully to the artistic problems of an *artiste
manqué,* and develops further the theme of *L'amore
coniugale*—that of the novelist trying to write a book.[9]
In the intimate manner we have come to expect of
Moravia's first-person narrators, Francesco Mancini
explains in the prologue that he wrote this diary in
order to use it as raw material for a novel. For ten
years he had been trying to avoid confronting reality
because of a sense of shame he felt for his past; but
now, by means of the diary, he will face reality as it is,
and thus will be able to use it as a vehicle for an
authentic work of art.

It is very easy to see Francesco's literary ancestors
in Moravia's earlier novels, especially in the narrators
of *L'amore coniugale, Il disprezzo,* and *La noia.* Francesco had rebelled against his class because of the
falseness he perceived in it everywhere, and he had
accepted the "myth of the lower classes" as a means of
attaining an authentic mode of being. He thus falls in
love with and marries a lower-class woman of whorish
tendencies named Cora. Happily married and not
obliged to work, thanks to an inheritance, Francesco
devotes his time to a novel he started writing when he
fell in love with Cora—a novel which is to be the story
of their relationship from the moment he met her
until their marriage.

In a twist on the situation of *Il disprezzo,* Francesco suddenly and unaccountably stops loving Cora a
year after their marriage; he begins to feel an unrea-
sonable aversion toward her and her illegitimate

daughter, Baba, whom he had adopted. He then discovers that his novel is unauthentic because it does
not reflect the truth of their relationship; ripping it
up, he throws the torn pages out the window. Francesco is now at the same point Dino was when he
slashed his painting and gave up art. He has lost all
sense of reality, and he feels estranged from his life;
eventually he escapes from it physically as well as
spiritually by working as a travel writer for a large
daily newspaper.

When Francesco, at the age of forty, decides to
return to his old life and keep a diary, it is because
once again he has come face to face with the problem
of authenticity. He has realized that he cannot have
an authentic relationship with himself or with others,
and that a novel is the only place where such a relationship is possible. His diary spans the period from
October 13 to December 17 (the epilogue dates from
some three weeks later). Once he begins to pay attention to all that he tried to escape, he quickly makes
some important discoveries, the most significant of
which are: that Cora supplements her income as a
dressmaker by acting as a procuress; that he is in love
with his stepdaughter, Baba, who seems to return his
love; that everyone is corrupted by the mask he wears
and by the identity that society forces on him; that he
had loved Cora while he thought of her as a whore,
and that he stopped loving her because she became a
middle-class lady after her marriage. But most impor-
tantly of all, Francesco soon begins to see that fiction
is freely mixed with fact in his diary, and that the
imaginary scenes which he inserts into his journal reflect a kind of truth that the objective facts he records
do not. Later he understands that this is the fictional
truth of the novelist.

The Oedipus legend is the accompaniment to Francesco's story, for he uses the Sophoclean tragedy to interpret his life and vice-versa. Francesco believes that Oedipus too had been "unauthentic," because he had tried to be "inattentive" (*disattento*) to the reality of his life so as not to be forced to recognize his guilt in corrupting his family through incest. A second important motif, which is also prominent in Moravia's later short stories and plays, is that of the dehumanization of man and his debasement to the level of an object. Baba's story is intimately tied to both the Oedipus and the dehumanization motifs. Her life was drastically altered after she underwent the experience of being treated as an object to be bought and sold when, at the age of fourteen, she was taken by Cora to a whorehouse to be sold to a man. (Francesco admits only very late in the novel that he was the first man to whom she was to be sold, and that he ran away the moment he recognized her.) At that point in her life, the old Baba died and a new Baba was painfully born —one slowly created by Baba herself. This new Baba consciously chose which roles she would play—the good student, the fiancée of a medical student, the loving daughter—and then played them in full awareness, without losing consciousness of the underlying truth of her nature.

Baba is thus an authentic person in her own right, which cannot be said of the other characters we meet in the novel. Neither Cora nor Francesco qualifies as an authentic person, for both try to hide their true nature, not only from others, but also from themselves. At the farthest extreme from Baba is Francesco's old journalist friend, Consolo, who is only the facade and mask of the role he plays—that of an editor-in-chief; underneath he has no existence. The

quick sketch Moravia gives us of him is a minor mas-
terpiece, but there are also other good ones of characters who are totally corrupted by roles chosen or imposed: Francesco's brother who has fully espoused the
materiality, crassness, and sensuality of his class;
Cora's parents, simple peasants who at one time possessed a kind of purity, but who have become fat and
artificial, having been completely undone by Cora's
money and by the new middle-class life they lead in
Rome.

Once Francesco introduces the Oedipus theme in
his diary, he begins thinking in terms of a *deus ex
machina*. Moravia thus sets up a situation in which
the reader becomes more and more conscious of the
artistic form and structure of his novel. Francesco discovers that there is no need to act in life, for life itself
does the acting, and it is enough merely to allow it to
go on. When life can do no more, it will pull out the
deus ex machina of death and all will fall into place.
Moravia had used precisely that particular *deus ex
machina* in other postwar novels such as *Il conformista* and *Il disprezzo*. As usual, the *deus ex machina*
works on schedule, for in the epilogue Cora dies of
cancer, and Francesco is finally rid of the one who
represented the shame of his past which he so keenly
felt.

It is after Cora's death that Francesco looks at his
diary and sees that it consists of two distinct, unequal
parts: one of essay and fiction, the other a record of
events that actually occurred. And he realizes that the
novel he meant to write is already written—it is the
diary. (A full explanation of why the diary is a novel
and how the intent to write a novel caused Francesco
to fictionalize in the diary is given on the last page of
the book.) Francesco ends by affirming the "truth" of

dreams, lies, and illusions. He tells us that he wrote in order to discover why he was writing, just as he always believed he lived in order to discover why he was living. One might say the same of Moravia—that he, too, has been writing in order to come to an understanding of reality.

Francesco's conclusions sound very much like a watered-down version of what Gide revealed in *Les Faux-Monnayeurs* (*The Counterfeiters*), 1925. Indeed, Édouard, the protagonist in Gide's important and subtle novel had already arrived at those same conclusions. One can only wonder whether Moravia is once again parodying another writer as well as himself. If Francesco's final statements about the relationship of fiction and reality represent Moravia's beliefs, then one is forced to conclude that Moravia has here adopted certain Gidean themes, fresh and significant in 1925, and reduced them to a distressingly banal level.

However, if in *L'attenzione*, as in *La noia*, Moravia is not a profoundly original thinker, he once again reveals himself to be a master of description, and a skillful teller of tales.

8

Io e lui

With *L'attenzione* a developmental phase came to an end—a phase that began with *L'amore coniugale* in 1949. It is as if Moravia had reached a terminal point in subject matter and technique. He had fully explored the problems of the creative artist, the mystery of the relationship of the couple, the nature of man's contact with reality. In doing so he had developed as far as he could a theatrical structure within the novel. As he himself stated: "*L'attenzione* is a turning point in my career, a self-critique of my own work . . . In a way I know now there are certain things I can no longer do; I do not think I could write another realistic novel, for example. The theater, I believe, is today the only medium left to me for expressing my ideas."[1] He did not publish another novel until some six years later—*Io e lui (Two)* in 1971.

While no different in essential ideas from Moravia's other novels, *Io e lui* (literally, I and He) is almost entirely devoted to satire and self-parody. There are so many striking similarities between Petronius' *Satyricon* and *Io e lui* that it would be surprising if Moravia had not found a principal source of his inspiration in the Roman author's famous satire. This is true despite the statement on the inside cover blurb telling us that "there are no precedents, or rather, from another point of view, there is Diderot's *Les Bijoux indiscrets*." Federico Fellini produced a film version of the *Satyricon* in the late 1960s, and Moravia published his *Io e lui* shortly thereafter. Fellini's movie and Moravia's novel are both monuments to a decadent society for which both artists had been tolling the bell over a period of many years.

In their fragmented, picaresque form as well as in spirit and content, the first-century *Satyricon* and *Io e lui* bear resemblances. Although Petronius' narrator,

Encolpius, and Moravia's narrator, Federico, have exactly the opposite problem (Encolpius has a non-functioning sexual organ, while Federico's functions only too well), they share a number of common experiences. In both works there are, for example, scenes in which the narrator becomes enraged at his sexual organ and beats it, in which each man fails in attempts to perform in bed with a woman and is harshly abused by her as a consequence, in which religion and religious rites are parodied, and in which a banquet provides the means for satirizing the decadence, vulgarity and grotesqueness of the rich.

Io, the narrator Federico (Rico), is a thirty-five-year-old rich, middle-class would-be film-writer-producer, another of Moravia's *artistes manqués*. He describes himself as short, stubby-legged, paunchy, bald, and as having a serious face that looks haughty, and even majestic at times, despite the bags under the eyes. Federico's only claim to fame is, as he tells almost everyone he meets, that he has been "exceptionally well-endowed by nature." This endowment is his sexual organ which he has named Federicus Rex and calls *lui*, his alter ego with whom he converses and quarrels. It is *lui* whom he blames for his failure to become a creative artist, and for making him "cut a bad figure" in front of other people.

Rico spends much of his time worrying about being "desublimated" while ardently desiring to be "sublimated." Although the book is partly a parody of Freudian psychology (Rico's Freudian psychologist friend, Vladimiro, is a skeletal, faded failure in life), one suspects that the author half believes in the ideas he is mocking. Moravia presents his protagonist as being a split consciousness: raw sexual exigencies (the Id) are represented by *lui*, while the artistic, creative, rational forces are those of *io* (the Ego). Rico believes that in order to be creative he must become fully "sublimated," that is, he must totally repress his sexual desires. He greatly fears loss of sperm which he equates with loss of creative energy (reminiscent of Silvio in *L'amore coniugale*). In order to avoid sexual activity, he has left his wife and has gone to live in a small, barren apartment, where he spends his time trying to write a script for a film about young revolutionaries.

Such repression does not, of course, work. *Lui* becomes even more troublesome than before, and although Rico hasn't been to bed with a woman for six months, he has lost a good deal of sperm during that period. In fact, much of the action of the novel involves erections and ejaculations, and most of the rest of it is dialogue with *lui*. We are given countless descriptions of *lui* in all his splendor—his size, weight and color, habits, likes, and dislikes. These repetitive descriptions were probably intended to be comic, but most often they seem merely tedious.

A fragmentary and episodic novel, *Io e lui* has only a skeletal plot: the narrator's attempt to become "sublimated" by giving up sex, writing a successful filmscript, espousing a revolutionary cause, and entering into a Platonic relationship with a woman whose only form of sexual expression is autoeroticism. At the end, Rico is forced to admit that he is hopelessly "desublimated" and always will be. *Lui* gives him a final talking to, philosophizing about the futility of trying to repress one's instincts, and proclaiming the necessity of accepting one's sexuality. Rico then returns to his wife and gives up his dreams of being an artist. As always, everything is clearly spelled out for the reader, so that there is no question about the reasons for Rico's return home.

In the novel, society is presented as consisting of a collection of freaks who inhabit a kind of madhouse. Apart from the two main "characters," *io* and *lui*, there are many other grotesques: Rico's mother, with her enormous fat head and skinny body looks like a ripe fruit on a dead plant; Rico's wife, Fausta, who is an ex-prostitute, has a ham-like face and breasts like a cow's udders; Protti, the rich film-maker is sexually deformed, and Malfalda, his wife, looks astonishingly like a brontosaurus. Even Rico's infant son, Cesarino, is an ugly little brute who is flabby, ill-proportioned, washed-out and paunchy. The only beautiful person is a woman named Irene, but she has the grave defect (in Rico's eyes) of being an autoerotic who wants nothing to do with men. A few bearded, long-haired revolutionaries and their girl friends round out the picture; their only interest is "the cause" and all their thoughts and emotions are regulated by their ideology (at group meetings a traffic light tells them when to boo and when to applaud).

Moravia's usual motifs are woven into this novel too: religion and religious rites are associated with middle-class values, with money, banks, and food. Women are either prostitute types; rich middle-class females who have become asexual through adoration of money; young, sexless revolutionaries; or sexual deviates. Men are impotent intellectuals, or virile, overbearing success figures. The revolt against capitalist middle-class society this time is portrayed in the ridiculous attempt of thirty-five-year-old Rico to buy his way into an organization of young revolutionaries.

The idea of a talking sexual organ which reveals

hidden truths and which embarrasses its owner might
well have been inspired by Diderot's *Les Bijoux indiscrets*, but apart from that one can find only tenu-
ous similarities between the work of the eighteenth-
century French author and that of Moravia. Both
indulge in occasional polemics against aspects of their
times and devote considerable space to psychological
and philosophical discussions in an essayistic manner.
But Diderot's intent is not satiric or parodistic. Just
how successful *Io e lui* is as a satire remains question-
able. A long and repetitious novel, it might have been
far more interesting as a shorter work. As it is, it appears to be a grossly self-indulgent piece of writing
which was intended to be humorous but which missed
the mark. It may be that such Freudian frolics were
far too outdated by 1971.

9

*The Short
Stories*

The early short stories, written between 1927 and 1952, are for many critics and readers some of Moravia's finest works. They fall into two general categories: the neo-realistic stories which include the collections *La bella vita* (1935), *L'imbroglio* (1937), *L'amante infelice* (1943), the stories published with *L'amore coniugale* (1949), and a few separate pieces. The second category is made up of satiric and surrealistic tales, principally those of *I sogni del pigro* (1940) and *L'epidemia* (1944). Nevertheless, Moravia regularly combined characteristics of both types in all his stories including his later ones. As the distinguished Italian critic Francesco Flora has pointed out, when Moravia is naturalistic and realistic in the details and framework of his story, the content is fantastic or nightmarish in its events; and when Moravia works in the surrealistic dimension in structure and detail, the content of the stories is realistic.[1]

With the two volumes of *Racconti romani* (1954 and 1959), Moravia moved into a new phase of short-story writing, one in which plot, brevity and lower-class protagonists are the outstanding features. Later, with *L'automa* (1964), *Una cosa è una cosa* (1967), and *Il paradiso* (1970), the earlier distinctions between neo-realistic versus surrealistic and satiric tend to become more blurred as the stories all become fragmentary and dreamlike within their realistic world.

Several of the early stories were collected in a thick volume and published in 1952 under the simple title of *I racconti* (in English, selections from the *Racconti* volume may be found in *Bitter Honeymoon* and in *The Wayward Wife and Other Stories*). More often than not, these early stories are captivating and memorable psychological sketches of a character caught in

a well-defined situation that has just reached a point
of crisis. We watch as the protagonist struggles with
himself during a critical moment in his life, most frequently to be beaten down by his experience. Only
rarely does a character seem to get control of his situation and gain the upper hand for even a brief moment. In this respect, these early pieces faithfully reflect Moravia's cruel fictional world where almost
everyone seems to lose except vulgar or brutal people.
It is a world where no one wins anything—if winning
there is—except at the expense of someone else, by
fraud, trickery, deceit, torment, cruelty, or an act of
violence.

Like so many small versions of situations and
themes of Moravia's novels and novellas, these stories
deal mainly with the author's view of middle-class life
as dehumanized and meaningless, and with the lone-
liness of the individual in a society controlled by the
rich middle class. The struggles with self against guilt
or sexual desire, against feelings of hopelessness and
worthlessness which often lead to the temptation of
suicide are at the heart of the moment of crisis in the
stories. And the drama is played out in an atmosphere
of a stifling enclosure where there are no windows that
open to the outside. A great many stories are about
adolescents or inexperienced adults, although there
are several which are concerned with the theme of
aging and which have protagonists who note with
panic the inexorable approach of middle age.

The earliest of Moravia's stories, "Cortigiana
stanca" ("Tired Courtesan") and "Delitto al circolo
di tennis" ("Crime at the Tennis Club"), both date
from 1927. "Cortigiana stanca" is the story of a young
man who struggles with the conflict between his sexual desires and the financial necessity of giving up his

aging mistress. He spends a tormented afternoon and evening with her, unable to accept what he must do, while she bemoans her own fate and chronic lack of money. Finally he slips from her bed while she sleeps and goes to the movies, telling himself: "To the devil with Maria-Teresa," thus affirming his youth and banishing his torment with a devil-take-all attitude. "Delitto al circolo di tennis" is a tale of violence about a society ball and the systematic torture by a group of young men of an aging, unattractive countess who would like to appear young and beautiful. At the height of their cruelty and excitement, one of the young men hits the countess on the neck with a bottle and she dies instantly. After a moment of panic, they decide to return to the dance, pretending that nothing has happened, and to dispose of the body later. Thus Moravia exposes in this story the hypocrisy, violence, corruption, and inhumanness which he saw about him.

Perhaps the best known and most admired story is "Inverno di malato" ("A Sick Boy's Winter"), which dates from 1930. Sickness, the anguish of adolescence, and the clash of middle-class and lower-class life are the threads with which the delicate fabric of this story is woven. It also contains a number of autobiographical elements. Girolamo, a middle-class adolescent who suffers from tuberculosis of the leg bone, is being treated in a sanatorium in the mountains. His roommate, a lower-class, middle-aged man named Brambilla, seconded by a staff attendant named Joseph, torments him incessantly during the eight months they are together. Girolamo decides that he must experience the sexual delights he has so often heard about from Brambilla (who has frequently teased him because of his innocence), and so he seduces a willing

fourteen-year-old English girl, Polly, who is also a pa-
tient. Thereafter, Girolamo's condition worsens, as
does Polly's, and eventually their sexual relationship
is discovered. Despised by Brambilla instead of admired as he had hoped, and tormented by guilt and
shame, Girolamo no longer sees any hope in the future. At the end, still far from cured, he is left alone
to continue his therapy.

The compassion of the author for his character, so
evident in "Inverno di malato" is rare in Moravia's
other works. And yet, this story is typical in many
ways of Moravia's subsequent fiction: the intellectual
middle-class protagonist is pitted against a vulgar,
dominating rival; there is an unsatisfying sexual relationship with a female who is a hybrid of an innocent
child and a provocative sensual creature; the protagonist is unable to act (here because of his age and
illness), and he is excruciatingly lonely in his tightly
closed world.

Succeeding stories of this early period take up the
themes of the above three, with an occasional foray
into a Balzacian type story (such as "L'avaro") or into
Flaubert's world ("La provinciale"). Many of the stories which date from the 1940s bear the imprint of war
on Moravia's traditional themes. Thus "Andare verso
il popolo" ("Going to the People"), 1944, shows the
literal stripping of a young middle-class couple by
peasants who had lost everything to the Nazis and
who now were forced to rob or die of hunger and
exposure; "Ritorno al mare" ("Back to the Sea"),
1945, portrays the alienation of an ex-fascist government official who is despised by his wife after the fall
of the fascists, and who so despises himself that he can
do nothing except walk into the sea and drown himself. "L'ufficiale inglese" ("The English Officer"),

1946, gives a glimpse into the life and emotions of a woman who struggles against her sexual tendencies but succumbs to them each time a man moves to pick her up on the street. And "Il negro e il vecchio dalla roncola" ("The Negro and the Old Man with the Bill-Hook"), 1948, tells of a young man who attempts to seduce his date on the beach only to see her led off, not entirely unwillingly, by a huge Negro soldier. When the young man runs away in fright, the girl is rescued by an old fisherman who silently menaces the soldier with a bill-hook until he backs off.

Unfortunately, several of the stories from the original collections (some of them very good ones) do not appear in the *Racconti* edition. But not even all those from the *Racconti* collection have been translated into English. Thus a number of Moravia's best stories remain unavailable to the English-speaking reader.

Other stories which have not been available in English are the surrealistic and satiric tales. In 1944, these were reissued in a single volume containing the fifty-five stories from *I sogni del pigro* (A Lazy Man's Dreams) and *L'epidemia* (The Epidemic), which was used as the title of the new volume. These are in general much shorter pieces than the neo-realistic stories, and many contain sharp political satire in addition to the usual social satire. But there are also brief, incisive psychological studies, and miniature philosophical tales.

Some interesting representatives of the above types include the title story, which is a surrealistic and satiric parable of fascism. A number of people suddenly begin to stink from the head. At first they are somewhat troubled by it, but later their stench becomes perfume to their own noses. Another bitingly satiric story entitled "Primo rapporto sulla terra dell' Inviato speciale dalla luna" (First Report on Earth of the Special Envoy from the Moon) is a discussion by a middle-class man of poor people and how perverted they are since they obviously do not like the better things of life and prefer filth, discomfort and rotten food.[2] "Il coccodrillo" (The Crocodile) is a strange story about a new fashion of the rich—the wearing of a crocodile on one's back. Despite the obvious discomfort she witnesses in the faces of wearers and the fact that she finds the whole thing senseless, a middle-class lady decides that she, too, simply must have her crocodile. One of the most striking psychological tales is "Il mare" (The Sea), a study of the problem of guilt in adultery, which is here symbolized by the tide that floods the bedroom where the adultery is about to take place, besmirching the woman's family photographs. The tide slowly ebbs when the adulterous intentions of the would-be lovers have been abandoned.

On the philosophical level, "Antico furore" (Ancient Passion) is a story about Lucretius who is portrayed as being oppressed by boredom (*noia*). When it is time for him to die, he expires in the throes of passion after drinking a love potion, thus rendering back unto nature the love he had found. "I sogni del pigro" (A Lazy Man's Dreams) shows life as a dream for a protagonist who finds reality too unsatisfying. Because of his laziness he finds it easier to fantasize his life away rather than to take action. Thus Moravia has portrayed an intellectual who has managed to come to terms with life—such as those terms are.

Beginning with the 1954 volume of *Racconti romani*, Moravia's short stories become more fragmented and considerably shorter. This is understandable when one considers that almost all of them from this point on were written for newspaper columns. Following the development of the stories through the fifties and sixties, one can note Moravia's increasing concentration on the dehumanization of modern life and the alienation of the individual.

The *Racconti romani* are published in two volumes: the 1954 collection consists of sixty-one stories, and the *Nuovi racconti romani* of 1959 contains sixty-nine stories. (Selections from the two volumes were translated into English as *Roman Tales* and *More Roman Tales*.) All of the tales were originally published as a regular feature in the Milan daily, *Corriere della Sera*, beginning in 1952, and charmed readers all over Italy, but especially the Romans themselves. Each of these brief sketches has a Roman lower-class male narrator who tells of some personal drama from which he can often draw a moral. Thus an ambulatory fruit seller in "Il concorenza" (Competition) understands, after spending months in prison for having tried to beat up a butcher, that the butcher won the girl both of them were courting because he was the stronger competitor. In "Il naso" ("The Nose"), the narrator has a friend whose nose seems to spell ill-fortune. He can thus only blame himself when he and his friend land in prison after a thwarted burglary attempt, for he had failed to follow his instincts and avoid contact with that ill-starred friend.

The tales tell of attempted crimes, happy outings that turn sour, relationships that become sources of torment, couples who break up, friends who betray friends, ventures that fail—in short, they tell of people getting their comeuppance in life whether it be deserved or not. None may be said to end happily, although occasionally a narrator seems to gain some relief from an unbearable situation. By that time, however, he has of course paid for whatever he gets.

Although Moravia was still using in his tales the same kinds of crisis situations he had written about previously, the old psychological problems look like remnants from an earlier evolutionary phase. The struggles with self are now played out on a pre-conscious level with an individual aware for only a fleeting anguished moment of what is going on within him. Having been acted upon rather than acting, a narrator ends his story with a shrug of his shoulders and continues on his way. Although the tales cannot be read in any great number at one time, they provide, especially for a foreign reader, fascinating glimpses of what is presented as the everyday life of the little people who live in Rome.

The next three volumes of short stories Moravia published are all far more forgettable than the previous ones. The themes and problems they deal with are essentially the same, and no new insights into them are incorporated. Moreover, these brief sketches of psychological anguish are more fragmented, less satisfying variations on Moravia's usual subjects.

L'automa (*The Fetish and Other Stories*) is a collection of forty-one stories published in 1963. The title story of the Italian edition is typical of the others in the volume and, as far as Moravia's ideas are concerned, is also one of the most revelatory. (The title for the English translation was taken from another, less appropriate story.) In "L'automa" ("The Automaton"), a middle-class man, described by his wife as a good provider, husband, and father from whom one need fear no surprises, feels vaguely dissatisfied with himself and his life. One Sunday he idly puts a record on his automatic turntable. For the first and only time the mechanism fails to function properly and ruins

the record. Shortly after that he takes his wife and two
small children on a Sunday outing. As he drives along,
he notes a number of things which seem interesting,
but their significance escapes him. Then suddenly he
has a sense of illumination in the form of a desire to
drive the car off the top of a hill into the abyss. He
struggles to resist the temptation and stops the car
only to be overcome immediately by a feeling of close-
ness and stagnation whereas he had experienced a
sense of clarity and light just a moment before. When
he had mentioned the record player incident to his
wife, she had jokingly answered that "machines sometimes get sick of being machines and want to show
they're not machines."

According to the stories in *L'automa*, people are
becoming increasingly like machines because they are
being forced to act like machines, although they may
occasionally rebel for a brief moment. Furthermore,
human communication is steadily breaking down, and
people treat each other more and more like objects.
The result is the greater alienation of the individual.

The 1967 collection, *Una cosa è una cosa*, illustrates even more explicitly the message of *L'automa*
(twenty-seven of the forty-four stories of *Una cosa è
una cosa* were translated into English under the title,
Command and I Will Obey You). All of these short
pieces are related by first-person male narrators (except for the last, Kafkaesque story which has a dog as a
narrator). The title story, "A Thing Is a Thing," bears
witness to Moravia's increasing interest in the problem of language, and his love of tautologies which
becomes a mannerism in his works of the sixties. In
this story, a man begins to see his wife as merely one
of the many objects around him that crowd in on his
mind demanding attention. Agostino tried to see his

mother as "nothing but a woman," but the narrator
here goes one step further and sees his wife as nothing
but a thing. At the end, he slips out of their bedroom
where she is crying hopelessly because of his treatment
of her. "Il mostro" ("The Monster") explains how a
person can act in a robot-like manner without being
aware of what he is doing. And "Celestina," another
story, tells the tale of a robot—a computer born of a
middle-class couple—who falls in love with a water
heater and gives birth to a monster.

Il paradiso (*Paradise and Other Stories*), 1971,
consists of thirty-four very brief stories recounted by
women of both the lower and middle classes. Many of
the tales are unbelievable, some are grotesque, and
others puzzling or simply outrageous. Sexual psychopathology is the norm in this collection. One finds, for
example, a woman who purposely enrages her husband so as to be beaten almost to death in order to
achieve a special kind of orgasm. Another plays at
being a prostitute one afternoon a week in order to
see herself as an object; but when her clients try to get
what they have paid for, she pretends to have a heart
attack. She is thus able to sell herself without giving
herself. And one girl, while waiting on the street to
meet her boyfriend, turns into a whore; we later discover that it was all a daydream she had while riding
in a car with her boyfriend. In another story a girl
engaged to a young man decides instead to marry his
father because she is so strongly attracted to the father's prodigious ugliness.

The usual Moravian themes are there, but apart
from the eccentric sex, one is most struck by the writer's transparent tricks, the worn-out narrative devices,
and the melodrama that prop up these stories. It is a
sure sign that this mine has been exhausted and that

it is time, once again, for Moravia to try to move on to new fields. Since the early nineteen-fifties, it is apparent that Moravia has had only one purpose in writing his short stories, only one tune to play: the dehumanization of the individual and his increasing alienation from life.

10

Essayist,
Playwright,
Travel Writer

Perhaps the best summary of Moravia's thought and artistic ideas is contained in a volume of thirty-three essays entitled *L'uomo come fine e altri saggi* (only eighteen of these are translated in the English version, *Man as an End*). This volume consists of literary criticism and essays on political, social, and moral subjects which Moravia had published from 1941 to 1963.

In his preface to the collection, Moravia explains his reasons for publishing it. *L'uomo come fine* is, he says, a defense of humanism at a time when anti-humanism—"which today goes under the name of neo-capitalism"—is in vogue. He further clarifies that the traditional humanism is long dead and that his essays represent "a cautious approach to the hypothesis of a new humanism."[1] He is quite proud of the continuity of thought and the tight unity of the essays. Indeed, Moravia's theory of one good tune is well illustrated here.

Many of the essays deal with literary questions, and Moravia's statements about them show that he is well aware of his own techniques and has clear reasons for writing what he writes. If many readers prefer his short stories to his novels, the reason may lie in the theory Moravia states in "Racconto e romanzo" ("The Short Story and the Novel"): ". . . while the short story comes close to being a lyric, the novel . . . has affinities with the essay or with the philosophical treatise."[2] (Moravia's novels, as we have seen, do read very much like essays.)

In these essays Moravia replies to some of the objections critics have raised to his fiction. Alienation, he says in several places, is of necessity the subject matter of contemporary art, and the theme of all his works. In "I miei problemi" (My Problems), he explains that since alienation is "the crisis of man's rela-

tionship with reality," and is "the fundamental phenomenon of the modern world,"[3] writers are, and
indeed must be, concerned with it.

As a self-proclaimed antiromantic, Moravia has
drawn fire from a number of critics because of his
emphasis on sex. Many readers see it as merely a de-
based form of the love which dominated the romantic
novel. The most frequent adjective used in describing
the sexuality in Moravia's fiction has been "squalid."
But Moravia sees his use of sex as quite a different
matter. "Sex in literature . . . should be an act of
penetration into a cosmic and superhuman order," he
states in "Erotismo e letteratura" ("Eroticism in Literature"). "From this point of view, sexuality is in
effect something higher, more mysterious, more complete than love; especially if love is interpreted as the
simple physical-sentimental relationship between a
man and a woman."[4] But whatever the proclaimed
intentions of the author, no such cosmic or superhuman order is visible in his fictional world, and the
sex Moravia writes about remains depressingly earth-
bound. A number of Moravia's other statements in
this volume are open to serious questioning; however,
the essays are always provocative, stimulating and interesting, if sometimes outrageous.

Little attention has been given by critics to Moravia's plays, perhaps because he began publishing
them long after he was known as a writer of novels,
stories, and essays. If not among his best works, several
of the plays are interesting as embodiments of themes
that are not always as fully explored in Moravia's fiction.

The list of his published theatrical pieces includes *La mascherata* (The Masked Ball) and *Bea-*

trice Cenci, published together in a volume entitled *Teatro* (1958); *Il mondo è quelle che è* (The World Is What It Is) and a one-act play, *L'intervista* (The Interview) were published together in 1966; *Il dio Kurt* (God Kurt) appeared in 1968, and *La vita è gioco* (Life Is a Game) in 1969. Of these, *La mascherata* is an adaptation of the novel of the same title, and *L'intervista* is an adaptation of a short story in the *Epidemia* collection, both essentially unchanged as plays.[5]

Beatrice Cenci is an historical play set in 1598 and based on a well-known story of cruelty, parricide, and punishment. However, the play is pure Moravia, with a few echoes throughout of Shakespeare (especially *Julius Caesar*). In *Beatrice Cenci,* boredom (*noia*), defined as the inability to feel that one is alive, is what leads Beatrice's father, Francesco, to extreme cruelty against his guiltless daughter. As for Beatrice, she is shown as being driven to parricide by an overwhelming desire to vindicate her lost innocence. After her father's death, however, she feels that she must atone for her crime and thus makes no attempt to escape punishment.

Moravia's treatment of the story contrasts sharply with that of other writers, for example, Shelley and Stendhal. In his baroque-style play, Shelley was interested in following Beatrice's presumed states of mind to the point where she is led away to execution. His is a romantic Beatrice, torn by surging, conflicting emotions. On the other hand, Stendhal, in his short story, begins where Moravia ends, for he is interested in recounting the torture of Beatrice and her stepmother, Lucrezia, during their imprisonment, and in portraying them at the moment of their death. He underscores the great heroism of Beatrice by emphasizing the weakness and tears of the others condemned with her.

In Moravia's version, trickery and deceit are the basis for relationships, and both Francesco and Beatrice have a single purpose. They both want to escape from life as it is and from themselves; both fail in their attempt. Francesco does not attain a satisfactory reality of self through cruelty, and Beatrice does not feel vindicated for her lost innocence after her crime; in fact, she is still seeking to return to a state of innocence at the end of the play.

Il mondo è quelle che è is a two-act play based on the language theories of Wittgenstein.[6] A group of persons staying at a villa agrees to participate in a language therapy experiment directed by an unemployed philosophy teacher. The point is to ban "sick words," that is, all those which have meaning and can inspire emotions, and to use only "healthy words," such as nonsense words or meaningless phrases. Tautologies such as the title of the play are particularly favored because such repetitions are seen as very strong medicine.

Thus Moravia here explores, in what is essentially a comic context, the problem of language, and how words relate to our judgments, ideas, and concepts of the world. His avowed purpose in writing the play was to give expression to the theories of Marx and Wittgenstein, that is, to contrast the idea of the necessity of acting on the world with that of acting on language in order to bring about the happiness of man.

Il dio Kurt, a tragedy consisting of a prologue and two acts, is a gruesome story of a Nazi S.S. commander who conducts an experiment in which Sophocles' Oedipus story is re-enacted by Jews in a concentration camp. Structurally it is a play within a play, a tragedy on both levels, for the actors are not merely playacting. They are unknowingly forced to relive the Oedipus story; they then step out of it to act within the larger tragedy of the concentration camp. *Il dio Kurt* is, of course, a bitter monument to Nazi atrocities. But it was also a vehicle for the exploration of the incest theme that had fascinated Moravia for years, surfacing here and there for a moment in the earlier works before becoming an integral part of the action of *L'attenzione* in 1965.

   La vita è gioco, the most existentialistic of Moravia's works, appeared in 1969, one year after *Il dio Kurt*. Its tone and ideas are largely those of the French existentialist theater of the 1940s. But it is also a satire of contemporary consumer society where everything is bought and sold—including people— and of aging revolutionaries who try unsuccessfully to elicit the support of uninterested lower-class youth. These two currents, existentialism and social satire, are joined in the central character, Berengario. In a communist party style meeting, he urges a group of young people to reject all models proposed to them by 'heir society, especially those of Jesus and of advertising. They should, he tells them, "play" with their lives. "Playing," he explains, "means doing what you want in a disinterested way."[7]

   The summary statement that accompanies the text gives us more explicit information. Playing and freedom are synonymous, it explains; and although such freedom is dangerous and exacts a high price, it is the only freedom without negative qualities. "Playing, in fact, does not mean being free *from* something. It simply means being free." This idea is amply illustrated in the play through two figures: Berengario, a middle-aged, rich former industrialist, and Federica, his wife. Berengario's attempt to gain freedom and turn his life into a game leads to his death at the hands of three young people who play at being kidnappers. Because he had also taught his wife to play, she takes her game to the limit after Berengario's death, shoots the other three remaining characters, and then points the gun at herself. Thus playing, which is freedom and life, leads to death.

All the characters in this play are extremely shallow and lack even the depth of those in *Io e lui*. Because they are mere stereotypes that act in a highly stylized manner and express ideas which belong to literary and social history, the interest of a play like this is extremely limited.

The travel books occupy a significant place in Moravia's works, for they permit him to break out of the entrapment of continually writing about the middle and lower classes of Italian society. They allow him to be an observer without constraining him to be a bitter satirist. If as a travel writer Moravia has been most concerned with objective reality, paradoxically, it is in the travel books that he most plainly reveals himself to be a dreamer and an idealist.

Obviously captivated by the places he visits and writes about, Moravia gives us fascinating and often warmly human accounts of his observations and experiences. These pages—impressions of the Soviet Union, India, China, Africa, and glimpses of people and life styles—are among the best in his writing. The weakest parts are those in which Moravia gives us a highly personalized, capsule version of the history of a country, allowing his biases and prejudices to have free rein. Such parts often have an annoying academic and didactic quality, and are frequently structured in a highly stylized manner: Moravia often asks himself a question and then answers at length. Most of the "chapters" that make up the travel books were originally published as newspaper articles, although in some cases Moravia has added an introduction and has included previously unpublished materials.

In *Un mese in U.R.S.S.* (A Month in the U.S.S.R.), 1958, we accompany the author as he visits tourist sites in various countries within the Soviet Union, meditating on the historical, economic, and social aspects of Russia. Although the least original of Moravia's travel books, it nevertheless contains vivid descriptions and some thought-provoking ideas.

In a chapter dealing with provincialism and industrialization, Moravia describes the U.S.S.R. as a "Victorian society." By Victorian he means "any society that holds an image of itself which is as far from reality as possible." Such a society in Russia, he theorizes, resulted from "the social and psychological censure created by two revolutions and various terrible and victorious wars."[8] Russia is a country of peasants, he tells us, two-thirds of whom live in rural areas, and one-third in cities. But, "the face of the Soviet Union," in his eyes, "is the austere, gray, serious face of laboring humanity."[9]

The "sterility" of pain and grief is the subject of another chapter in which Moravia advances an hypothesis to explain why, in his view, Russia's arts and economy had not made significant progress. Overbearing pain and grief began in Russia in 1917, he explains, whereas in Europe they surfaced some fifteen years later. In Russia, the pain and grief were unbearable and excessive. The great purges, bloodbaths, and the unflinching oppression killed something in the survivors and left them with what Moravia identifies as a "poisoned torpor," "an incapability of reacting," "a kind of insensitivity, dismay, feeling of impotence, and elegiac resignation."[10] Although the pain and grief ended, the effect was the general sterility of art and literature, and of Soviet life in general as Moravia saw it throughout his travels.

Un'idea dell'India (An Idea of India), 1963, consists of an introduction and twelve articles on such subjects as the Hindu religion, the social caste system, Indian cities, and the traces of colonialism left on the Indian landscape. It also includes an interview with Nehru and fascinating discussions on art, temples, and the illusionary quality of India. But it is perhaps the excellent descriptions of people and of everyday scenes from Indian life that stand out most of all. In the article, "Tanjore," for example, Moravia describes the train stations of India which are as vast as temples:

Indian railway stations are always full of people who rarely show impatience, or at the most show only that slight tension which is typical of someone who is going away. Indians in a railway station don't seem to be waiting for the train; the most important thing doesn't seem to be the arrival of the train, but rather just being in the station . . . In fact, it is just like the temples, where people don't pray, but live.[11]

The last article, on Khajuraho, deals with Moravia's favorite theme—sexuality. But here, contrary to his use of it in his fiction, sexuality is presented in cosmic terms. The erotic sculptured figures on the temple of Khajuraho illustrate an exuberant sexual concept of life, which in Indian thought is balanced by a concept of the strictest chastity and asceticism. As we leave the temple with Moravia, the last image we see is that of a Guru, a man devoted to a life of absolute chastity, who lives in the temple a mere two feet away from some of the most erotic art ever created. For Moravia, these two contrasting concepts of life are essential for an understanding of Indian culture; they represent the two means of annihilating the individual and of rendering "the human, historical world void of any importance or meaning, reduced to nothingness"[12]—the essence of Indian thought as Moravia sees it.

The dialogue between A and B which constitutes the introduction to *La rivoluzione culturale in Cina* (*The Red Book and the Great Wall*), 1967, ranges over a variety of topics. Moravia himself admits at the end of this introduction that he has strayed far from the subject of the book, and that it was really a pretext for a discourse on various things that interested him, such as poverty, humanism, the human condition, sexuality and chastity, and the inhumanity and abnormality of capitalist society versus the humanity and normality of Chinese society. This dialogue with self is curiously reminiscent of medieval debates between body and soul; here B represents the earthy, materialistic and sensual self, while A is the austere, spiritual and puritanical soul.

The fourteen separate pieces in this volume present one man's thoughtful view of revolutionary China. Perhaps the best aspect of the book is Moravia's sense of the revelatory detail: the innocence and ignorance of the Red Guard which remind him of the Children's Crusade of 1207; the statues of Mao in the style of Soviet realism which are surrounded with fresh flowers, appearing very much like the cult of a saint; the Red Book carried by everyone in an ostentatious manner, like a breviary, in order to prove that one has it.

Moravia was continually struck by the quality of uncertainty, ambiguousness, and mystery (which he identified as part of the Chinese character and way of life), by the religious and puritanical character of the revolution, and most of all by the practice of poverty as a positive value. From his observations, Moravia concludes that it is a revolution of very traditionalist origins, and a means of re-establishing conservatism on a natural basis. He sees the hatred of the past and its monuments as an attempt to replace the sense of beauty by a sense of the good.

While not entirely free from mannerisms (annoying tautologies slip from Moravia's pen all too often), this book is extraordinarily well written and sensitive, and seems fresher in its outlook than any of his other works of the 1960s or 1970s. And there are a number of unforgettable scenes: the amusing Red Book debate between Moravia and a Chinese writer, with each man in turn searching furiously through his Red Book for a quotation from Mao to back up his position; the highly stylized Peking-duck dinner in the only restaurant operating in Peking, and the sense of guilt which accompanies the succulent food eaten there; the visit to the Great Wall, whose vastness overwhelms despite its present state of decay. Moravia sums up as follows the difference as he sees it between Europe and Asia: "Europe is the continent of unstable states, ephemeral dynasties, numerous revolutions. But Asia is the continent of states and dynasties that last for centuries and centuries, of single revolutions that become permanent."[13]

More than twice as long as any of the previous

travel volumes, Moravia's book on Africa, *A quale tribù appartieni?* (What Tribe Do You Belong To?), 1972, is also of more uneven quality than the others. The thirty-eight articles contained in it span a ten-year period, 1963–72, during which Moravia made extended journeys through various parts of Africa.

The earliest pieces in the volume are the least interesting, for they concentrate to a great extent on the author's obsession with social and economic concepts, and are devoted to discussions of slavery, colonialism, and neo-capitalism—the great scourges of Africa, according to Moravia. He sees very little hope for the future of the vast continent, and predicts that in from ten to thirty years it will be completely spoiled by the neo-capitalistic forces that are exploiting it.

The Africa that interested Moravia is a prehistoric land full of mystery. For him, Africa has until recently existed totally outside of history, living its own vital and natural life of tribal communities, wild animals, and uncultivated, rampant vegetation. It is this prehistoric, mysterious Africa that he tried to penetrate during his travels, but never quite succeeded, or so it seems from his accounts. A profound sense of unease runs through most of the articles, as if Moravia were never comfortable plunging into the primitive mysteries he was seeking.

The countryside he passes through is monotonous, endless and unpleasant, whether it be plains, forest or brush. The skies he sees are continually ugly and cloudy, or blindingly bright, and the air is humid and oppressive, often heavy with a mist that hangs over everything. What he liked were the animals—the lions, zebras, gnus, hippopotamuses, crocodiles; but it was especially the giraffes which most of all for him symbolized black Africa. He describes all the animals with a warmth, enthusiasm and admiration that are lacking in his other descriptions.

His feelings about the people he meets are quite complicated. Like the animals, they are a part of Moravia's prehistoric Africa; but unlike the animals, they tend to be disturbingly unpredictable. Despite the many examples he gives of spontaneous friendliness on their part, the gulf between him and the African people was apparently too great to be bridged. The explanation may lie in the prehistoric quality of Africa itself as he identified it—the irrational and primitive other half of rational and civilized Europe.

11

Conclusion

Looking back on the forty-odd years of Moravia's writing, one can fully agree with him when he says that he has remained faithful to himself. He has followed very personal lines of development, reaching the goals he set for himself. He has tenaciously used the same themes again and again, keeping them basically unchanged in all his works, with only the settings updated now and then. While it is certainly laudable for an author to follow his own line of artistic development without regard for literary fashion, such an attitude can also have its pitfalls. When it means that a writer "discovers" for himself literary devices and truths about the nature of man which had been introduced in the literary world some twenty-five to forty years before by such writers as Gide, Svevo or Pirandello, one can only wonder about the contemporary value of such discoveries. Indeed, Moravia's personal artistic development has often led him to the rediscovery of truths that were already commonplace in European literature.

Moravia's characters have not changed either; no significant evolution or growth can be seen in them. They have remained variations of Michele, Carla, the Mother, Leo and Lisa from *Gli indifferenti*, with an occasional illuminated figure in the form of an Agostino, an Adriana (*La romana*) or a Cesira (*La ciociara*). All in all, the male characters have been more satisfactory creations than the females. In fact, almost all Moravia's women have been depressingly shallow and unbelievable creatures. Perhaps Colette put her finger on part of the problem when she asked herself: "Why is it that a man can never talk about a woman's sexual nature without making incredibly stupid remarks?"[1]

In answer to objections from critics concerning

his highly personal fictional world, Moravia has always maintained that he is not a realist, and that in any case reality is an extremely subjective matter. However, he has also often stated that his fiction reflects "the world we live in." In response to a critic who accused him (and other contemporary writers) of fabricating "alienation" in order to provide themselves with a literary theme to use over and over, Moravia flatly stated: "We, too, are tired of continually saying the same things. But it isn't possible to do otherwise; this is the world we live in, there is no other world, nor can there be one. At the most, we can contribute to the formation of a new world in which, however, we will not have the opportunity to live."[2]

It is clear from the above quotation and from statements in many of Moravia's works that his art has been oriented toward a goal. A master of plot and of concise description, he has tried to reflect the world we live in; but he has also hoped to effect a change in our world by exposing what is wrong with it. Perhaps this intent helps to explain why, in the final analysis, Moravia partakes more of the journalist than the artist, more of the essayist than the novelist, more of the social commentator and satirist than the creator who provides new insights into the nature of man.

Notes

Translations of titles of Moravia's works that have been published in English are given in quotation marks or in italics. For works not translated into English, a literal translation of the title has been provided. All translations appearing in the text are my own.

1. The Man, His Thought and His World

1. *The New Yorker*, May 7, 1955.
2. Luciano Rebay, "Moravia: storia e strascichi di uno 'pseudonimo,' " *Forum Italicum*, IV (1970), 16–22.
3. *The Guardian*, May 31, 1962.
4. "L'uomo come fine," in *L'uomo come fine e altri saggi* (Milan: Bompiani, 1964), p. 214.
5. *The Guardian*, May 31, 1962.
6. *La rivoluzione culturale in Cina* (Milan: Bompiani, 1967), p. 26.
7. *L'attenzione* (Milan: Bompiani, 1965), p. 20.
8. *The Guardian*, May 31, 1962.
9. For a thorough discussion of the *impotente-prepotente* motif in Moravia's fiction see Donald Heiney's very helpful book, *America in Modern Italian Literature* (New Brunswick, N.J.: Rutgers University Press, 1964), pp. 202–20.

2. Style, Form and Imagery

1. "Differenza tra artista e intellettuale," *Corriere della Sera*, November 5, 1972.

2. See especially "Ricordo de *Gli indifferenti*," "Note sul romanzo," "Risposta a 9 domande sul romanzo," and "I miei problemi," in *L'uomo come fine*.

3. *The Guardian*, May 31, 1962.

4. Ibid.

5. Giuseppe Gioacchino Belli (1791–1863), a Roman poet who wrote more than 2,000 sonnets. His satirical poems present a vivid picture of life in Rome in the early nineteenth century. It was his *Sonetti romaneschi* in particular with their splendid descriptions of people and observations of Roman life that inspired Moravia's *Racconti romani*.

6. "Ricordo de *Gli indifferenti*," in *L'uomo come fine*.

7. Notably, those of Shakespeare, Ibsen, Chekhov and Pirandello, as well as the comic devices of Molière and Goldoni.

8. "Ricordo de *Gli indifferenti*," in *L'uomo come fine*.

9. *Three Greek Romances*, trans. and intro. by Moses Hadas (New York: Doubleday Anchor, 1953), p. 11.

10. Dominique Fernandez, *Le Roman italien et la crise de la conscience moderne* (Paris: Bernard Grasset, 1958), pp. 56–7.

11. *The Guardian*, May 31, 1962.

12. Ludwig Wittgenstein, an Austrian-British philosopher who was born in 1889 and who died in 1951. His philosophy aimed at solving once and for all the central metaphysical problems of the nature of reality. He saw language as the key, for it expresses what we think about reality. Language, he believed, was composed of logical pictures in which words are substitutes for objects, and their order in sentences reflects the way things are arranged in reality. He later repudiated this metaphysical picture of a formal correspondence be-

tween language and reality, but still emphasized the
importance of language in our view of reality.

3.   The Early Novels

1. *The Guardian*, May 31, 1962.
2. *Gli indifferenti* (Milan: Bompiani, 1970), Ch. 5, p. 51.
3. See "L'uomo e il personaggio," in *L'uomo come fine*.
4. *Gli indifferenti*, Ch. 16, p. 342.
5. Ibid., Ch. 16, p. 342.
6. Ibid., Ch. 9, p. 199.
7. Ibid., Ch. 16, p. 349.
8. Ibid., Ch. 15, p. 325.
9. "Ricordo de *Gli indifferenti*," in *L'uomo come fine*, p. 63.
10. Ibid., p. 65.
11. Ibid., p. 66.
12. *Le ambizioni sbagliate* (Milan: Mondadori, 1949), Pt. II, Ch. 9, p. 279.
13. Ibid., Pt. III, Ch. 8, p. 457.
14. Ibid., Pt. III, Ch. 8, p. 461. The sexual symbolism in this passage is obvious.
15. *La mascherata* in *Romanzi brevi* (Milan: Bompiani, 1964), p. 9.
16. Ibid., p. 41.

4.   Agostino and Luca

1. *Agostino* in *Romanzi brevi*, Ch. 1, p. 145.
2. Ibid., Ch. 1, p. 160.
3. Ibid., Ch. 2, pp. 194–5
4. Ibid., Ch. 4, p. 216.
5. *La disubbidienza* in *Romanzi brevi*, Ch. 3, p. 248.
6. Ibid., Ch. 3, p. 249.
7. Ibid., Ch. 3, p. 252.

8. Ibid., Ch. 16, p. 346.
9. Ibid., Ch. 15, p. 340.

5. *Two of Moravia's Women*

1. *La romana* (Milan: Bompiani, 1953), Pt. I, Ch. 6, p. 147.
2. Ibid., Pt. I, Ch. 9, p. 214.
3. Ibid., Pt. II, Ch. 3, p. 295.
4. Ibid., Pt. I, Ch. 1, p. 15–16.
5. Ibid., Pt. I, Ch. 7, p. 178.
6. For a discussion of Moravia's carefully plotted corre-spondences of seasons and events in Adriana's life, see my Chapter One.
7. *La ciociara* (Milan: Bompiani, 1957), Ch. 4, pp. 163–4.
8. Ibid., Ch. 11, p. 411.
9. Ibid., Ch. 11, p. 414.
10. Ibid., Ch. 6, p. 241. Moravia used the same idea ex-pressed here by the lawyer in his satirical short story, "Primo rapporto sulla terra dell'Inviato speciale della luna," from *L'epidemia.* Later he adapted that story for the stage as a one-act play entitled *L'intervista.* In both story and play Moravia presents the oppression of the lower class as being the result of a hypocritical belief on the part of the rich middle class: poor people, ac-cording to middle-class spokesmen, actually enjoy liv-ing in poverty and filth.

6. *Three Postwar Novels*

1. Moravia himself apparently believes in the principle of asceticism during creative endeavors. In an interview published in *The New Yorker* (May 7, 1955), he stated: "Beautiful as they are, women are bound to get in the way of one's work. There's an old Italian motto that

is ideal for writers. It goes: 'Dear Lord, permit us to remain chaste and to recount the loves of others.' "

2. *Il disprezzo* (Milan: Bompiani, 1956), Ch. 9, p. 112.

3. Ibid., Ch. 20, p. 226.

4. For a parallel situation see "Ritorno al mare," or "Back to the Sea," *I racconti*. Adriana of *La romana* (*Woman of Rome*) also dreams of purifying herself by drowning in the sea.

7.   *Two Novels of the Sixties*

1. This is in keeping with Moravia's concept of the novel as an essay, and with his statements that man's relationship with reality and alienation are the subjects of his fiction. See his collected essays, *L'uomo come fine,* especially, "La presenza, la prosa," "Note sul romanzo," and "I miei problemi."

2. *La noia* (Milan: Bompiani, 1962), p. 108.

3. It is interesting to compare Dino's definitions of *noia* with statements Moravia made in an interview published in *The New Yorker*, May 7, 1955: "I am an addict of boredom. I understand it so well. It is a frightful thing, yet a great creative force. A necessary poison. No one who is not bored can create anything."

4. *La noia*, p. 98.

5. "I pittori malati di Verona," *Corriere della Sera*, September 6, 1959. Reprinted in *Saggi italiani* (Milan: Bompiani, 1960), p. 44.

6. *La noia*, p. 56.

7. Ibid., p. 304.

8. For a discussion of Moravia's use of the snake as a principal female image, see my Chapter Two.

9. Throughout *L'attenzione*, affinities can be noted with Proust's *A La Recherche du temps perdu*, and Gide's *Les Faux-Monnayeurs*. The manner of investigation, the interrogation of the past, and the revelations of

memory seem Proustian, while the conclusions reached
by Francesco are those of Gide.

8. *Io e lui*

1. Quoted by Luciano Rebay in *Alberto Moravia* (New
    York: Columbia University Press, 1970), pp. 44–45.

9. *The Short Stories*

1. Francesco Flora, *Scrittori italiani contemporanei* (Pisa:
    Nistri-Lischi Editori, 1952), p. 228.
2. Moravia later adapted this story and published it in
    1966 as a one-act play entitled *L'intervista*.

10. *Essayist, Playwright, Travel Writer*

1. *L'uomo come fine*, pp. 5–6.
2. "Racconto e romanzo," in *L'uomo come fine*, p. 278.
3. "I miei problemi," in *L'uomo come fine*, p. 379.
4. "Erotismo e letteratura," in *L'uomo come fine*, p. 359.
5. See my Chapter Three for a discussion of *La mascher-
    ata* as a novel, and Chapter Nine for a résumé of
    "Primo rapporto sulla terra dell'Inviato speciale della
    luna," from *L'epidemia*, the short story from which
    L'intervista was adapted. Moravia has also written a
    number of plays which have been performed but which
    are not available as published texts.
6. Ludwig Wittgenstein, see Ch. II, n. 12.
7. *La vita è gioco* (Milan: Bompiani, 1969), Act I, p. 49.
8. "Provincialismo e civiltà meccanica in U.R.S.S.," in
    Un mese in U.R.S.S. (Milan: Bompiani, 1958), p. 48.
9. Ibid., p. 51.
10. "Sterilità del dolore," in *Un mese in U.R.S.S.*, p. 67.

11. "Tanjore," in *Un'idea dell'India* (Milan: Bompiani, 1962), p. 117.
12. "Lo scandalo di Khajuraho," in *Un'idea dell'India*, p. 156.
13. "Il libro," in *La rivoluzione culturale in Cina* (Milan: Bompiani, 1967), p. 49.

11. Conclusion

1. Colette, *Duo*, in *Oeuvres* (Paris: Flammarion, 1960), II, 595.
2. "I miei problemi," *L'uomo come fine*, p. 382.

══

Bibliography

1. Moravia's Works

A. NOVELS AND COLLECTED SHORT STORIES

Gli indifferenti. Milan, Editrice Alpes, 1929. (*The Time of Indifference.* New York, Farrar, Straus and Young, 1935.)

La bella vita. Lanciano, Editore Carabba, 1935. (Contains: "Cortigiana stanca," "Delitto al circolo di tennis," "Apparizione," "Una domanda di matrimonio," "Inverno di malato," "Visita crudele," "Lo snob," "La bella vita," "La noia," "Morte improvvisa," "Fine di una relazione.")

Le ambizioni sbagliate. Milan, Mondadori, 1935. (*The Wheel of Fortune.* New York, Viking, 1937. Also *Mistaken Ambitions.* New York, Farrar, Straus and Young, 1955.)

L'imbroglio. Milan, Bompiani, 1937. (Contains: "L'imbroglio," "La provinciale," "L'avaro," "L'architetto," "La tempesta.")

I sogni del pigro. Milan, Bompiani, 1940.

La mascherata. Milan, Bompiani, 1941. (*The Fancy Dress Party.* New York, Farrar, Straus and Young, 1952.)

L'amante infelice. Milan, Bompiani, 1943. (Contains: "Il ritorno dalla villeggiatura," "L'equivoco," "La soli-

151

152   *Alberto Moravia*

tudine," "La caduta," "L'avventura," "Malinverna,"
"L'amante infelice.")

L'epidemia: Racconti surrealistici e satirici. Rome, Documento, 1944. (Includes the stories from *I sogni del
pigro.*)

Due cortigiane e Serata di Don Giovanni. Rome, L'Acqu-
ario, 1945.

Agostino. Milan, Bompiani, 1945. (Included in *Two Adolescents.* New York, Farrar, Straus, 1950.)

La romana. Milan, Bompiani, 1947. (*The Woman of Rome.*
New York, Farrar, Straus, 1949.)

La disubbidienza. Milan, Bompiani, 1948. (Included as
Luca in *Two Adolescents.* New York, Farrar, Straus,
1950.)

L'amore coniugale e altri racconti. Milan, Bompiani, 1949.
(*Conjugal Love.* New York, Farrar, Straus and Young,
1951. Italian edition contains: *L'amore coniugale,* "Ritorno al mare," "La casa è sacra," "Delitto al circolo di
tennis," "La messicana," "L'ufficiale inglese," "Il negro
e il vecchio dalla roncola," "Andare verso il popolo.")

Il conformista. Milan, Bompiani, 1951. (*The Conformist.*
New York, Farrar, Straus and Young, 1951.)

I racconti. Milan, Bompiani, 1952. (A selection from this
book and from *L'amore coniugale e altri racconti* appeared in *Bitter Honeymoon and Other Stories.* New
York, Farrar, Straus and Cudahy, 1956. A further selection was published in *The Wayward Wife and Other
Stories.* New York, Farrar, Straus and Cudahy, 1960.
Italian edition contains short stories from previously
published volumes.)

Il disprezzo. Milan, Bompiani, 1954. (*A Ghost at Noon.*
New York, Farrar, Straus and Young, 1955.)

Racconti romani. Milan, Bompiani, 1954. (A selection from
this volume was translated as *Roman Tales.* New York,
Farrar, Straus and Cudahy, 1958.)

La ciociara. Milan, Bompiani, 1957. (*Two Women.* New
York, Farrar, Straus and Cudahy, 1958.)

Nuovi racconti romani. Milan, Bompiani, 1959. (A selection from this volume was translated as *More Roman Tales*. New York, Farrar, Straus & Giroux, 1964.)

La noia. Milan, Bompiani, 1960. (*The Empty Canvas*. New York, Farrar, Straus, 1961.)

L'automa. Milan, Bompiani, 1963. (*The Fetish and Other Stories*. New York, Farrar, Straus & Giroux, 1964.)

L'attenzione. Milan, Bompiani, 1965. (*The Lie*. New York, Farrar, Straus & Giroux, 1966.)

Una cosa è una cosa. Milan, Bompiani, 1967. (A selection of twenty-seven of the forty-four stories was translated as *Command and I Will Obey You*. New York, Farrar, Straus & Giroux, 1968.)

Il paradiso. Milan, Bompiani, 1970. (*Paradise and Other Stories*. London, Secker and Warburg, 1971.)

Io e lui. Milan, Bompiani, 1971. (*Two: A Phallic Novel*. New York, Farrar, Straus & Giroux, 1972.)

Un'altra vita. Milan, Bompiani, 1973.

NOTE: The following films have been adapted from Moravia's fiction: *The Wayward Wife*, directed by Mario Soldati (1955); *Too Bad She's Bad*, directed by Alessandro Blasetti (1955); *Woman of Rome*, directed by Luigi Zampa (1956); *Two Women*, directed by Vittorio De Sica (1961); *The Empty Canvas*, directed by Damiano Damiani (1964); *Le Mépris (Contempt)*, directed by Jean-Luc Godard (1964); *Time of Indifference*, directed by Francesco Maselli (1965); *The Conformist*, directed by Bernardo Bertolucci (1970).

B.   THEATRE, COLLECTED ESSAYS AND TRAVEL BOOKS

Teatro. Milan, Bompiani, 1958. (Contains: *La mascherata* and *Beatrice Cenci*. Only one of the plays has been translated: *Beatrice Cenci*. New York, Farrar, Straus & Giroux, 1966.)

Un mese in U.R.S.S. Milan, Bompiani, 1958.

Saggi italiani (with Elemire Zolla). Milan, Bompiani, 1960.

Un'idea dell'India. Milan, Bompiani, 1962.

L'uomo come fine e altri saggi. Milan, Bompiani, 1964. (A selection of nineteen of the thirty-four essays was translated as *Man as an End.* New York, Farrar, Straus & Giroux, 1965.)

Il mondo è quello che è; L'intervista. Milan, Bompiani, 1966.

La rivoluzione culturale in Cina. Milan, Bompiani, 1967. (*The Red Book and the Great Wall.* New York, Farrar, Straus & Giroux, 1968.)

Il dio Kurt. Milan, Bompiani, 1968.

La vita è gioco. Milan, Bompiani, 1969.

A quale tribù appartieni? Milan, Bompiani, 1972.

C. INTERVIEWS, ARTICLES AND ESSAYS

La speranza. Rome, Documento, 1944.

"Perché ho scritto *La romana*," in *Fiera letteraria*, March 13, 1947.

Interview, *The New Yorker*, May 7, 1955.

"I pittori malati di Verona," *Corriere della Sera*, September 6, 1959.

Interview, *L'Express*, December 31, 1959.

Interview, *Avanti*, January 1, 1961.

Interview, *The Guardian*, May 31, 1962.

"Differenza tra artista e intellettuale," *Corriere della Sera*, November 5, 1972.

II. Works on Moravia

Bergin, Thomas G. "The Moravian Muse," *The Virginia Quarterly Review*, XXIX (1953), 215–25.

Dego, Giuliano. *Moravia.* Edinburgh and London, Oliver and Boyd, 1966.

Del Buono, Oreste. *Alberto Moravia.* Milan, Feltrinelli Editore, 1962.

De Michelis, Eurialo. *Introduzione a Moravia*. Florence, La Nuova Italia, 1954.

Fernandez, Dominique. *Le Roman italien et la crise de la conscience moderne*. Paris, Bernard Grasset, 1958, pp. 9–138.

Flora, Francesco. *Scrittori italiani contemporanei*. Pisa, Nistri-Lischi Editori, 1952, pp. 197–231.

Heiney, Donald. *America in Modern Italian Literature*. New Brunswick, N.J., Rutgers University Press, 1964, pp. 202–20.

————. *Three Italian Novelists: Moravia, Pavese, Vittorini*. Ann Arbor, University of Michigan Press, 1968, pp. 1–82.

Kenelm, Foster. "Alberto Moravia," *Blackfriars*, XLIII (1962), 221–30.

Kibler, Louis. "Imagery as Expression in *Gli indifferenti*," *Italica*, XLIX, No. 3 (1972), 315–34.

Lewis, R. W. B. "Alberto Moravia: Eros and Existence," in *The Picaresque Saint*. New York, Lippincott, 1956. Reprinted in *From Verismo to Experimentalism*. Ed. Sergio Pacifici. Bloomington and London, Indiana University Press, 1969.

Limentani, Alberto. *Alberto Moravia tra esistenza e realtà*. Venice, Neri Pozza Editore, 1962.

Longobardi, Fulvio. *Moravia*. Florence, La Nuova Italia, 1969.

Mastrangelo, Aïda. "Alberto Moravia as Dramatist," *Quarterly Journal of Speech*, LIII (1967), 127–34.

Pacifici, Sergio. *A Guide to Contemporary Italian Literature*. New York and Cleveland, Meridian Books, 1962, pp. 29–56.

————. "Alberto Moravia's *L'automa*: A Study in Estrangement," *Symposium*, XVIII, (1964), 357–64.

Radcliff-Umstead, Douglas. "Moravia's Indifferent Puppets," *Symposium*, XXIV (1970), 44–54.

Ragusa, Olga. "Alberto Moravia: Voyeurism and Storytelling," *The Southern Review*, IV (1968), 127–41.

156 *Alberto Moravia*

Rebay, Luciano. "Carteggio inedito Moravia-Prezzolini 1935–1965," *Forum Italicum,* III (1969) 567–84.

——————. "Moravia: storia e strascichi di uno 'pseudonimo,'" *Forum Italicum,* IV (1970), 16–22.

——————. *Alberto Moravia.* New York and London, Columbia University Press, 1970.

Rimanelli, Giose. "Moravia and the Philosophy of Personal Existence," *Italian Quarterly,* XI, No. 41 (1967), 39–68.

Ross, Joan and Donald Freed. *The Existentialism of Alberto Moravia.* Carbondale and Edwardsville, Southern Illinois University Press, 1972.

Sanguineti, Edoardo. *Alberto Moravia.* Milan, U. Mursia & C., 1962.

Index

Globalization and Catching-up in Transition Economies

WITHDRAWN
UTSA Libraries

Rochester Studies in Central Europe

(ISSN 1528–4808)

Senior Editor: Ewa Hauser, Director,
Skalny Center for Polish and Central European Studies,
University of Rochester

Globalization and Catching-up
in Transition Economies

Grzegorz W. Kolodko

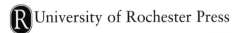
University of Rochester Press

Copyright © 2002 Grzegorz W. Kolodko

All Rights Reserved. Except as permitted under current legislation,
no part of this work may be photocopied, stored in a retrieval system,
published, performed in public, adapted, broadcast, transmitted, recorded,
or reproduced in any form or by any means, without the prior permission
of the copyright owner.

First published 2002

University of Rochester Press
668 Mt. Hope Avenue
Rochester, NY 14620   USA

and at P.O. Box 9
Woodbridge, Suffolk IP12 3DF
United Kingdom

ISBN 1–58046–050–X
ISSN 1071–9989

Library of Congress Cataloging-in-Publication Data
has been applied for.

British Library Cataloguing-in-Publication Data
A catalogue record for this book is
available from the British Library

Designed and typeset by Cornerstone Composition Services
Printed in the United States of America
This publication is printed on acid-free paper

Library
University of Texas
at San Antonio

Preface

Since the terrorist attack on the United States on September 11, 2001, almost everyone agrees that the world has changed and never again will be the same. Definitely, there have been major changes since the attack on New York and Washington, and on the U. S. A. as such, but some things will remain the same. And that is so because the world had already changed before the atrocities of September 11 and the reactions to these events.

The world has already changed in a remarkable way because of ongoing globalization and post-communist transformation. These two all important features of the turn of Twenty First century are discussed in this book, especially from the perspective of the Great Transition Depression, which—fortunately—is already in the past, and the fast long-term growth, which—hopefully—is still in the future.

It is strange, but globalization and transformation are often not considered in the same context, or as two interrelated aspects of one bolder process. Yet they should be, because there is a clear feedback between these two phenomena. Aside from the internal forces and external mechanisms, globalization acts as a galvanizing factor, which pushes forward and accelerates the process of post-communist transformation. On the other hand, globalization would be incomplete if the post-communist economies were not integrated into the global economy. After all, the latter would not even deserve to be called "global" unless it encompassed such a large part of the world as the post-communist countries of Eastern Europe. They constitute a large part of the world in terms of population (about one fourth) and land (about one third), but not in terms of contribution to the world economic output.

But—as we know—much has changed and the world, from an economic viewpoint, never will be the same again. The postcommunist economies seem to be coming out from the most difficult period of early stages of transformation and in the long-term future they have an excellent chance to grow fast, much faster than the world economy on average and for certainly faster (perhaps even twice as fast) than the advanced economies of the West. The Chinese accomplishments during the decades of the 80s and 90s have proven this already and now the question arises: will it be possible for other countries emerging from the legacy of centrally planned economy and communist state to also grow as fast economically? Of course, East Central Europe is very different from China, as are also the former Soviet republics. Yet in the latter case relevant differences sometimes are not that significant.

In the chapters that follow I try to argue that indeed a scenario for a significant step forward—without any unnecessary shocks, but with all needed therapy—is likely and fast growth of post-communist markets is feasible. Basically, it will depend on the quality of implemented policies and, to have such, they must be based on a correct theory. Hence the debate about the theoretical explanation of the post-communist transformation in the wider context of globalization must continue. The more it is needed, the more new questions are lying ahead.

This is the second book which I have written and published within the Rochester Studies in Central Europe. The previous one (Volume 1)—released by the University of Rochester Press in November 2000—is entitled *Post-Communist Transition. The Thorny Road.* The road remains thorny indeed to transform the former centrally planned economies, state-controlled societies and non-democratic regimes of East Central Europe and the former Soviet Union into the free market economies, civic societies and political democracies.

These issues are elaborated in a systematic and comprehensive way also in one of my earlier books, namely in *From Shock to Therapy. The Political Economy of Postsocialist Transformation* published in 2000 by Oxford University Press. Together with this work—*Globalization and Catching-up in Transition Economies*—these three books make a kind of trilogy on the politics and economics of the fast post-communist changes, not only in East Central Europe and the former Soviet Union, but also in the Asian countries going through vast process of changes including, of course, China.

Therefore, the considerations and conclusions presented here seem to be relevant to as many as about 30 countries in Europe and Asia (and soon also in Cuba) and to 1.7 billion people living there. They have the right to expect a better future and certainly some of them may be able to catch-up with the more economically advanced countries. This, however, depends on the chosen strategies for development and policies for reforms. Globalization, being itself an indispensable process, ought to be seen in this context as an additional factor, which must be taken carefully into account in a search for such strategies. Globalization—that is liberalization and integration of several autonomous markets into one global market of free flow of information, technology, goods and capital (and, to a lesser extent, labor)—creates both an additional risk and additional chances for the emerging markets and democracies, including the post-communist ones.

Yet the question remains: to what extent and by what means will they use these chances to their advantage? And how much can they accelerate the rate of economic growth and the scope of the progress vis-à-vis social development, and to what extent will they be able to overcome the risk brought by intensifying competition within the global market? It seems that in this changing world—which indeed has neither been the same since the end of the Cold War and collapse of the Berlin Wall, nor will be the same in the future due to irreversible globalization—there are more new chances than risks for the post-communist countries' development. It is up to them to maximize the former and neutralize the latter.

Professor Grzegorz W. Kolodko
John C. Evans Scholar in Polish and European Studies
Department of Political Studies, University of Rochester, Rochester, New York
And
Professor and Director of T I G E R
Transformation, Integration and Globalization Economic Research
Leon Kozminski Academy of Entrepreneurship and Management (Waspish),
Warsaw, Poland
http://kolodko.tiger.edu.pl

Rochester, October 2001

Contents

Tables

Figures

Chapter One

Introduction

The historical endeavor of the transformation from a statist-controlled economy to new institutional arrangements of a free market economy is a unique undertaking. Ongoing transition in the former centrally planned economies of Eastern Europe (EE) and the former Soviet Union (FSU)[1] is an indispensable part of globalization. Without this transition globalization would fall short of its full dimension, comprehensiveness and dynamism. Leaving aside the political and ideological concerns, the main argument in favor of transition to a market system has been a wide conviction that the introduction of a market economy should improve competitiveness and efficiency. Hence—after some short period of transitional contraction—the new system is supposed to lead to recovery and, later, to fast growth. However, for a number of reasons it has not occurred. Transitional recession lasted much longer than expected, contraction was deeper than assumed earlier, and the recovery was not—and in several cases still is not—as smooth as envisaged both by the relevant governments and the international organizations. Actually, instead of a rapid recovery and robust growth, the lasting recession rather turned into the Great Transitional Depression, continuing in some countries over the whole decade of the 1990s. Moreover, it is important that such a great depression happened to its full extent in the two biggest transition economies, Russia and Ukraine, with a population of about 200 million, or about a half of all the people in the countries in transition to a market system.

While after the first decade of transition, i.e. 1990–99, the index of average (weighted) gross domestic product (GDP) for the twenty-five countries

---

1. Henceforth—unless otherwise stated—the Baltic republics, i.e. Estonia, Latvia and Lithuania, though they belonged to the former Soviet economies, are counted as the East European countries. In recent years this has been a common practice, including among international organizations. Thus we are dealing with two major groups of transition economies, that is Eastern Europe, including the three Baltic states (EE), and the twelve former Soviet republics, that is the Commonwealth of Independent States (CIS). China and Vietnam are not taken into consideration in this context, since these countries are rather aiming still at reforming the existing economic system than at replacing it by an entirely new institutional set-up.

of EE and CIS stands at around 65 percent of pre-transition output, it is as low as around 54 percent for the CIS economies and still below the level from 1989—around 95 percent—in the case of the EE economies (Figure 1).[2] By all means that was not expected at the onset of transition. Furthermore, the surprise stemming from these unforeseen developments causes significant differences vis-à-vis the interpretations of occurring events. It is true both for the explanations of the causes of such a long-lasting contraction and, later, the sources of fast growth (in those countries where it has indeed happened) are concerned. Thus it is worth looking for the patterns underlying these processes in transition economies, especially from the viewpoint of policy options for the future and their political and technical constraints.

Consequently, after the Introduction, chapter 2 briefly discusses the links and feedback between globalization and transition to a market economy. In chapter 3 the scope and dynamism as well as the general causes of deep transitional recession are presented. Chapter 4 describes various paths of recession, recovery and growth, because these processes evolve along quite different routes in certain countries and regions of the EE and FSU. Chapter 5 elaborates on policy responses towards the challenge of prolonged transitional depression, while especially stressing the meaning of institutional vacuum and the importance of the following institution-building. Chapter 6 brings into consideration the problem of market imperfections and their implications for the redesigning of the government's role. In chapter 7 the issue of small versus 'big government' returns, and the link between the size of the government and the pace of economic growth is reconsidered. In chapter 8, on one hand, the implications of globalization and external shocks upon the recovery and growth are discussed and, on the other hand, the chances and mechanisms of the catching-up with highly developed industrial economies are examined. Chapter 9 presents both the passive scenarios of alternative growth paths in transition economies as well as the active policies aiming for growth acceleration and its sustainability in the long term. Finally, in chapter 10, the policy conclusions are presented for further debate.

---

2. The evaluation of GDP for Yugoslavia (Serbia and Montenegro) and Bosnia-Herzegovina is not taken into account here, due to the lack of reliable and consistent data. Yet if they were included, it would only change the overall picture for the worse. Data for 1994–99, based upon the evaluation of international organizations and PlanEcon (1999b) is presented in Table 3. Also the Mongolia's GDP—equal to about 1 billion current USD and thus matching only about 0.1 percent of total aggregated GDP for all transition economies—is not taken into account here; however doing so would not change an overall picture.

Figure 1: Index of Real GDP 1999 (1989=100)

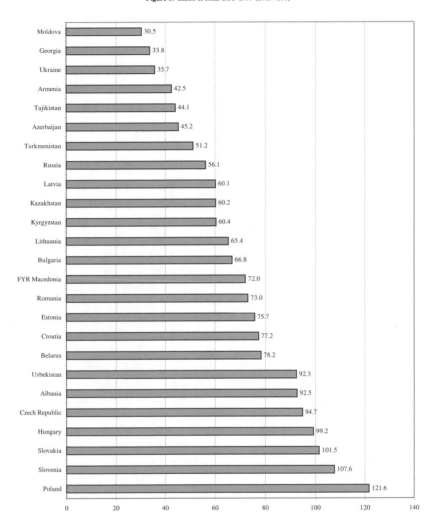

Chapter Two

Globalization and Postsocialist Transformation

The last decade of the twentieth century has been marked by immense changes in the world economy. The new phase of technological revolution occurring within the countries and continents' borders, on the one hand, and far-reaching internationalization of capital flow, on the other, have changed the patterns of economic performance. Broad trade liberalization, accompanied by growing liberalization of the financial and capital markets, has brought new prospects and new challenges. These challenges must be tackled not only by governments and various international organizations, but to an even greater extent by the private sector and non-governmental organizations (NGOs). Hence, on the eve of the new century, there are not only old structural problems that are increasing, but also several new issues that must be addressed properly by theoretical considerations as well as by sound policy response.

First, the private sector ought to be not only the main beneficiary of the fruits of globalization and transition, but it must be engaged more than up to now in crisis management. The role of private business is growing worldwide, both in advanced market economies and in developing and formerly centrally planned economies—in the latter mainly owing to vast privatization taking place there. The private sector, hence, must bear larger responsibility for the outcomes of the crises when they occur. To be sure, from time to time they will do so, regardless the efforts taken to avoid them. The private sectors in advanced industrial countries—including various financial intermediaries, investment banks and funds, the hedge funds, and still further merging multinational corporations—while getting involved more and more in business on the global scale, must also be more concerned about sharing the responsibility and the costs, when the international flow of capital fails to deliver positive results.

Second, the international organizations—including regional development banks and institutions dealing with particular aspect of international and global economic activities (i.e. IMF, WB, WTO, UNCTAD, ILO, etc.)—must coordinate their actions in a well-orchestrated way. Despite advancing liberalization, or in some sense because of it, there are certain intertwined processes being monitored by different organizations that are not capable of coordinating their policies sufficiently. Many problems on the global economic scene, including its postsocialist theatre, have evolved because of a lack of such coordination. A good example here is a risky situation of unregulated flow of short-term capital, which could help and facilitate economic growth in emerging markets, but might also make it more difficult. Unfortunately, in the late years of the last decade the latter was often the case. If the risk evolving from rampant trade liberalization is augmented by the risk coming from radical financial liberalization, these risks escalate critically, particularly in economies with weak institutions. And this is often the case in emerging markets, especially among the postsocialist countries.

Third, the international NGOs are going to play a much more important role on the global scene, including the economic part of it, than they have done so far. Thus they must be seen as the strategic partner for the private sector, the governments, and their international organizations. The recent case of coordinating the actions (if not yet the policies) towards debt reduction for highly indebted poor countries (HIPC) is a good example of such work and may turn out to be a good message for the future too. If the leading developed countries from the G-7 group, as well as the International Monetary Fund and the World Bank, work out the challenge of the debt burden together with some NGOs, like Oxfam and Jubilee 2000, then the effects will be visible. The future will definitely bring more initiatives of a similar type, in particular regarding investment in human capital and natural environment protection, on the one hand, and, on the other, counteracting poverty and inequality, which are still rising on a global scale. Transition economies also will be increasingly involved in these types of endeavors. It will work on behalf of their ability to develop faster, since these activities are linked to the learning process and to more favorable participation in the global economic interchange.

Fourth, the systemic transition to a market economy occurring in postsocialist countries has a significant meaning for globalization. Some of these countries are clearly on the path towards a full-fledged market economy. Some others—while still attempting to reform their existing economic system, for example, China—will most likely join this process soon. All three aspects of transition, that is, liberalization-cum-stabilization, institution-building, and the restructuring of industrial capacity, are related to the internationally occurring processes (Kolodko 1992b).

Liberalization-cum-stabilization is linked to the process of opening up previously relatively closed economies. That is reflected not only in the fact that, due to higher participation in international division of labor, their imports and exports are growing faster (or, during contraction, falling more

---

1. The World Bank (1997c) has seen the share of the transition economies' exports growing from 3.0 percent in 1992 to 3.6 percent in 2020 and the share of imports growing respectively from 3.4 to 3.9 percent. It is supposed to occur in the future due to the growth of the former at an average rate of 6.2 percent and the latter at an average rate of 5.9 percent over the entire period of 28 years.

slowly) than overall output.[1] It means also free entry to and exit from liberally regulated businesses for both domestic and international entrepreneurs. In addition, capital flow has been liberalized as well, thus making the infant capital markets of those countries a part of the global integrated financial and capital markets very quickly. International investors enter especially the financial and utilities sectors. This not only causes progress as far as quality of services provided by these sectors is concerned, but also a risk of a kind of 'dependent capitalism' (Poznanski 1997). Such risk stems from the asymmetry between the scope of capital being invested by transnational corporations and foreign investors in these countries, on the one hand, and the lack of ability of these countries to raise enough capital to invest into foreign markets, since they are short of capital to meet their own needs, on the other hand. This challenge can be overcome only in the long run, assuming that financial stabilization is accomplished, the fundamentals are sound, and the growth is fast.

Institution-building, especially through new laws and organizations facilitating the market-based allocation of recourses, is linked to globalization too. There are several institutional arrangements that are at the same time intensively a part of international and global institutional order, for example, regulation vis-à-vis trade liberalization agreed within the framework of the WTO, or standards and policies aimed at protecting the natural environment. An indispensable part of globalization—and not a contradiction to it—are the processes of various regional integration, for example, with (and later within) the European Union and, after initial disintegration, within the CIS. During globalization the national economies' institutional arrangements are becoming more similar to each other and the more similar they become, the easier it is to enhance the process of integration and globalization.

All these reforms lead to microeconomic restructuring of the existing industrial capacity. To a large extent it takes place simultaneously with the expanding involvement of multinational corporations. Thus a growing part of the production and distribution processes in transition economies can be seen simply as a fraction of the global economy. Increasing inward foreign direct investments (FDI) are making important contributions to this process. Nonetheless, the crucial meaning for future growth will have a propensity higher that that achieved so far to save and, consequently, a higher capability for domestic capital formation (Kolodko 1999b).

From this perspective, a sustained influx of FDI must be seen only as an addition to a healthy flow of domestic capital. Owing to globalization it should continue, even after the privatization process, which had been so strongly attracting the internal FDI expansion in the 1990s, is completed. Therefore, it ought to be expected that in the future the FDI will also be targeting microeconomic restructuring and thus will contribute to rising competitiveness in the long run. All these ought to enhance still further the growth ability in transition economies.

Chapter Three

Transitional Recession and the Great Depression of the 1990s

Before the historic endeavor of transition to a market economy has been launched, the formerly centrally planned economies were growing. Indeed, they were growing fast. Over the four decades preceding the 1990s the annual rate of growth had averaged from 4.8 percent in the former Czechoslovakia to 8.2 percent in Romania.[1] With such a pace of growth the national income was doubled in sixteen years in the former case, and in less than nine in the latter. However, growth under a centrally planned system had numerous specific features. At least five of them are worth mentioning in the context of the method of reasoning relevant in these considerations.

First, despite stubborn attempts of the governments—or indeed quite often because of their intervention in economic matters and owing to the bureaucratic allocation of resources—there were specific growth cycles (Bauer 1978, Kolodko 1976 and 1986). Although the output was growing systematically, the medium-term rate of growth was fluctuating up and down. There were periods of accelerated growth, and then—due to too extensive investment drive and the necessity to allocate more resources towards consumption's upgrading—there were periods of correction, during which the growth slowed down. Later, another expansion was launched and the sequence, by and large, was repeated (Table 1). These two features—the endogenous mechanism of periodical fluctuation and the relatively regular character of these changes—justify the interpretation of those processes as of a cyclical nature.

Second, the growth was of a 'bad quality', since even in relatively better performing economies the shortage syndrome was never eliminated entirely. That in turn was causing serious economic and political stress. Price distor-

---

1. There might be certain doubts and concerns about the reliability of data from that period. It could happen that, owing to methodological reasons as well as because of the political bias, the data about the pace of growth for some periods is not accurate. If it is not, then it is surely exaggerating the range of growth than underestimating it. However, if there are certain errors involved, it should make neither the long-term analyses, nor the comparisons between particular countries impossible. The conclusions drawn from these analyses must be taken with a proper care and reservations. So they are.

Table 1. Economic Growth Cycles in Centrally Planned Economies, 1950–89

Years/Growth rate in net material product, percent

Bulgaria

na	1953–56	1957–59	1960–63	1964–67	1968–71	1972–75	1976–80	1981–85	1986–88	1989
	6.5	14.0	6.0	9.1	7.4	8.3	6.4	3.5	5.2	0.5
	–	+	–	+	–	+	–	–	+	–

Czechoslovakia

1950–52	1953–56	1957–61	1962–65	1966–69	1970–75	1976–78	1979–84	1985–88	1989
10.0	6.5	7.4	0.8	7.2	5.3	4.7	1.8	2.4	1.9
–	–	+	–	+	–	–	–	+	–

GDR

1950–52	1953–56	1957–59	1960–63	1964–69	1970–75	1976–86	1987–88	1989
18.0	6.7	8.7	2.2	5.0	5.7	4.4	3.3	2.5
–	–	+	–	+	+	–	–	–

Hungary

na	1951–53	1954–56	1957–60	1961–65	1966–69	1970–74	1975–78	1979–85	1986–88	1989
	9.3	2.0	11.0	5.4	7.2	6.2	5.0	0.9	1.6	0.4
	–	–	+	–	+	–	–	–	+	–

Poland

1950–53	1954–57	1958–63	1964–68	1969–70	1971–75	1976–78	1979–82	1983–85	1986–88	1989
9.8	9.1	5.4	7.1	3.7	9.8	4.9	–2.7	4.9	3.9	0.2
–	–	–	+	–	+	–	–	+	–	–

Romania

na	1951–53	1954–56	1957–59	1960–62	1963–66	1967–70	1971–76	1977–79	1980–84	1985–88	1989
	17.0	5.0	10.6	7.6	10.5	7.0	11.5	7.7	4.0	5.4	–5.8
	–	–	+	–	+	–	+	–	–	+	–

Soviet Union

1950–51	1952–53	1954–56	1957–63	1964–68	1969–73	1974–78	1979–88	1989
16.0	8.2	11.6	6.0	8.2	6.5	5.0	3.3	2.6
–	–	+	–	+	–	–	–	–

Sources: Central Statistical Office (GUS), Warsaw, various years, and author's calculations.

'+'—acceleration. '–'—slowdown.

tions were leading to additional obstacles to sustaining a high and stable rate of growth. At the later stage, in some countries the shortages became accompanied by open (i.e., price/wage) inflation. Thus so-called 'shortageflation' syndrome had emerged (Kolodko and McMahon 1987). Consequently, growth was associated with lasting disequilibrium (Kornai 1986). Under the statist economy and central planning allocation that was just opposite to what was expected by the authorities.

Third, despite a high rate of growth the living standard was not improving fast enough. The socialist model of development had been based upon firm expansion of heavy industries and the investment drive, so consumption was always slowing down. Owing to the cyclical nature of growth, the rate of consumption growth fluctuated too, yet the highest variation was vis-à-vis the investments. Nevertheless, too slow (at least from the people's expectations perspective) improvement of standard of living was causing increasing social dissatisfaction, which in turn was causing a further loss of momentum. This factor, together with the discomfort of shortages, or even shortageflation, explains why the sociopolitical system was also becoming unbalanced, despite the fact that the rate of growth of production was not that low.

Fourth, there was a 'growth fatigue' (Poznanski 1996). The pace of growth was slowing. Especially at the later stages, after the initial rapid growth in the 1950s and less in 1960s, the rate of growth significantly declined. This happened even though investments were growing faster than overall production, what shows that, once again contrary to the expectations of the governments and policymakers, efficiency was shrinking. As labor productivity was growing slower and slower, in the late 1980s growth was coming close to stagnation and in 1989 it became even more sluggish. Thus the potential for growth was fading away. Yet before the quick growth could resume, output had collapsed by unexpectedly great extent. Unfortunately, together with the arrival of transition, the recession started too. Still worse, before critical financial stabilization could be established, inflation accelerated significantly. Thus these countries, although to different degree and for a different period of time, had shifted from one malaise—that is, the shortageflation under a dying centrally planned regime—to another one— that is, the slumpflation under the emerging market order (Kolodko 1992a).

Fifth, the catching-up process was already taking place under the centrally planned system. Especially in the early years, the countries at a relatively lower level of development, for example Bulgaria and Romania, were growing much faster that the countries enjoying a relatively higher level of production and hence a better standard of living, for example Hungary and the former Czechoslovakia (Table 2). The same can be said about the pattern of growth within the former Soviet Union, where Caucasus and Central Asian republics were growing significantly faster than the East European republics did, and about the former Yugoslavia republics, where this

Table 2. Average Rate of Growth (NMP) in Centrally Planned Economies,
1950–89 (percent)

	1950–89	First Phase of First Cycle	Last Phase of Last Cycle
Romania**	8.2	17.0	5.4
Bulgaria*	6.9	>10.0	5.2
Poland	6.7	9.8	3.9
Soviet Union	6.5	16.0	3.3
GDR	5.9	18.0	3.3
Hungary**	5.0	9.3	1.6
Czechoslovakia	4.8	10.0	2.4

Source: Central Statistical Office (GUS), Warsaw, various years and author's calculations.
* Average for 1953–89
** Average for 1951–89
NMP—Net Material Product

phenomenon, though to a lesser extent, had taken place too, for instance if one compares the rate of growth of Macedonia and Slovenia.

And then the year 1989 arrived and the transition began.

Transitional recession lasted from three years in the best case—i.e., Poland from mid-1989 until mid-1992—to as many as 10 years in the worst case, i.e., in Ukraine from 1990 until 1999. In the former, GDP contracted by about 20 percent and then started to recover and grow. In the latter, output (in terms of GDP) fell by over 60 percent and is believed to start to grow only in the year 2000.

While only four countries—in addition to Poland in 1996, Slovenia in 1998, Slovakia in 1999 and Hungary in 2000—have been able to recover the pre-transitional output, at the other end of the spectrum there are countries doing, from this angle, even worse than Ukraine. In Georgia and Moldova GDP in 1999 was at about one-third of its 1989 level and in another four FSU republics it was significantly below half that level. Among the EE economies, in six countries GDP was hovering around or below three-fourths of the 1989 output (Table 3).

Thus the great slump is a fact. However, it must be emphasized that the data for transition economies is far from perfect. Of great significance here is the bias stemming from the existence of vast informal, i.e., neither officially registered, nor taxed sector. The problem is that the informal activities indeed do alter upward the official statistics for both output and employment, but they do not necessarily raise the rate of growth or mitigate the rate of contraction. In other words, it is obvious that in transition economies the factual output and thus GDP is significantly—in the range between 15 and 30 percent—higher than the one officially acknowledged (Kaufman and Kaliberda 1996).

Table 3. Recession and Growth in Transition Economies. The Rates of GDP Change, 1989–99

	1989	1990	1991	1992	1993	1994	1995	1996	1997	1998	1999	Real GDP 1999 1989=100
Poland	0.2	−11.6	−7.0	2.6	3.8	5.2	7.0	6.1	6.9	4.8	3.8	121.6
Slovenia	−1.8	−4.7	−8.9	−5.5	2.8	5.3	4.1	3.5	4.6	3.9	3.5	107.6
Slovakia	1.4	−2.5	−14.6	−6.5	−3.7	4.9	6.9	6.6	6.5	4.4	1.9	101.5
Hungary	0.7	−3.5	−11.9	−3.1	−0.6	2.9	1.5	1.3	4.6	5.1	4.2	99.2
Czech Republic	1.4	−1.2	−11.5	−3.3	0.6	3.2	6.4	3.8	0.3	−2.3	−0.3	94.7
Albania	9.8	−10.0	−27.7	−7.2	9.6	9.4	8.9	9.1	−7.0	8.0	7.1	92.5
Uzbekistan	3.7	1.6	−0.5	−11.1	−2.3	−4.2	−0.9	1.6	2.4	3.3	3.9	2.3
Belarus	8.0	−3.0	−1.2	−9.6	−7.6	−12.6	−10.4	2.8	10.4	8.3	1.5	78.2
Croatia	−1.6	−7.1	−21.1	−11.7	−8.0	5.9	6.8	6.0	6.5	2.3	−0.7	77.2
Estonia	−1.1	−8.1	−13.6	−14.2	−9.0	−2.0	4.3	3.9	10.6	4.0	0.0	75.7
Romania	−5.8	−5.6	−12.9	−8.8	1.5	3.9	7.1	4.1	−6.9	−7.3	−4.1	73.0
FYR Macedonia	0.9	−9.9	−7.0	−8.0	−9.1	−1.8	−1.2	0.8	1.5	2.9	0.6	72.0
Bulgaria	0.5	−9.1	−11.7	−7.3	−1.5	1.8	2.1	−10.1	−7.0	3.5	1.4	66.8
Lithuania	1.5	−5.0	−6.2	−21.3	−16.0	−9.5	3.5	4.9	7.4	5.2	0.0	65.4
Kyrgyzstan	4.0	3.0	−5.0	−19.0	−16.0	−20.0	−5.4	7.1	9.9	1.8	0.0	60.4
Kazakhstan	−0.4	−0.4	−13.0	−2.9	−9.2	−12.6	−8.2	0.5	2.0	−2.5	−1.7	60.2
Latvia	6.8	2.9	−10.4	−34.9	−14.9	0.6	−0.8	3.3	8.6	3.6	1.5	60.1
Russia	2.6	−4.0	−5.0	−14.5	−8.7	−12.7	−4.1	−3.5	0.8	−4.6	1.5	56.1
Turkmenistan	−6.9	2.0	−4.7	−5.3	−10.0	−18.8	−8.2	−8.0	−26.1	4.2	17.0	51.2
Azerbaijan	−4.4	−11.7	−0.7	−22.6	−23.1	−19.7	−11.8	1.3	5.8	10.1	3.7	45.2
Tajikistan	−2.9	−1.6	−7.1	−29.0	−11.0	−18.9	−12.5	−4.4	1.7	5.3	5.0	44.1
Armenia	14.2	−7.4	−17.1	−52.6	−14.8	5.4	6.9	5.8	3.1	7.2	4.0	42.5
Ukraine	4.0	−3.4	−11.6	−13.7	−14.2	−23.0	−12.2	−10.0	−3.2	−1.7	−2.5	35.7
Georgia	−4.8	−12.4	−20.6	−44.8	−25.4	−11.4	2.4	10.5	11.0	2.9	3.0	33.8

Table 3. *(Continued)*

	1989	1990	1991	1992	1993	1994	1995	1996	1997	1998	1999	Real GDP 1999 1989=100
Moldova	8.5	-2.4	-17.5	-29.1	-1.2	-31.2	-3.0	-8.0	1.3	-8.6	-5.0	30.5
Bosnia-Herzegovina	na	na	na	na	na	na	-5.7	58.9	50.1	19.4	6.6	x
Yugoslavia	na	na	na	na	na	2.5	6.1	5.8	7.6	1.5	-37.3	x
GDP-weighted average*												
EE-13	-0.2	-6.6	-10.7	-3.6	0.4	3.9	5.5	4.0	3.6	2.4	1.7	99.3
CIS-12	0.6	-3.7	-6.0	-14.2	-9.3	-13.8	-5.2	-3.5	0.9	-3.5	0.3	54.3
EE and FSU-25	0.3	-5.0	-8.1	-9.5	-5.0	-6.0	-0.5	-0.2	2.0	-1.2	1.07	1.3

Sources: EBRD 1999. Data for Russia for 1989 is for Soviet Union; source as in Table 1. Preliminary data for 1999 also from PlanEcon 1999a and 1999b, and from available national statistics. Data for Bosnia-Herzegovina, and for Yugoslavia from PlanEcon 1999b.

*The weights used are the EBRD estimates of nominal dollar-GDP for 1996.

na—data not available.

Though it changes only the basis from which the pace of growth should be counted, it does not change the rate of growth as such. Accordingly, contemporary—in 2000 and beyond—overall GDP as well as GDP per capita (and consequently GDP absorption, e.g., private consumption and investment) are both higher than it may be read from the official data provided by particular governments and international organizations. The reason for this otherwise good news is not faster than registered economic growth, but higher output at the point of departure. Hence these observations might change the understanding and interpretation of the absolute level of output, but not its dynamism.

It must also be admitted that, in some cases, the range of decline of output could be exaggerated at the onset of transition. It might be so, since part of the factual production did not vanish, but rather was transferred (most often together with the assets) from the official to the informal sector. Such particular form of privatization (since the official sector used to be state-owned and the unofficial became a private one) resulted in a pace of growth larger than the official figures. Often the output, which did exist before, yet was not registered, had turned out to be gradually recorded and thus counted in the official statistics.

Moreover, this process still continues and will continue as long as the informal economic activities are incorporated into the legal economy. Basically, that is due to further progress of financial stabilization and its consolidation into stability, on the one hand, and enhancement of institutional arrangements friendly to the market system, on the other hand. So, under such circumstances, the data suggest growth within some additional range, yet actually it is not taking place. Only what has been produced already earlier, now is counted in the national statistics.

Therefore, the phenomenon of the informal sector is bringing two types of bias to the real picture of initial contraction and recovery. First, it could happen that the real scope of contraction was exaggerated, but later the real growth could be exaggerated as well. Interestingly, in many analyses much more attention has been given to the former case than to the latter. The point is that in the longer run—say, in a period of a decade or two—the balance of these two contradictory phenomena may be neutral.

There was always a belief that growth would come sooner than indeed it did. For instance, in Poland, at the beginning of the transition, the government assumed that the contraction would last just one year and the fall of GDP would not exceed 3.1 percent. Actually, it lasted three years and was six times more severe.[2]

---

2. Despite the official statistics—accepted also by the international organizations, including the IMF, World Bank and EBRD—a dispute about the actual drop of output in Poland continues. There are authors (for example Berg and Sachs 1992, Czyzewski, Orlowski and Zienkowski 1994, DeBroeck and Koen 2000) trying to challenge the scope of transitional recession reflected in official data. However, the evidence seems to be clear that there was a drop within the range of about 20 percent over the period of three initial years of transition.

Gomulka (1990) was predicting the rate of growth for 4.7, 8.7 and 7.9 percent from 1991 to 1993, respectively, which altogether would bring sound expansion of about 22 percent in those three years, whereas actually the economy had contracted after the fall of about 12 percent in 1990 by an additional 7.0 percent in 1991 and then grew by just 2.6 and 3.8 percent in 1992 and 1993, respectively.[3]

Borensztein and Montiel (1991), though assuming better policy response and structural reforms, had forecast a 6.5 percent rate of growth, on the average, from 1991 to 1995 for Hungary and Poland and 3.25 for the former Czechoslovakia.

Summers (1992) expected that the Polish economy would turn around already in 1991 (2.0 percent growth) and thereafter would soar by five or six percent yearly. He had foreseen the positive growth in case of Hungary, Poland, Romania, and Yugoslavia since 1992, and in the case of Bulgaria and Czechoslovakia since 1993, with the acceleration of non-weighted mean rate of growth for the whole EE going up from 0.8 percent in 1992 to about 4 percent by the end of decade. On the contrary, it shrank by an additional 3.6 percent in 1992 (after a drop of about 17 percent in 1990–91), and at the end of decade, i.e., in 1998–99, it was expanding by only about two percent.

Not only were the individual experts wrong, but so were the governments and respected international organizations. The International Monetary Fund in its *World Economic Outlook 1991* had been expecting GDP growth for EE already since 1992. After predicting a contraction of only 1.5 percent in 1991 (contrary to the actual collapse of output by 10.7 percent in that year) the GDP growth was forecast at 2.8 percent for 1992 and at 4.4 percent for 1993 (IMF 1991), yet it dropped in the former by 3.6 percent and then increased by just 0.4 percent in the subsequent year.

And then the pendulum of expectations shifted to the other extreme. In the October 1992 issue of *World Economic Outlook*—under the influence of the data showing for 1991 a severe contraction of 10.7 percent in the EE economies and 6.0 percent for the FSU—the forecast had been changed significantly. For the EE countries, instead of earlier expectations of 2.8 percent growth in 1992, there was a forecast of 9.7 percent recession. As for the FSU economies, the forecast for that year was minus 18.2 percent, yet actually GDP contracted 'only' by 14.2 percent.

---

3. Interestingly, despite such bitter experience with greatly exaggerated and too optimistic predictions—and in addition to the deep slowdown of 1998–99, when the rate of GDP growth in Poland had declined from 6.3 percent, on average, in 1994–97 to 4.8 and about 4.0 percent in 1998 and 1999, respectively—he forecasts for 2000 a rate of growth within the range of 6.0 to 7.0 percent (Gomulka 2000). Other, more realistic, forecasts foresaw GDP growth for this year within the range of 4.2 to 5.2 percent. For instance, the former was the forecast of Citibank Poland and the latter was the official target of the Polish government. In reality the GDP growth was 4.0 percent in 2000 and a meager 1.5 percent in 2001

There have been, of course, a number of reasons that the early forecasts turned out to be overoptimistic, i.e., wrong, and that the expectations were not met. The range of uncertainty vis-à-vis especially the early transition and towards the results of the then ongoing vast and comprehensive change upon the level of output and its dynamic was indeed huge. Thus it was not that difficult to be wrong because of the substance of the process. Yet the issue is that the true mistakes had been much more about the policies and their theoretical foundation than simply about the forecasts. The latter were not accurate, because the former was mistaken (Kolodko 1991 and 1999d, Nuti 1992, Poznanski 1996, Stiglitz 1998a). Thus what has caused such a deep contraction that in so many cases has turned out to be a decade of lasting depression of economic activity at the very basic level?

By all means it is not possible to explain the Great Transitional Depression of 1990–99 either by the legacy of the past, or by the external shocks exclusively (Mundell 1997). This set of factors, of course, does play a meaningful role; however they are not to be blamed for all that misfortune, since it is indeed a great misfortune to lose a half or so of GDP over a decade. The crucial role in these events had been played by the policy and that policy was often wrong. Among the weakest part of this incorrectness was the initial negligence of the role of the institutional aspect of building a market system. Emerging market economy performance depends much more on the institutional arrangements than simply on overall economic liberalization.

Therefore, the discussion on the platform 'too fast versus too slow' liberalization and privatization has been led along the lines of the wrong alternative (Kolodko and Nuti 1997, Stiglitz 1998a). The theoretical question and pragmatic challenge were not about the pace either of liberalization or privatization, but about the ways these two processes were designed and coordinated (or, more precisely, often not coordinated) with institution-building.[4] If the institution-building was not enhancing the former processes, then there was a lack of compatibility among the elements of the multi-track process of transition. As a result, instead of growing, the microeconomic efficiency was further eroding, leading to such a long and deep decline in output.

---

4. In the extreme cases of both the large economies, such as Russia, and the small, such as Albania, it had happened that with an even bigger private sector (in terms of contribution to GDP) than in other countries, as for example in Poland or in Slovenia, the overall performance was much worse. Hence, the scope of the liberalization and the range of the private sector were not decisive in the changes of efficiency, but the institutional vacuum in the former countries and relatively sound arrangements and good policies in the latter.

Chapter Four

Different Paths of Contraction, Recovery, and Growth

There is a further strong, although indirect argument convincingly proving that policies that have been actually executed are of critical importance for recession and growth, not the legacy from the past, or bad or good luck. The legacy sometimes may help, but in the postsocialist economies it more often hinders. Yet whatever is such a legacy, the policies do decide. This argument is based on the fact that, despite many structural, institutional, geopolitical and cultural similarities between these countries, they have been moving along quite different paths over the first decade of transition (EBRD 1999, Kolodko 2000a, Blejer and Skreb 2000). These paths have been (and are going to continue to be) much more shaped by the policies than by any other factors. And that is the main cause that whereas in certain countries the transitional recession lasted just three to five years, in some others it continued over the entire 1990s. Therefore, the current, i.e., the 2000 level of output, is a function of two occurrences. First, it is a result of the seriousness of output decline during the particular years of recession. Second, it is a consequence of the numbers of such years.

In some countries the contraction lasted for a shorter period of time, yet altogether it was deeper owing to more severe decline of output during that time. In some others the recession lasted for a longer period, yet it was milder because production dropped to a lesser degree in subsequent years. In the two countries most deeply affected by the Great Transitional Depression—that is in Moldova and Georgia—in 1999 GDP stood at about one third of pre-transition level. Whereas it is the outcome of eight years of contraction and two years of growth in the former case, in the latter it is the result of six years of contraction and four years of growth. Whereas there are countries, like Armenia, suffering recession for a period of only four years though it was enough to bring their national income down to about 40 percent of pre-transition level, there are also countries like Romania, where the output had been falling for seven years, nevertheless by 1999 it was brought down just to 76 percent (Table 4).

Transition is a unique process by its very nature and substance. So even more is the transitional recession, depression and recovery. There are ex-

Table 4. Duration of Recession and Growth in 1990–99 (in number of years)

	Transitional Recession	Recovery	Second Generation Contraction	Growth	Total Contraction	Years of Growth
Albania	3	4	1	2	4	6
Armenia	4			6	4	6
Azerbaijan	6			4	6	4
Belarus	6			4	6	4
Bulgaria	4	2	2	2	6	4
Croatia	4	5	1		5	5
Czech Republic	3	5	2		5	5
Estonia	5			5	5	5
FYR Macedonia	6			4	6	4
Georgia	5			5	5	5
Hungary	4			6	4	6
Kazakhstan	6	2	2		8	2
Kyrgyzstan*	5			4	5	5
Latvia*	3	1	1	4	4	6
Lithuania	5			5	5	5
Moldova	7	1	2		9	1
Poland	2			8	2	8
Romania	3	4	3		6	4
Russia	7	1	1	1	8	2
Slovakia	4			6	4	6
Slovenia	3			7	3	7
Tajikistan	7			3	7	3
Turkmenistan*	7			2	7	3
Ukraine	10				10	0
Uzbekistan*	5			4	5	5

Source: Author's compilation based on data from Table 3.

In countries labeled with * there was growth until 1990 and transitional recession started only in 1991.

treme examples of annual drop of GDP in excess of 50 percent (Armenia in 1992) and growth of 17 percent (Turkmenistan in 1999). It is possible to spot huge differences between the highest rates of contraction and growth for the same year; in the most extreme case such gap exceeded 55 percentage points and that was in 1992. Even in the tenth years of transition, i.e., in 1999, this difference was still larger than 20 percent. Altogether, there are as many as fifty-seven cases of years with two-digit rate of contraction, but (not surprisingly) only seven cases of years with two-digit rate of growth. To be sure, after the initial collapse of output, the more the transition process had been advanced, the lower had been the fluctuations of the rates of growth (or contraction, if the growth had not come yet). Thus the processes ongoing vis-à-vis production activities are becoming less hectic and more easily manageable from the viewpoint of macroeconomic policy.

The worst of all those years was 1992, when only Poland—due to the recovery, which had taken off already since the middle of that year—had modest (2.6 percent) rate of growth. All other countries were suffering deep contraction within the range from minus 2.9 percent in Kazakhstan and minus 3.1 in Hungary to as much as minus 44.8 percent in Georgia and minus 52.6 percent in Azerbaijan. For the whole group of countries, the recession that year was fairly deep and accounted for minus 9.5 percent. And that had occurred when the transition was going peacefully and, unfortunately, there were local (military) conflicts in certain minor regions. Of course, in the latter case the explanation of such dramatic contraction is obvious, since these conflicts did contribute to further distortions, thus to output that dropped still further and to growing economic and social hardship.

So far the best year was 1997, that is the year when the early fruits of structural reforms had started already to ripen, but still before the East Asian contagion and the fallout from Russia's financial crisis were making their impact upon the region's economic activity (Montes and Popov 1999). In this year production fell only in five countries (including a drop of 26.1 percent in Turkmenistan, unusual for this stage of transition), whereas it was growing in remaining 20. The highest rate of growth was recorded in Georgia and Estonia—11.0 and 10.6 percent, respectively. For the entire region the rate of growth of weighted GDP on average was 2.0 percent. And then, in 1998, it fell again by 1.2 percent. It is possible and even likely that that was the last year when the contraction was reported for the whole region of both the EE and the FSU economies.

Hence, thus far there is not any clear pattern of the sequence of contraction, recovery and growth in transition economies. The first decade of this historical endeavor must be seen as a very untypical period of time, which has neither a parallel to anything in the past, nor should be expected to be repeated with similar characteristics in the foreseeable future—if ever at all. This is due to a number of specific factors influencing the developments in this regard.

First, the moment the output began to decline was somehow different in the different countries. In a few of them, for example Latvia and Uzbekistan, it occurred only at the end of 1991 and at the beginning of 1992, because of postponed and inconsistent liberalization. However, for the same reasons—that is, due to delayed structural reforms—production had already started to fall in 1989 in countries like Turkmenistan (within the FSU), or in Croatia (within the former Yugoslavia), or in Romania (within the former Comecon). Although they belonged to the same group of formerly centrally planned economies, they were not alike, though in all of them the distortions were mounting. The institutional arrangements of that time were inadequate for the challenge of the incipient globalization. Such a lack of institutional compatibility influenced economic efficiency in a negative manner. However, the initial impulse of contraction was not identical in each of the transition economies. In some of them contraction happened because transition to a market system was just initiated, whereas in certain others it happened because it was not yet launched.

Second, the depth of the recession was different in different countries. That was, on the one hand, due to the initial distortions associated with the late centrally planned economy, and, on the other hand, due to the applied policies. The more severe those distortions were—for example, the burden of non-performing foreign debt, the rate of open inflation and the scope of shortages, the range of price subsides, the array of inefficient state companies, etc.—the deeper the following contraction was. But during the early years of transition, the range of contraction was also larger in the countries that tried to exercise more radical liberalization policy. Therefore, if both these occurrences took place simultaneously—and that was precisely the case in, for example, Poland in 1989 and Russia in 1992—the early contraction was deeper (Figure 2).[1] The opposite example—that is the case without the distortions typical for a partly reformed statist economy and with a gradual shift towards liberalization—does not exist. Nevertheless, the Chinese and the Vietnamese experiences of the 1990s show that, if there is not too much of the first characteristic and not too little of the second, afterward the growth can be fast and, at least for the time being, sustainable.[2]

Third, the duration of transitional contraction was shorter in these countries, which were able to reform their economies under the previous system. The more the economic and financial mechanism of the centrally planned economy was reformed, the shorter was the period of introduction of the critical mass of new arrangements. Consequently, it has taken less time to improve allocative efficiency and hence to return to the path of growth. This is clearly the case in Hungary and Poland as well as Slovenia.[3] This

---

1. However, the case of Russia is quite different than Poland's. In the former, the GDP fell by 8.8 percent already in 1990–91, i.e., before substantial liberalization occurred. In the latter, there was growth until mid-1989, when the pace of liberalization was fundamentally accelerated, and only since then did the output start to fall during the subsequent three years. Considering the magnitude of distortions, no doubt it would have fallen also if the liberalization-cum-stabilization attempt was not undertaken, but under such circumstances the characteristics and consequences of recession would have been different. In Poland—owing to overshooting the stabilization policy and a trade liberalization that was too radical—GDP contracted in 1990 by as much as 11.6 percent and then, in 1991, by another 7.0 percent. Hence, it happened to be much more the result of policy mistakes than of the legacy inherited from the past. To the contrary, this legacy—that is the hybrid system that had been to a degree reformed and liberalized under previous institutional arrangements—did contribute significantly to the shortening of the period of transitional contraction. Nonetheless, in such a case three years is an extremely short period of time and under better policies it could have been even shorter.

2. The opposite tendencies vis-à-vis recession and growth in China and Russia should be seen as the most striking event in the world economy in the last decade of the twentieth century. Whereas GDP was doubled over a period of ten years in the former, it was halved in the latter. That has significant geopolitical implications for the future developments.

3. Slovenia was not as seriously affected by the regional conflicts as the other countries of the former Yugoslavia. When only such a conflict ceased to harm Croatia, this country too

Figure 2: Recession and Growth in Poland and Russia, 1989-99 (1989=100)

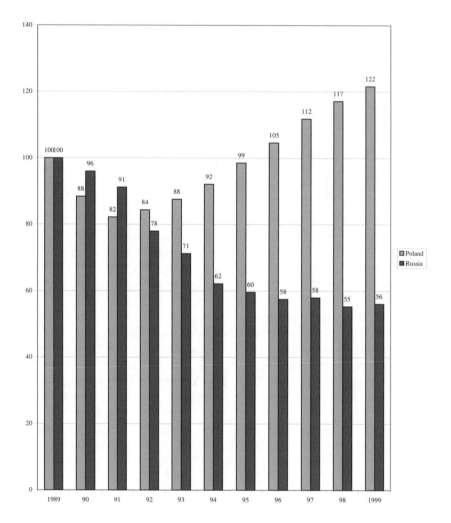

had taken off, enjoying 6.3 percent average rate of GDP growth in 1994–97 (same as Poland at that period). That was basically the outcome of gradual liberalization executed in the course of the 1990s, but also of the reforms carried before transition was fully launched. Later, in 1998–99, Croatian economy slowed down again, especially in 1999, owing to the new wave of regional conflict in the aftermath of the Kosovo crisis. Clearly, if not the regional conflicts, the republics of former Yugoslavia would do much better. Although suffering high inflation, a decade ago they were less distorted and better prepared than any other former centrally planned economy (along with Hungary and Poland) for the introduction of full-fledged market system. Only non-economic factors caused that it has not been the case.

claim is also supported by the experience of Estonia, where certain market-oriented reforms were also executed relatively earlier than in other countries of the FSU.[4] Such observation does not contradict the conclusion that these limited reforms, exercised prior to the transition, did contribute to growing financial destabilization as well. Therefore, this mixed outcome was also creating a mixed impact on the propensity to have first contraction and then expansion. Again, the best examples here are Hungary and particularly Poland. In this country, on the one hand, the inconclusive reforms of the 1980s led to fiscal and monetary instability. Yet on the other hand—and in the longer run it has been proved to be a much stronger factor—those changes contributed to a higher flexibility and ability to adjust. Thus, the derivative of both these contradictory tendencies for future growth turned out to be a positive one. The recovery came sooner and growth was faster, particularly from 1994 to 1997.

Fourth, even when there is a recovery following the period of contraction, it does not mean that the transitional recession and depression are over altogether. During the decade of the 1990s there were at least ten cases of returning contraction after the economy had alreadybegun to recover. So far, six cases of such 'second generation transitional contraction' have lasted for more that just one year. These events are not caused solely by the external shocks, but are happening as well due to a lack of both sound fundamentals and strong institutions that are supposed to uphold the growth when it comes. In other words, in transition economies, even more than in mature market economies, continuing growth is never a given just because it has already begun. It must be maintained by good policy, and also that might not be enough, if good institutions do not support good policy. Undoubtedly, just for that simple reason it must be expected that the future will also bring instances of falling output. Some of them will result from failure of the policies; some just form the work of business cycle mechanism. However, as far as the cases of the 'second generation transitional contraction' that have occurred recently are concerned, they have been mostly the results of wrong policies or negative external shocks, or the coincidence of both. The business cycle mechanism had not been yet set fully in motion, since it is a function of the strength of market mechanism, which is just being introduced during the transition.

Fifth, it must be remembered that if the national income was lost in the past due to the failure of the policies, its current and future growth is not a

---

4. Although prior to 1990 the systemic differences were much smaller among the FSU republics than they were between the EE countries, some economies within the former Soviet Union were more reformed than some others. This was most visible in the Estonia's instance, which was allowed to experiment with liberalization a little bit more than other republics, because it was the smallest of all of them. Thus, it was accepted also that the experiments with limited market-oriented arrangements could take place there relatively more vividly, without a great impact upon the whole country.

compensation for such loss. Only in the instances when the later growth is a function of the previous fall in output (happening because of structural reforms) can such a contraction be seen as a specific 'investment' necessary for gaining the fruits in the form of later growing output. Otherwise—and this is mostly the case in several transitional economies—contraction and recession simply means unrecoverable lose of welfare (Nuti 1992). Of course, such interpretation is a kind of oversimplification, since the inter-genera-tion redistribution of income is also taking place. Thus, some people are the losers, and some others are the winners, yet at a different time span. In the very long run it does not matter that much, but the very long run al-ways consists of very many short runs.

The first decade of transition in the EE and FSU economies has come to an end with the aggregate GDP for the whole region matching barely about 70 percent of the pre-transition level. With this evaluation in mind, the individual countries are compared from the point of view of their current output in relation to their output at the onset of transition and, of course, to the other countries' relative production (see Table 3 and Figure 1). How-ever, it may be very revealing to take a look at their aggregated output over the whole decade of the 1990s. If a certain country has succeeded in recov-ering the pre-transition level of output and another country was not able to do so, most often it is interpreted that the former is doing better than the latter, at least as far as the growth process is concerned. But it may happen that in the latter case the output—in relative terms—was higher over the entire period of ten years than it was in the former country.

Consider the hypothetical four-year sequence of recession, recovery and growth in two countries. In the first, the output fell by 10 percent during the second year of that sequence and then, in the third year, returned to the previous level. In the fourth year it was still growing, yet, say, by only 2.0 percent. As a result, it was overcoming the pre-transitional level by this very fraction. Thus, the sum of output over a period of four years is equal to 392 units (100+90+100+102). In the second country, the output con-tracted by only one percent and then again by one percent, and then again by one percent. So, at the end of that period it stood at 97.03 percent of the level of the starting year. Thus, the sum of output over a period of four years in this instance is 394.03 (100+99+98.01+97.02). It means that, de-spite the fact that currently, i.e., at the end of the whole sequence of con-traction–recovery–growth, the production (a one year flow) is larger in the first country (i.e. 102 units), the total aggregated production—if only the whole time span is taken into account—is larger in the second country, where the current production (again one year flow) stands at about 97 units. In the latter, with current output smaller by five units (i.e. 102–97), the sum of the four years output is by two units (i.e. 394–392) larger.

This, for instance, was the case of Slovakia and Uzbekistan. The index of 1999 GDP, when compared with 1989, is equal to 101.5 and 92.3 percent, respectively. However, in the former the GDP amassed for the whole decade is equal to 883 percent of the 1989 GDP, whereas in the latter it is equal to 901 percent of the output from that year. The illustration of relevant sums of the GDP, combined over the period of entire decade of the 1990s for all twenty-five transition countries, looks interesting (Figure 3).

The message is mixed again. In certain instances, while the relative aggregate GDP counted for the entire decade is larger, simultaneously the current relative level of GDP is smaller (Table 5).

Table 5. Ranking of GDP in Transition Economies in 1999 and 1990–99 (1989=100)

	Index of Real GDP 1999 1989=100	Total GDP for 1990–99 1989=100	Ranking Index	Ranking Total	Difference between two rankings
Poland	121.6	988.3	1	1	0
Slovenia	107.6	937.2	2	2	0
Slovakia	101.5	882.6	3	6	-3
Hungary	99.2	887.3	4	5	-1
Czech Republic	94.7	920.9	5	3	2
Albania	92.5	777.8	6	9	-3
Uzbekistan	92.3	901.1	7	4	3
Belarus	78.2	783.0	8	8	0
Croatia	77.2	723.3	9	12	-3
Estonia	75.7	715.7	10	14	-4
Romania	73.0	810.8	11	7	4
FYR Macedonia	72.0	739.5	12	10	2
Bulgaria	66.8	734.6	13	11	2
Lithuania	65.4	672.5	14	18	-4
Kyrgyzstan	60.4	684.3	15	16	-1
Kazakhstan	60.2	720.8	16	13	3
Latvia	60.1	637.8	17	19	2
Russia	56.1	685.1	18	17	1
Turkmenistan	51.2	696.9	19	15	4
Azerbaijan	45.2	540.8	20	22	-2
Tajikistan	44.1	565.4	21	20	1
Armenia	42.5	462.7	22	24	-2
Ukraine	35.7	558.4	23	21	2
Georgia	33.8	402.7	24	25	-1
Moldova	30.5	500.3	25	23	2
GDP-weighted average*					
EE-13	99.3	894.6	1	1	0
CIS-12	54.3	673.2	2	2	0
EE and FSU-25	71.3	760.6	x	x	x

Sources: EBRD 1999 and author's calculation. Preliminary data for 1999 also from PlanEcon 1999a and 1999b, and from available national statistics.

*The weights used are the EBRD estimates of nominal dollar-GDP for 1996.

Figure 3: Index of Aggregated GDP for the Decade 1990-99 (1989=100)

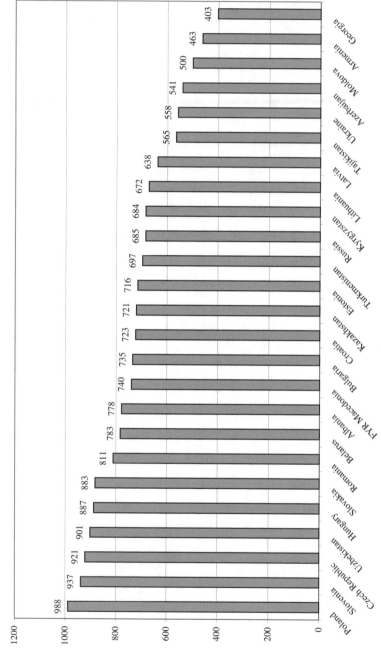

Source: Author's calculation based on data from Table 3.

Who therefore is better off? Is it a country with higher current level of GDP compared against the pre-transition output, though the sum of GDP for the entire transition period is relatively lower than in an alternative case? Or is it a country where the GDP amassed over the whole transition decade is relatively larger than the other country, although the current production is still relatively lower if compared to the other country? It depends. The issue is that from the formal point of view (leaving aside important structural changes), the same category of GDP is concerned. From another point of view, though, the somehow changed society is taken into account. Once again: today's higher income is not always a compensation of yesterday's loss. This is because some other people had lost and some other had gained. Such an outcome may cause social stress and political tensions, making economic policy and the structural reforms that facilitate it more difficult. Thus, what is important in this regard is a fluctuation of the rates of contraction and growth. It seems that what is more favorable is a less hectic and volatile fluctuation of these rates and a smoother process of quantitative change vis-à-vis output.

The differences are not striking, yet they are not negligible either. As for the end of the list, the same group of six countries, i.e., Azerbaijan, Tajikistan, Armenia, Ukraine, Georgia and Moldova (and all these countries belong to the FSU) are closing both rankings, although in a slightly different order. As for the beginning of the list, among the group of first six countries, as many as five are on both lists. While Poland and Slovenia are ranked with the same position, that is the first and the second, respectively, the remaining four countries are occupying only slightly different places.

Obviously, in several cases the position on both lists varies and the differences sometimes are quite significant, which illustrates more hectic changes vis-à-vis the alteration of recession and recovery, on the one hand, and the duration of these particular periods, on the other. In utmost instances, the difference is matching four points in either direction. Thus, Estonia and Lithuania are ranked four places worse on the list according to the amassed GDP for the 1990–99 period than vis-à-vis their 1999 GDP compared to the 1989 GDP. On the contrary, Turkmenistan is positioned four notches lower on the former than on the latter.

The most striking difference is between the two FSU republics. Whereas Estonia—acknowledged always as a leader among this group of transition economies—is followed immediately by Turkmenistan from the perspective of aggregated ten-year GDP (respectively 716 and 697 percent), her position from the perspective of the current GDP flow compared with the 1989 GDP (respectively 75.7 and 51.2 percent) is as many as nine positions higher. Therefore, the advantageous position accomplished through this latter criterion almost vanishes if only the total ten-year output is considered as an alternative criterion. But while looking forward, for obvious reasons Estonia is better, because from now on she may enjoy the growth stemming from the higher basis, hence bringing also a larger increment of production in absolute terms. In another words, if Estonia's GDP grows now by 10 percent, it makes an increment of about 7.5 percentage points of her 1989 GDP. If Turkmenistan does so, it makes an increment of merely about 5 percentage points.

In total, over the period of last decade, the whole group of twenty-five postsocialist transition economies produced barely 7.6–fold what they were able to produce in 1989. The corresponding index for the CIS stands at 673 percent and for the EE at 895 percent (see Table 5). It means that in Eastern Europe it takes as many as eleven years to produce the GDP matching the 11–fold 1989 GDP. It is the same from a formal viewpoint, as there would not be a recession, but just stagnation lasting eleven subsequent years— from 1990 until 2000.

Hence, such diversified paths of first recession and then recovery, and then growth (and, unfortunately, in some instances then once again recession) are of a unique nature. This is already the past, although transition will continue into the future for a long time. There are some lessons that ought to be learned from the experience of transition up to now, yet as far as the growth policy is concerned, the bygones are more and more the bygones.

At the current stage of transition, this group of emerging markets indeed has more in common with other emerging markets than it had only some years ago. Then it was often believed that these countries were supposed to be tackling similar problems as other distorted regions of global economy, particularly Latin America. That was neither the case then nor it is now, despite growing similarities between structural and institutional challenges that all these countries are facing. Nonetheless, whilewe consider the policy options from the viewpoint of future growth, the specific features of postsocialist economies still must be taken into account very seriously. Of crucial importance here is the process of institution-building.

Chapter Five

Policy Response and the Role of Institution-Building

From an economic perspective, the statist centrally planned system had come to the end because of the lack of ability to adjust. The changing environment of the world economy became a more demanding and thus rigid, inflexible system, enmeshed in numerous distortions, proved to be unable to improve its competitiveness. Whereas on the one hand globalization brought a threat for countries unable to adjust, on the other hand it brought also a chance to overhaul an inefficient system. In addition to growing internationalization of economic links, the ongoing technological progress together with vast political changes were critical catalysts in deciding that the time for comprehensive transition had arrived. Otherwise it would have been difficult (if possible at all) to adjust to growing development challenges and to take advantage of increasing chances for long-term expansion. Therefore, two issues have emerged.

First, initially the policies must tackle these new challenges within the framework of inherited old institutions. The institutions, i.e., the rules and the organizations that help to comply with these rules, always matter in economies in transition to a market system. But, within the wider concept of the meaning of institutions, the market culture and behavioral aspects of market economy ought to be looked at also. Hence, in transition economies—even if the law regulating the rules of an emerging market economy has been already adopted, and even if the organizations assisting the observance of these laws have been established—there is still a challenge of market culture and behavior, which are lagging behind the requirements of a sound market system. This culture is also a function of learning by doing, and it takes time everywhere, including the postsocialist societies. Yet it must be admitted that on a historical scale this process of learning by doing is going reasonably fast.

Second, as time is elapsing, these very institutions must be changed for the purpose of facilitating the policies. While in the long run the quality of institutions, and thus their short-term ability to support the course of actions, is a matter of policy, in the short run time the institutions are given. Hence, the policies carried out must be performed within the limits imposed by the existing institutional arrangements. In another words, there were—and to a degree still are—policies that cannot be implemented in transition economies because of institutional weakness. This claim, so obvious at the end of the first decade of postsocialist transition, was not a common wisdom at the onset of it; quite the contrary. Nonetheless, already at the beginning of transition there were also serious warnings pointing to this institutional dimension of the process.[1]

Not surprisingly, weak institutions—either tailored earlier for the needs of the outgoing statist system with the dominance of the government sector and bureaucratic control, or later only emerging from nothing—were also weakening the efficiency of policy. As for the real economic processes, considering such institutional weakness, there were various reactions that should have been expected, yet often they were not anticipated, precisely because of the negligence of institutional arrangements.[2] The most important in this respect was the lack of an early positive supply response. Many policymakers and their advisors, including certain international organizations, expected that the output should start to grow soon after liberalization took place and some critical mass of privatization was executed.

However, despite quite rapid and far-reaching privatization, for a prolonged period of time there was no improvement of allocative efficiency, or—to be more precise—it deteriorated. It would be opaque to assume that it was happening because private assets are less productive than the ones owned by the governments—since they are not less, but more productive— although there was such a coincidence that privatization was followed by the contraction. Thus, sometimes, transitional recession and depression are associated with ongoing privatization, yet it must be mainly linked to the institutional drawback.

Another important observation is that within the same or similar institutional arrangements alternative sorts of policies might be implemented. That means that, regardless of the existing institutional arrangements at a given moment in time, the policies can be better or worse. The policy re-

---

1. A good example of such warning was, *inter alia,* the following opinion: "The reform of [a] tax system will take place under difficult economic, social, and political conditions. Successful tax reform is never easy, but, given the circumstances, it is likely to be especially difficult in these countries and to take longer than many observers have assumed. In taxation there cannot be a 'big bang' solution since required changes, even when mistakes are avoided, cannot be made overnight. Because of the different environment in which the tax reform will be enacted, there is no certainty that the final outcome will be as good as one would desire." (Tanzi 1991, p. 19).

2. While considering the institutional aspects of transition, Douglass C. North has pointed out that: "Western neo-classical economic theory is devoid of institutions, it is of little help in analyzing the underlying sources of economic performance. It would be little exaggeration to say that, while neo-classical theory is focused on the operation of efficient factor and product markets, few Western economists understand the institutional requirements essential to the creation of such markets since they simply take them for granted." (North 1997, p. 2).

sponse can be more suitable to tackling the issues in one country, or less suitable in another. Therefore, the different policy responses are delivering different results, though the institutions do not differ.

However, it is also possible that even within the framework of weaker institutions the outcomes are better than they might be in places with stronger institutions. And that is exactly the result of better policies. Thus, the institutions do matter, but so do the policies. It may happen that economic performance is healthier in a country with better or worse institutions, or in a country with a better of worse policy. To some extent these are complementary matters, to some extent they may substitute for each other. And this explains why, as far as economic growth is concerned, some countries, *ceteris paribus,* are doing better than others. It also explains why in some of them the performance may be more remarkable over one period and worse during another, despite the fact that in the meantime the institutional arrangements have been upgraded and improved.[3]

Of course, the best combination is to have sound policies and good institutions. And, no doubt, the worst one is to have the opposite, i.e., weak institutions and bad policies. From this perspective, unfortunately, in transition economies the latter alliance has happened more often than the former. So, not surprisingly the transitional recession became the Great Transitional Depression.

There is not any clear rule with respect to the combination of quality of institutions and quality of policies in early transition economies. Later, presumably, they start to facilitate each other vigorously. However, before that occurs, it may happen that relatively better institutions can demobilize the lawmakers and the policymakers from taking committed care of further structural reforms and continuing institution-building, since it is an everlasting process and not an episode. Or it may happen to go the other way around. Then the distortions, difficulties, tensions, crises, etc. are pushing the governments to reform the institutional orders still further. In short, although of great economic implications, this question is also of a great political nature. The answer to it depends on the ability of the elite to formulate the long-term development visions and is strongly involved in a feedback with the simultaneous process of political liberalization, i.e., democratization.

---

3. A fine example of this inter-relation is the Polish economy. In this country, due to gradual yet committed institutional building and because of sound policy, growth had accelerated after 1993, following the recovery that started in mid-1992. However later, since after 1997, the pace of growth did slow down significantly (and much more than expected). It had occurred despite ongoing advancement of institutional building over all these years as well as before and afterwards. To modest extent it was provoked by the external shocks, by mainly was caused by the deterioration of policy. The analysis just pointing to the external shocks falls short to explain the drop of the rate of GDP growth from as much as 6.7 percent in 1995–97 to only about 4.4 percent in 1998–99 and then to as low as 2.7 percent in 2000–01. The deterioration of policy does explain it.

Hence, the issues are quite complex. It is excellent when the progress with institution-building results simply from the wisdom of the people and the determination of their leaders. It happens. But experience shows too that quite often the institution-building gains momentum if the problems are mounting. Then a strong pressure appears and a need for structural reforms, coming especially from the emerging business sector, but also from the outside, increases. The international organizations—which provide technical and financial assistance based on the condition that a proper policy is executed and adequate reforms are put forward—contribute as well to such processes.

Chapter Six

Market Imperfections and the New Role of Government

As the debate continues about the policies that should be used to shift from state socialism to the market economy and from stabilization to growth, it has become the generally accepted opinion—if not a truism—that none of this can happen without proper government engagement (Fischer, Sahay, and Vegh 1995). Even extreme neoliberal zealots in government—not at all a rare occurrence in Eastern Europe—exercise vast amounts of interventionism.[1] The laissez-faire ideology remains where it belongs, in the world of words, in the sphere of ideas and illusions. In the world of real politics and true policymaking, laissez-faire is not and cannot be a viable approach. The work of the market is being seconded by the active policies of government in financial, economic, and social matters (Kolodko 1998).

Though arguing appropriately in favor of the market, some authors stress that until not so long ago government intervention played a very positive role in development. State control of the economy worked well for a long while in traditional capitalist countries. In reference to the statist policies adopted after the Second World War, Yergin and Stanislaw (1998, 128) ask,

'Who could deny the success of the experiment? From the end of the Second World War until the oil crisis of the 1970s, the industrial world enjoyed three decades of prosperity and rising incomes that sparked aspiration and dreams. It was an extraordinary achievement.'

And then they reach the conclusion (p. 129) that,

---

1. Some observers believe that the declared 'neoliberals' in Hungary and Poland, having already been taught by the experience of the early 1990s how the economy really works, are eager now to intervene in the market even more than the 'leftist' governments did (the leftists presumably having hesitated because they wished to prove that they were not 'postcommunists'). Though this is not true, the fact is that, whereas the gap between the words of the 'neoliberals' and the 'leftists' is like the Grand Canyon, the gap between their deeds is like a little ditch. Such pragmatism is a good sign for those who hope for the success of the transition.

'By the end of the troubled 1970s, a new realization had gained ground: More than daily management, it was the entire structure of the economy that had reached its limits. It was imperative to rethink government's role in the marketplace.'

If indeed the issue was the simple one of reaching the limits, then it is puzzling that almost the entire globe turned away from statism at almost the same moment, since at the time nations were at such varying stages of development.[2] But the world was also turning away from other old habits around them. Why? Simply because one must follow the leader. When changes are being undertaken in countries that are leading the course of events, soon afterwards they can (or must) be carried out elsewhere. If a step has already been accepted and executed by a leader, then it is much easier to push the case for such a step elsewhere. This is even more true in the midst of a vast process of globalization that is reaching well beyond economic and financial affairs alone. Thus, since a leader is getting rid of some old habits, during a period of globalization the old habits are being got rid of on a global scale. It is only a matter of time.

Of course, there is a world leadership, as well as local ones. The United States has unquestionably been leading the world since the end of the cold war, but there are also regional leaders taking steps that deserve to be followed. The social security reform implemented in Chile is catching on throughout South America. The way Poland has managed the transition is a model in Eastern Europe. Uganda is trying to find the path toward fast growth in Central Africa. The industrial policy of Singapore has imitators in East Asia.

If the impact of what is going on in the most advanced market economies is not always directly felt in the economies going through structural adjustment, then it is certainly very often felt indirectly. The best way to bring democracy and an open market economy to Paraguay is probably to do it via Chile, to Myanmar via Thailand, and to Belarus via Poland. This is well understood among world leaders, including the potential partners in the post-Washington consensus.

Aside from the geopolitical dimension, in trying to answer the important questions, one must take the historical perspective, too. For example, the United States has come to terms with the acknowledgment of the existence of minority rights quite late. Only a generation ago in some states there were still schools and other public institutions (including restaurants and public restrooms) 'for whites only'. So, the 1960s were not the best years for the US to complain and moralize about the civil rights of blacks in

---

2. This is also true of the former socialist economies. Hidden within the 'multi-republic' Soviet Union and the Yugoslav Federation were countries like Tajikistan with GDP per capita below $1,000 and countries like Slovenia with GDP per capita at 5 times that much.

South Africa or about the treatment of the Hungarian ethnic minority in Czechoslovakia. On another topic, Joseph E. Stiglitz (1998b, 70) writes that,

> 'It is hard to escape the irony between early drug wars—Western powers trying to keep China open to the flow of drugs—and the more recent equally adamant stands [of the Western powers] trying to stem the flow of drugs into their own countries. Only the lapse of time—and lack of knowledge of these historical experiences—softens what otherwise seem[s] an intolerable level of hypocrisy.'

Yet the hypocrisy is still there, even without the difference in historical time zones.

After years of insistence on trade liberalization, the U.S. House of Representatives—when a majority of emerging market countries in Latin America has finally accepted the idea and got keen to apply it—has denied the president the power to take the fast track in trade, and so trade has not turned out to be as free as the market zealots themselves have said it should be. Once more, it is a good idea to distinguish between the ideas and the words, the interests and the deeds.

And it is good to remember that hypocrisy exists, and that unfortunately it does matter in politics and politically motivated economic debates. In the real political world, including the international one, it so happens that the stronger partners really seem to expect the adage 'do what I say, not what I do' to be followed. If only what some are advising others to do were also being done by the advice-givers in their own countries, many problems would look quite different. For example, an upward adjustment of energy prices in the United States through the imposition of a special excise tax would have led to a decrease in the fiscal deficit several years ago. Likewise, if the advisers would only follow their own advice the EU bureaucracy in charge of agriculture policy would now be several times smaller than it actually is. Instead, today the energy prices in the United States are lower and the agriculture subsidies in Western Europe are higher than those in Eastern Europe.

When (or perhaps the question ought to be introduced by 'why') should one retreat from statism? It might be argued that the 'when' has arrived already, since the leaders of the global economy have already so decided and acted (albeit only to a degree). And they, for sure, know what they are doing and why. However, if state control has reached its limits in the advanced market economies (which is not certain), this is not necessarily the case in transition economies or in less-developed economies. Even at a time of deep structural crisis in Japan, one of the most developed countries, the most extreme of the neoliberal extremists have not expected markets to fix the problem, but have called on the government to do so.

In general, the state may retire from intervention in the economy when market mechanisms, market culture and behavior, and proper institutional arrangements exist to carry out the functions it performs. There seem to be two criteria for the withdrawal (never complete) of the state from intervention in the economy. First, there must be a reliable mechanism to sustain long-run growth that is impervious to minor external shocks. Second, if there is nonetheless a crisis because of an unfortunate coincidence of external shocks, then there must be an automatic mechanism that corrects distortions so that the economy can remain on track toward development. Even in the most advanced market nations, including Germany and the United States, these criteria are not met.

If the involvement of the state in economic matters was justified in the past in the development of the countries that are currently most advanced, it is at least equally well justified in countries currently lagging behind with respect to development and market sophistication. There may be good arguments for significantly less government intervention in the economy in Belgium and Italy today, but they do not necessarily apply in, say, Bulgaria or FYR Macedonia. What may be reasonable in the United States under President Bush may be irresponsible in Russia under President Putin. Even what is now feasible in Hungary and Poland should not be attempted yet in Kazakhstan or Ukraine because of the institutional gap among these emerging market economies.

If the transition to the market is to succeed, governments must be energetic in a number of areas of the economy. Governments in the postsocialist nations must intervene to manage transition policy and development strategy so that production can start to increase. Active government intervention is especially required to steer the economy toward recovery, but it is needed to achieve sustainable growth, too. Government policy engagement must be maintained even when the economy is expanding, because nowhere—and this is particularly true during transition—is economic growth a given. It must be supported and managed. To sustain rapid growth—if it is to contribute to equity and not harm the environment—may demand even much more policy attention than the early stages of liberalization and stabilization. During the later stages of transition, in the aftermath of the postsocialist crisis, even more government involvement may be justified. When liberalization and stabilization are the priorities, the 'invisible hand' of the market can be relied upon more, but during the shift from stabilization to sustainable, environmentally friendly, and equitable development the 'visible hand' of the policymaker has more to do.

Few people like to go to the dentist, but the dentist is essential if we wish to monitor the health of our teeth properly. The dentist reduces the risks by cleaning, filling cavities, and sometimes doing a little drilling. But we would be wise to choose our dentist carefully. Likewise, if the government putters with the market, it may augment the distortions, but by intervening wisely it can prevent crisis. The government can inadvertently boost the effect of the imperfections in the market, or it can counteract them to enhance the strengths of the market.

Even in contemporary liberalized economies, governments and markets must complement each other.[3] There is all the more reason why this should be so in postsocialist economies, where automatic mechanisms have not yet evolved sufficiently to enhance the institutional arrangements on which the market must depend if it is to function efficiently and contribute to the welfare of the nation.

Market imperfections, as well as governments, can cause serious economic problems and foster crisis. The expansion of the role of government is not a sure remedy for market imperfections, nor is the extensive liberalization of the market a sure remedy for the failures of government. The cure-all is a 'partnership' between the market and the policymaker. What is needed to mend market imperfections is not less market and more government, but a better and stronger relationship between the market and the government.

The collapse of state socialism was a result of the failure of the state for the simple reason that under state socialism there was no market. The Great Depression of 1929–33 was caused by the failure of both the market and the state. The Great Transitional Depression of 1990–99 in postsocialist countries was likewise due to the fact that neither the state nor the market was able to clean up the mess. Now, in the aftermath of this depression, neither the state alone nor the market alone is going to be able to achieve recovery and sustainable growth. The transition is thus an ongoing search for the proper mix of market and government.

The market must evolve, and the government must assist in the process, but as the market evolves, so must the role of the government. Only a combination of these two regulatory systems, the one led by the market and the other by the state, will be able to deliver sound supply responses. Market institutions must be designed by the state and then allowed to evolve in such a way that they promote efficiency and competitiveness. Meanwhile, as the market evolves, the state must redesign its interventions to correct market imperfections and assure equity and long-term development. Only coordination between these two processes can secure increased capital formation and growth.

The danger of too-thoroughgoing government interventionism is especially high at the early stage of transition, when the burden of old policy instruments and weak institutions is greatest. The neoliberal solution is the withdrawal of government ('the best policy is no policy'). But then there is also no growth, or, if there is growth, it is sluggish, unsustainable, and inequitable. Some segments of society benefit, but most people suffer more. Thus, the non-approach of 'the best policy is no policy' has been compromised (and not only in transition economies).

---

3. Obviously, the debate on this issue is far from over. For example, see World Bank 1997b.

The constructive solution is a new style of engagement of the state, not the withdrawal of the state. A convincing argument in favor of this approach has already been provided through the experience of a number of growing economies, including reformed socialist economies and transition economies. The approach represents a foundation for the post-Washington consensus, and this is very important, for it can affect economic policies worldwide. Indeed, almost the entire globe is turning away from the neoliberal bias and seeking a new role for the state, and the effort would have a better chance of paying off in Myanmar, Paraguay, or Belarus if it were well understood elsewhere, for instance among the potential partners of the post-Washington consensus.

The fact is that the contemporary world is so complicated because there are so many global links, and national economies need government-led policies and government intervention more than ever. Yet, the involvement must be of a different sort, especially in postsocialist countries. The core of the transition process is a liberalization that releases spontaneous market forces, but this should be matched by an effort to establish sound financial fundamentals, develop infrastructure, secure investments in human capital, introduce necessary structural reforms, and set new institutional arrangements. This effort should be serious enough that the state seeks to restructure its interventions in the economy, not eliminate them.

In industrial nations the share of public spending in GDP jumped from about 12 percent in 1913 and 18 percent in 1920 to 28 percent in 1960 and 45 percent in 1990. There were several reasons for this phenomenon, but it would not have occurred if there had not been strong and constant political pressure and a good economic rationale for so much public expenditure. In part, it was also due to an evolution in social values, especially the growing conviction that development must be equitable and that the market system was unable to guarantee this equitability. The expansion seemed to be justified by traditional needs such as defense, infrastructure, and administration, but also by the widespread belief that only the state can furnish adequate education, health care, and social security for all. So, the new state and 'big' government emerged.

The insistence on an expansion in government spending can be reexamined only at a higher stage of development, when there are sufficient private resources to ensure that the requirements in education, health care, and social security can be reasonably met, and when the institutions exist to manage these resources without direct state participation. The recent drive in advanced market countries to alter the decades-old tendency toward ever bigger government can be explained by the fact that they possess a positive alternative. Indeed, it may be necessary to contain or downsize big government for the sake of competitiveness, capital formation, and growth potential.

The situation is not the same in transition economies, and the same considerations are therefore not necessarily justified. The postsocialist nations are poorer, and their level of development is far from adequate. While the more advanced and the relatively rich among them have somewhat more resources, even these do not have private institutions able to provide the services only the state has supplied so far.

Because of the long experience in some regions it is being realized that development also depends on the 'visible hand' of the government rather than exclusively on the 'invisible hand' of market forces. In the mid-1960s the level of development was similar in Africa and East Asia. In 1990 Africa was still backward, but East Asia was 'newly industrialized'. Without appropriate state involvement and government policy backing, market forces in Africa have not been able to deliver durable growth. Paradoxically, the late 1990s Asian crisis, manageable neither exclusively by market forces nor only by governments, is another argument in support of the claim that even at the *fin de millénaire* there is room for more and better government engagement, but not for government retirement.

The active role of the state must be redefined, not abandoned, during systemic transformation, whether the reform of a socialist regime or the postsocialist transition. The process of privatization demands a different type of partnership between government and the private sector. The new circumstances call for a fresh regulatory environment, not only 'deregulation', but 're-regulation'. The government must take on the burden of a proper policy to encourage competition. It must fight monopolies. Even if just for this one cause, the old state may not be needed anymore, but the new one is very much required, at least until the competitive environment is established and efficient product markets appear.

During transition the state changes the scope of its activities and also the instruments it uses to implement its chosen strategies.

'The market itself cannot deliver broad-based improvements in the standard of living without an active state which establishes the right conditions, responds to change, and which, together with the market, provides for the delivery of health, education, infrastructure, and social protection, which the market cannot provide by itself. The way in which the role of [the] state is defined, and in which services are delivered, is probably the most important determinant of the standard of living of the community over the long-run term.' (Stern and Stiglitz 1997, 27)

These are still more important reasons because they are here being listed by the former and the new chief economists of the World Bank, and a successful shift from depression to recovery to sustained growth in the transition economies depends to a considerable extent on the financial and technical assistance of these and other financial organizations, mainly the International Monetary Fund and the European Bank for Reconstruction and Development.

The world is so very diverse that it is quite strange that there is a tendency to draw general conclusions and give advice that is supposed to meet all challenges. What works in some circumstances is not necessarily appropriate in other circumstances. One size does not fit all. This is as true of shoes and socks as it is of the level of involvement of the state in managing recovery after a crisis. If the downturn in the business cycle in an advanced market economy is of the normal variety, then of course market forces and the government should react normally. But if there is long-lasting depression and extensive structural crisis, then a 'new deal' in government economic policy and in institutional responses may be required. This is true not only of the postsocialist transition and development, but also of the serious economic challenges being faced elsewhere in the world. The 'new state' is as much needed in Africa as it is East Asia.

According to the World Bank (1997b), there are five crucial functions that should be fulfilled by the state because the market and private institutions cannot perform them. These functions are related to legal foundations; the macroeconomic policy framework; investments in basic social services, in human capital, and in infrastructure; the comprehensive safety net for the vulnerable in society; and the protection of the natural environment.

The problem is that these five key functions are policy declarations or policy directives rather than conditions that are respected in the advice of international financial organizations and in the policies being executed in developing and transition economies. They have not really become performance criteria, and thus they are not considered so decisive in actual policy packages. Yet, financial and technical assistance would do well to focus greater attention on these five functions, which ought to be performed by the modern state in an emerging market economy.

Furthermore, lending by the World Bank and the EBRD should be based much more on conditionalities that recognize these five key domains of state activity and should definitely not support policies or programmes that may weaken or ignore them. This calls for a revision of the qualification procedures for financial assistance and especially a revision of the method of monitoring the countries being provided with lending by international organizations, so that much more serious attention is paid to the fulfillment of these five essential state functions.

However, for the sake of fiscal prudence and monetary stability, policies that disregard these functions are being supported, too, especially stabilization and structural adjustment measures which, unfortunately, often lead to falling output and growing inequality and thus to spreading poverty, rising unemployment, divestment in human capital, a frazzling safety net, and weaker environmental standards.

There are contradictions between the means and the ends of policies, and there are thus also contradictions among the excessively numerous priorities on the agenda. So, the World Bank postulates firm financial reasons for one course of action, but these turn out to be secondary in the confrontation with the IMF over sound financial fundamentals.

Despite the significant structural and institutional changes of the 1990s, the redefined functions of the new state in transition economies are all quite similar. But 'similar' does not mean 'identical'.

Chapter Seven

Small versus Big Government and the Quest for Equitable Growth

It is often claimed that the shortest way to recovery and growth following transitional contraction is to diminish the role of the state. As proof of this, mainstream neoclassical economists cite a few carefully selected examples of successful nations with small governments and fast growth. However, in light of experiences in the world economy, the supposed alternative between big government and a lower rate of growth or small government and a higher rate of growth does not really seem to be an entirely valid one. If there were such a clear choice, then small government might be a better option, even at the cost of a temporary dropoff in public services. In fact, in the real world, such a solution may sometimes be appropriate, but the opposite situation is more likely to emerge: a positive correlation between the size of government and the pace of growth.

In transition countries, 'small government', that is, a relatively lower amount of income redistribution through the public finance system and the relatively minor involvement of the state and the public bureaucracy in economic affairs, usually means that institutions are weaker and that the shadow economy is larger. Meanwhile, 'big government' means that the state is more active and redistributes a relatively larger chunk of income through the government budget.

Government expenditure can accelerate the pace of growth, particularly if it is directed at institution-building, the upgrading of infrastructure, and human capital investment, especially education, health care, and research and development. Government expenditure can hinder growth if the bulk of state expenditures flows toward the bureaucracy, defense, and subsidies for non-competitive activities. In short, outlays can be productive or non-productive, investments can be oriented toward the future or toward current consumption, and expenditures can be well targeted or miss the target. The trick is to determine the proper mix between management by the state and management by the market.

Orthodox neoliberal economics suggests that a reduction in the size of government facilitates growth. However, during the early transition something quite different happened. Owing to the complexity of the changes, it is not possible to identify exactly the nature of the correlation, but there can be no doubt that during the early transition there was a causal relationship between the rapid shrinkage in the size of government and the significant fall in output. The sudden withdrawal of subsidies caused a financial squeeze, and the radical stabilization measures led to a credit crunch. The initial shocks were thus followed by recession. Only later, after output is back on the path of growth, can the positive effects of the pruning in government be seen, if indeed they occur, for this depends more on the quality of development policy than on the pace and scope of the decrease in government expenditure.

Consequently, even if to some extent under certain conditions it may be true that smaller government can foster long-term growth, the issue is not really whether less government is better, but how to get from here to there and how long is 'long-term'. Is it 15 years or 50? This is at least as important here as it is in a marriage. The challenge in transition economies is not the overall paring of government expenditures, but a change in the structure of government expenditures so that a greater portion of outlays contributes to faster growth and fairer income distribution.

It is almost impossible to prove that public services are more effective if there are fewer of them (that is, when government is smaller), but the attempt is still being made (*The Economist* 1997). However, it is clear that the various components of government expenditure change during transition. Since the type of government is new, with new targets and instruments, new friends and enemies, and, especially, new sets of problems, expenditures in some areas must climb, but in others they decline. Nonetheless, an across-the-board reduction in the size of government by reining in expenditures, often those directed at infrastructure and human capital investments, can erode not only current levels of consumption and living standards, but also growth and the standard of living in the future. The belief that there is a strong inverse correlation between the size of government and the rate of economic growth can thus exert pressure for spending decreases that are too far-reaching not only in countries with unsustainable fiscal deficits, such as Russia and Ukraine, but also in those with a sound fiscal position, such as the Czech Republic and Hungary.

Analogous conclusions about the danger of excessive curbs on government expenditure have been derived from an extensive study conducted on the issue of humanitarian emergencies in a sample of 124 developing nations by the World Institute for Development Economics Research (WIDER). The number of such emergencies rose from 20 to 25 per year in the early 1990s to 65 to 70 more recently.[1] 'External pressure by the World Bank,

---

1. Among transition economies there have been humanitarian emergencies in Armenia and Azerbaijan (due to the conflict over Nagorny Karabakh), Bosnia-Herzegovina, Cambodia, Georgia (due to the conflict over Abkhazia), and most recently in Albania and the Yugoslav province of Kosovo.

International Monetary Fund, and Western donors to cut the size of the state in order to encourage economic stability in practice triggered increased competition for governmental resources and ended up contributing to greater instability' (Nafziger 1998).

During the early transition, the share of GDP redistributed through the government budget dropped by 3 to 5 percentage points. This means that the participation of the state and its institutions in the absorption of national income diminished by a factor of about one-tenth and in some cases even more.

At the end of the cold war, simply due to plummeting defense outlays, the share of public expenditure in GDP was slashed. This represented a very healthy form of government downsizing. Of the twenty-eight countries involved in postsocialist transformations, only in one, Croatia, was defense expenditure increased, while in half it fell by about 10 percentage points.[2]

The absolute and relative declines in defense spending and in subsidies, another major area of reduction, were one-time measures and cannot be repeated. They were executed in a radical manner, and this caused substantial modifications within the structure of public expenditures in a very short time. Meanwhile, the portion of public expenditures going for human capital and infrastructure investment rose, though the absolute level dropped significantly here, too. Whereas in 1991 military expenditures still exceeded combined education and health disbursements by 14 percent in China and by 32 percent in Russia, now these states invest more in human capital than they do in unproductive armaments.[3] The relatively low military expenditures in China and Russia reflect a clear policy choice: defense has been subordinated to the reforms and to transition.[4] This is indeed an important shift in the pattern of income distribution through taxation and government spending. In the contemporary world there is no analogy for such a tremendous GDP redistribution in peacetime.

Yet, these quickly shrinking items (in absolute terms) on the expenditure side of the public finance balance sheet have been replaced by other quickly climbing items. A special burden is being imposed by the mushrooming costs of social security. The burst in unemployment and the mounting outlays to support the pension system are taking their toll. To maintain or curtail the relatively high levels of government spending is hardly a policy

---

2. They certainly rose also in Bosnia-Herzegovina and Yugoslavia, which are not included in this accounting.

3. By comparison, in the same year military expenditure exceeded combined education and health care disbursements in Israel by 6%, in Pakistan by 25%, and in Iraq by 171% (UNDP 1997).

4. In the case of China, rapidly growing income means that there has been more flexibility in identifying spending priorities. In Russia the collapse of fiscal revenue has forced military expenditures downward, so that the 'choice' has been more like an economic constraint.

possibility as long as the reform of social security systems has not been completed. Only when an alternative method of financing pensions is in place can additional thinning out in overall government expenditures be considered. This will not be for quite some time.

Meanwhile, the public provision for social security will not only remain high, but must grow. Populations in the postsocialist countries are ageing. The share of people over 60 is expected to exceed 25 percent by 2030 (IMF 1998). However, by that time, pensions will no longer be financed through the old pay-as-you-go public systems, so relative government spending will have had (perhaps) an opportunity to diminish.

Government expenditures can also be trimmed across the board without so much attention to the composition and structure of the reductions, especially if the need is urgent or the external pressure is great. Often overlooked in such a situation is the lack of services or funding sources to replace those eliminated because of the cuts. What has so far been provided by the state through the budget is now supposed to be supplied by the private sector through market allocation. This is a very difficult part of the transition exercise, and through it the importance of the coordination between transition policy and development strategy can be clearly seen (Kolodko 2000c).

Only in a growing economy do households have a chance of finding alternatives to these services, and then only if they have enough income. To change the system is therefore only feasible if the economy is expanding; it is ill advised to push through the relevant structural reforms at a time when their implementation will lead to a deterioration in living standards.

A study prepared at the World Bank (Commander, Davoodi, and Lee 1996) finds that a country with a proper combination of small government and good institutions may be able to double GDP in about two decades, but that a country with a bad combination of big government and poor institutions would need two and a half centuries to accomplish the same thing. This sounds impressive, but it looks more like mumbo-jumbo than economics. Fortunately, no modern nation anywhere anytime has needed 250 years to double its GDP, and this is not going to happen in any of the transition economies either. Anyway, the transition is not going to last that long, so there will be no chance to run the experiment. Even if the relative size of their governments is bigger than that of some of the most advanced market countries, the leading transition economies may be able to double their output in a matter of just one decade.[5]

What the study does point to correctly is the strong correlation between the rate of growth on the one hand and, on the other, the size of government and the appropriateness of institutional arrangements. The unfavor-

---

5. This is what the World Bank envisages in another forecast (World Bank 1997c). If a transition economy is able to enjoy a 7% GDP growth rate over two decades, this would not be a doubling in output, but would represent a growth of nearly four times over the 20 years.

able combination of big government and low-quality institutions is a serious threat in postsocialist economies, as it is in several less-developed market economies. Such a combination favors ill-advised interventions of the weak state bureaucracy in market affairs. This may lead to improper allocations of public expenditure. It can also delay the adoption of new laws and needed market regulations.[6] It can fuel corruption, which takes resources away from the official economy.

Regulations which are transparent—especially vis-à-vis financial and capital markets, banking, privatization, and public-sector procurements—should be introduced and enforced as soon as this is feasible. The implementation of effective regulatory measures requires the sound commitment of the government. It also calls for a strong, not a weak state, and such a state must have already been redefined and redesigned.

It may be that at least part of the debate about the role of the state stems from a confusion between small and big government on the one hand and strong and weak government on the other. A lot of the confusion—if it exists—may be due to a false supposition that 'big' means 'inefficient' and that 'small' means 'efficient'. In fact, for instance, Turkmenistan has a big, strong government, which, however, is not very efficient. Meanwhile, Croatia also has a big, strong government, but it happens to be rather efficient. Whereas Latvia has a small, strong, and efficient government, Albania has a small, weak, and inefficient one.[7]

The best (worst) example is Russia in the 1990s, with its informal institutions and very poor regulatory framework. From time to time the government makes very serious attempts to push through sound structural reform, but the attempts quickly fail. The problem seems to be not that the government is too big, but that there are too many of them. There is a lack of transparency. What is the role of the government? What is the responsibility of the Kremlin, that is, the President's Office? What is the attitude of the parliamentary majority toward the executive branch? What indeed is the position of the informal institutions (starting with the financial and industrial 'tycoons' and the news organizations they seem to control), which often behave as though they were another government?

In short, the government must first be strong enough to carry out its new role, and this ability is not a simple function of its size. The real choice is

---

6. Catch-22–type situations sometimes arise. In Ukraine in 1998 a budget amendment could not be adopted until the summer, although it was a crucial provision required for numerous structural reforms. This occurred not because of any inability to obtain the support of a majority for the reforms or the budget amendment, but because parliament could not agree on a speaker. It failed to chose one in eleven attempts: very democratic, but very counterproductive.

7. From a purely mathematical viewpoint, leaving aside any nuances or subtleties in terms of the specific conditions within countries, there are eight possible combinations of the words 'big' or 'small' government, 'strong' or 'weak' government, and 'efficiency' or 'inefficiency'.

between the kind of regulations and the range of budgetary redistribution in efficient countries, like Hungary or Slovenia, and those in inefficient countries, like Belarus or Romania. Hungary and Slovenia have shown that, even if they do not have small governments, they do have experience, good institutions, and wise policies, and they have enjoyed good overall economic performance and an early recovery. Thus, the main challenge for the nations lagging behind in growth and development is not a reduction in the size of government, but the need to overhaul government and put it in order. This may call for downsizing, or it may not. A government can be too big, or it can be too small, but it can never be too good.

The issue is not the need to decrease state expenditures, but the need to improve the allocation and efficiency of these expenditures.[8] In several nations, because of the resistance of the government bureaucracy, financing for schools and health care has been pared instead of controlling the excessive outlays for the bureaucracy. In many cases, crusades aiming at containing the size of the bureaucracy have ended up by containing only the number of teachers and doctors or adding to the arrears in salaries owed to teachers and doctors. The impact of such policies on growth and equity must be taken very seriously.

If the public finance system needs reform, this should be accomplished in a way that contributes both to growth and to equity. If the approach favors growth over equity or equity over growth, then we are back with the debate between liberalism and populism, and we already know that both these adversaries are wrong. If the government curbs its expenditures and its revenues simultaneously, then it is downgrading its financial effort to meet the needs of some parts of the population while boosting the net incomes of other parts of the population. So, the public finance system is redistributing resources from some individuals and groups to others.

Basically, this is a redistribution by the state to the private sector with as many implications as the number and kinds of services being affected. It might help movie theatres, but it might fail to improve health care. It may do no harm to the circulation of newspapers, but lead to the elimination of symphony orchestras. It may be justified vis-à-vis reduced support for postgraduate university studies, but it may not be justified in terms of the fall in secondary school enrolments. Perhaps postgraduate university studies can and should seek to survive without state help, but secondary school enroll-

---

8. The belief which says that the remedy lies in lower expenditures dies hard. 'The IMF will press Kiev to slash some 1,000 tax exemptions as a key condition for handing over the loan to the cash-strapped government. . . . [T]he Fund has also asked the government to cut planned expenditures in the remaining half of the year by 30 per cent, or $2.1 billion' (*Development News* 1998). However, even in a situation of robust growth and healthy performance, it is extremely difficult to reduce expenditures by such a huge margin; to require this in such wretched circumstances is simply unrealistic.

ments will be able to rise again only after long and painful adjustments in education at the expense of the future.

If such policies are applied, perhaps the private sector will be able to expand more quickly, but those groups will suffer that cannot now afford to pay for the services that used to cost so little when they were provided by 'big' government. Hence, even before output has started to grow, inequity has already risen a great deal. The roots and the fruits of this sort of redistributive policy, undertaken merely because of a curbstone opinion about the role and the size of the state, represent serious political challenges, not strictly economic and financial issues.

If a 'big' government economy is defined as one with public spending exceeding half of GDP (like Belgium, Italy, the Netherlands, Norway, and Sweden), and a 'small' government economy is defined as one with public spending below one-third of GDP (like Australia, Japan, Switzerland, and the United States), then the two possess similar characteristics. In 1997, the per capita output (adjusted for purchasing power parity, PPP) in the five former nations was over $21,000 and in the latter four nations around $23,000. The average annual rate of growth in 1960–95 in both cases was almost identical, equal to about 2.5 percent. Gross fixed capital formation is also about the same, that is, 20.5 percent and 20.7 percent of GDP, respectively. The rate of inflation does not differ by much and from 1986 to 1994 was at 3.9 percent in the first group and 3.7 percent in the second. Life expectancy at birth is 78 years in the former and 77.8 years in the latter. The respective infant mortality rates are 6.7 and 6.4 per 1,000 live births. The secondary school enrollment rate is 92.8 percent in the big government sample and 89 percent in the small government sample.[9] According to the composite school-enrollment ratio calculated by the UNDP, the weighted share of children of various ages attending schools in the former is 85 percent and in the latter 82 percent. Illiteracy rates are similarly low in both groups.

With respect to the quality of human capital and the standard of living, the admittedly minor distinctions seem generally to favor the big governments. However, what really seems to distinguish these two groups of economies is not GDP level or rate of growth, but income distribution. The bigger the government, the more equitable seems to be income distribution, and the smaller the government, the larger the share of the income distribution goes to the richer part of the population. The debate therefore seems once again to be more about different interests rather than different theoretical concepts. The claim that small government is efficient government is

9. The infant mortality and secondary school enrolment rates for countries with 'small' government refer to nations in which public expenditures are below 40% of GDP. This sample clearly includes the countries mentioned above (Australia, Japan, Switzerland, and the United States), but is not necessarily limited to them.

not only an abstract intellectual argument, but it protects the interests of favored income groups, too. This last may even be the real aim of policies designed on the basis of the inaccurate statement that small governments better satisfy social needs and serve economic welfare. They satisfy social needs and serve economic welfare, but often mainly the needs and the welfare of the privileged in society.

The two poorest quintiles of the population receive 24.1 percent of the income distribution in countries with big governments, but 20.8 percent in countries with small governments (Tanzi and Schuknecht 1995, Tanzi 1997). In countries with small governments the most affluent quintile receives approximately 44 percent of the income, while the poorest quintile takes in only a little more than 5 per cent. At the other end of the spectrum, in countries with big governments the richest quintile gains about 37 percent of total income, while the poorest quintile gets 7.4 per cent. Thus, in countries with small governments the ratio of the income of the richest quintile relative to the income of the poorest quintile is approximately 8.3, while in countries with big governments it is about 5. That does make a difference.

There would be nothing wrong with these various ratios if they more or less reflected the contribution of the quintiles to a nation's wealth. But this is by no means clear, since the significant expansion in income dispersion in recent decades is the result of an unfair distribution and does not necessarily reflect the real value of the human capital involved.[10] Even this might somehow be acceptable, if the inequalities enhanced the ability of an economy to grow over the long term. However, the words of neoliberals notwithstanding, it does not work this way. The truth is that, whether they have big governments or small governments, the sample countries are growing at similar average rates. Thus, in terms of equity and in a context of growth-oriented policies, the best combination seems to be not small government and good institutions, but big government and good institutions.

In fact, big or small, the only really 'good' government is a capable government that can assure robust economic growth and a fair distribution of the results. There are examples of countries in which government involvement in economic and social affairs is relatively substantial and in which the quality of life is more favorable than it is in countries with less government intervention in these areas (Alesina 1998). This depends mainly on the structure of government consumption and is therefore essentially a function of the policies chosen. For instance, although Vietnam shows a lower level of income per capita than does Nigeria and has a relatively bigger

---

10. Inequality is growing internationally, too. Similar to the situation within countries, this does not reflect actual changes in the contribution of nations to global wealth, but results from the redistribution of income, this time on an international scale. Worldwide the ratio of the income received by the richest quintile relative to that of the poorest quintile jumped from an already unseemly 30 to 1 in 1960 to a shocking 59 to 1 in 1989 (UNDP 1992).

government, life expectancy at birth in Vietnam is 15 years longer, the chance of children surviving to the age of 5 is two times higher, and the illiteracy rate is two times less.[11]

Not surprisingly, whereas the human development index (HDI)[12] for Vietnam is 0.557, with GDP per capita at $1,208 (in PPP terms), the Nigerian HDI is 0.393, with GDP per capita at $1,351 (PPP). Consequently, the HDI rank minus the rank according to GDP per capita (PPP dollars) is 26 in Vietnam and 1 in Nigeria. China has a GDP per capita at only half the level in Brazil ($2,604 and $5,362, PPP, respectively), but life expectancy at birth is four years longer in China. The relevant differences between the HDI and GDP ranks are 3 and 0, respectively (UNDP 1997). This is so simply because countries like Vietnam and China spend relatively more via the public finance system on human capital than do other countries at similar levels of development.

Thus, the size of government should be a function of the purposes the government serves, not merely a function of general 'rules' which may identify what is better and what is worse regardless of complex local economic concerns and social reasoning. The size of government evolves according to many factors which tend in several directions at once. In fact, the composition of government spending itself reflects the development process in a complicated way. It may happen that big government is sometimes better for growth and development, or that small government is in some cases more appropriate for these purposes. In some nations, big government may turn out to be unsustainable because it is too costly, and it may have to be downsized only for this reason, even if the downsizing slows growth for a while. It may be that, even if a smaller (or bigger) government would under some circumstances promote faster and more equitable growth, an attempt at enlarging (or downsizing) it appreciably in the wrong manner and at the wrong time may cripple performance and thus harm equity and growth.

---

11. Data refer to 1995 (World Bank 1995d).

12. The human development index (HDI) calculated by the United Nations Development Programme seems to be a more relevant measure of improvement in society than is GDP, although, in general, over the long run there is a strong positive correlation between the level of GDP per capita and changes in the HDI (UNDP 1997, World Bank 1997a, Ravallion 1997). The HDI is a composite indicator and takes into consideration accomplishments in areas of basic human capability such as life expectancy at birth, educational attainment, and income. Hence the HDI is a more suitable measure of change vis-à-vis the ultimate target of development policy. The HDI is described by the UNDP (1997, 44) as follows:

'The HDI value for each country indicates how far the country has to go to attain certain defined goals: an average life span of 85 years, access to education for all, and a decent standard of living. The HDI reduces all three basic indicators to a common measuring rod by measuring achievement in each as the relative distance from the desirable goal. The maximum and minimum values for each variable are reduced to a scale between 0 and 1, with each country at some point on the scale.'

Nonetheless, there are upper limits to the effective size of government, just as there is a limit to the amount taxes can be raised without hobbling capital formation, investment, and expansion. Beyond some maximum, a rise in public expenditures is no longer accompanied by an increase in the quantity or an improvement in the quality of services provided by government. This 'maximum' is believed to hover around 40 percent of GDP. Thus, the governments defined earlier as 'big' (with public spending exceeding half of GDP) are probably too big, while the 'small governments' (with public spending below one-third of GDP) may be too small. If a drive toward further state expansion is too aggressive, government spending may pass the threshold beyond which additional increments become inefficient and no longer contribute to welfare. In countries where this has occurred, the challenge is turned around: first, how to contain state expansion and, second, how to cut non-productive public expenditure without causing erosion in the standard of living or in future development.

This is certainly not the case in postsocialist economies, where, after the initial sharp reduction in the size of government at the onset of transition, enormous efforts were undertaken to continue the process. Even the notion 'government consumption' is now being exploited to suggest that the state bureaucracy, not society, gains from government spending. If this stubborn push to downsize had permitted the sprouting up of a private sector able to use more efficiently the resources being released by the withdrawal of the state, then it might have been appropriate. However, allocative efficiency was not necessarily improving, and the more limited redistribution of GDP and the restrained fiscalism, instead of producing a positive effect, tended to aggravate the contraction and make it last longer than would probably have otherwise been the case. Moreover, the supply of social services began to dwindle, and the divestment in human capital was weakening the long-run potential for growth.

Unfortunately, policymakers were being misled by the half-baked piece of advice according to which the sooner government becomes small, the sooner the market economy can begin to rise and expand. Instead of focusing attention on the ends of policy, they burned a lot of energy attempting to adjust one important policy instrument. Thus, Jeffrey Sachs (1993) expressed the conviction that '. . . markets spring up as soon as central planning bureaucrats vacate the field.' So, bureaucrats vacated the field and moved to business, to the shadow economy, to policymaking, to cushy consultancy jobs, to organized crime, to countries with better economies, but the markets did not 'spring up'. What instead did happen was the Great Transitional Depression.

Healthy markets can expand quickly within institutionally mature systems, which have abandoned central regulations and which are guided by liberalized government industrial and trade policies. This could occur in a nation like Japan, for instance (though, no doubt, Japan possesses a big bureaucratic burden and a poor regulatory environment), but it has never happened either in developing countries, as for instance Nigeria, or in transition economies, as for instance Uzbekistan, with weak institutions. In transition economies, the problem is to furnish the new state with the ability to police the economy and develop market institutions, not instantly to liquidate central planning bureaucrats, no matter who the terminator may be.

Chapter Eight

External Shocks and the Catching-up Process

The strongest argument, both economic and political, behind the rationale to push towards postsocialist transition to a market system is a widespread conviction that such a system must bring better allocative efficiency and hence higher competitiveness. In due time it must bring higher output and eventually a better standard of living for the people. Yet to accomplish such a result, not only the pre-transition level of output must be recovered—and even reaching this target in some countries will take another decade or two of hard work—but these economies must be put on the path of quick growth.[1] Furthermore, it must be sustained for a long period of time. Only then there will be a chance for catching-up in transition economies. Catching-up means a gradual, long-lasting process of diminishing the development gap between the richer industrial countries and the transition economies that are lagging behind them, now even more than ten years ago.

While looking into the future, there is always a temptation to presume that it will be fine. Such optimism may seem reasonable from the policymakers' perspective, especially since they always assume that they well know what ought to be done and that unfavorable external shocks, making their ambitious plans impossible, will not happen. Unfortunately, quite often neither assumption holds. Consequently, the future seldom looks as bright as envisaged only a couple of years earlier. Despite such experiences, the optimistic expectations tend to be repeated time and again. And the postsocialist transition economies and their leaders are not exempt from this optimism. It might be added that international organizations are following this pattern of behavior as well, or at least they have done so for several years (World Bank 1997c).

---

1. To recover the previous level of output for a country were it shrunk by, say, 50 percent, one needs a decade with an annual rate of growth of 7.2 percent. In the case of output collapse by two-thirds, the full recovery needs two decades of annual growth of 5.7 percent. Under other circumstances it would be recognized as a remarkable pace of growth, yet in such case, for instance in countries like Georgia and Moldova, it would bring, from the production level viewpoint, a return only in 2020 for a situation dating back to 1990. And that is the time span of whole generation.

There would be nothing wrong with optimistic expectations, if only they were based on vast knowledge and true commitment to sound policies on the one hand, and if they were drawing the right conclusions from historical experience, on the other. Otherwise, too much optimism becomes too much ignorance, which always prevents fast growth and its sustainability. Therefore, the considerations about catching-up in transition economies should draw from both their own recent experiences and the characteristic of the growth process occurring elsewhere in the global economy.

As for these experiences, it must be clearly understood why a few countries—actually very few of them—in 1999–2000 produced more that they did in 1989–90, and many others are still not able to do so. There is a question to what extent the rate of growth in the future will differ between various emerging markets in the EE and FSU region? Can it differ as significantly as it did over the last decade?[2] This is hardly imaginable, because there were some unique reasons for such diversifity and it is very unlikely, if at all possible, that they will reappear in the future. Therefore, what kind of reasons were they?

First, there had been local military conflicts. Obviously, the countries affected by these misfortunes have lost a remarkable part of their production, which would not have happened otherwise.[3] Especially Armenia, Azerbaijan, Georgia, Moldova, and Tajikistan in the FSU region, and several Balkan countries in the EE region, have been harmed by heavy losses owing to military operations. In some places the situation is still unstable and, hence, unpredictable. As for the future, all predictions for the future have been presuming that there would not be such type of conflicts. Unfortunately, this has not been the case.

Nevertheless, if the transition process during next decades evolves peacefully—and all necessary attempts to secure such a course must be undertaken—it is reasonable to expect certain additional growth. It might be indirectly deduced from the 1990s data, when the output started to grow rapidly soon after the military conflicts ended. Yet if local or regional conflicts continue, the sluggish economic performance as well as stagnation and depression may last for several more years.

Second, there were other types of external shocks that made the transition exercise still more difficult. Especially for the FSU republics the initial shock following the collapse of the former Soviet Union was remarkable. For this reason alone the transitional recession was much deeper in the FSU

---

2. In the extreme cases, that is, in Poland and Moldova, the average annual rate of GDP growth in 1990–99 varied from plus 1.95 to minus 10.5 percent. Hence, at the end of the decade, these countries GDP were, respectively, 121.6 and 30.5 percent of the pre-transition level (see Table 3 and Figure 1).

3. It had indeed been a disaster to lose during the short period of just one year as much as 21.1 percent of GDP in Croatia in 1991, or 52.6 percent in Armenia in 1992, or 18.9 percent in Tajikistan in 1994, or 37.3 percent in Yugoslavia in 1999. This kind of single year damage needs more than a few years to recover the prior output.

economies than in the EE countries. The break of the former Yugoslavia was also a great shock for all five republics composing that country. Still meaningful, though of a smaller dimension, was the dissolution of Comecon, the late trade bloc of socialist countries. But all these shocks are already in the remote past and cannot be repeated.

However, as the recent trend following the 1998–2000 Russian financial crisis shows, the transition economies, especially the FSU republics, are very vulnerable for crises occurring in other countries, especially those with which they have strong trade links. Russia, of course, is here the most important country. The more these countries are exposed for trading with a large partner, the more vulnerable they are for the fallout from a crisis that may strike such a partner. Thus in the future the risk of external shocks will depend on the pattern of their trade and financial links.

Considering that the processes of diversification of the main trade partners and the directions from which the capital is flowing continue, there is a likelihood that this vulnerability will decline. Yet at all times there will be a risk of external shocks that can diminish the prospect of that growth. The answer for such a challenge is to maintain strong fundamentals and sound institutions, and to react through wise policy response. Thus, a shield against negative external shocks can and should be created.[4]

Third, certain events, both in the global economy and its postsocialist region, have good and/or bad effects, depending on who is the newsmaker and who is the newstaker. There are several economies, mainly among the FSU emerging markets, which rely to large extent on specific commodity prices. Natural gas and oil for Turkmenistan, oil for Azerbaijan, and cotton and gold for Uzbekistan are of great significance for these countries' income. So is oil for Russia. Without taking a closer look at the fluctuation of these prices, it is not possible to explain such shifts of rate of growth as from minus 26.1 to about plus 17 percent between 1998 and 2000 in Turkmenistan, or from minus 11.8 to plus 5.8 percent between 1995 and 1997 in Azerbaijan.[5]

When, a couple years ago, the prices of oil and gas were plummeting to the lowest level in twenty-five years, it was a negative external shock for the countries whose revenues depend to a great degree on export of these products. And, on the contrary, it was a positive shock for the importers,

---

4. In Poland, in 1994–97—during the implementation of structural reforms and development program "Strategy for Poland"—there was a special task force, led by the deputy premier and minister of finance, which was working on an early warning system and, if necessary, drafting proposals for policy response that would counteract a threat of negative external shocks, especially vis-à-vis risks stemming from the ongoing liberalization of financial markets.

5. Of course, there were some other specific causes for such huge shifts. In the instance of Turkmenistan, the lack of financial liquidity of certain trade partners contributed to drastic decline of oil and gas sold. In Azerbaijan local ethnic conflicts contributed also to deep contraction.

including a majority of transition economies. Through favorable influence on their terms of trade, it helped to accelerate the rate of growth. That was the case in several EE countries in 1995–97. Unfortunately for the latter group (and, of course, fortunately for the former) the trend turned around in 1999. In the future it will change several times both ways, and once again it is impossible to predict when and in what direction.[6] The remedy for the producers of these primary goods is to diversify their output and thus diminish the ratio of dependency on the revenue collected through export of such traditional commodities. The remedy for the importers is to advance their economies towards a less energy-consuming technology, which indeed is taking place, however not fast enough.

Fourth, in the postsocialist countries not only is a market economy emerging, but democracy is rising as well. Democracy is a value in itself, yet at the same time it is interlinked in a complex manner with the process of economic growth. There is not a clear relation neither between market and democracy (Alesina 1997), nor between marketization, that is, the process of transition to a market system, and democratization, that is, the process of transition to democracy (Kolodko 2000a). There are examples of economies growing fast and becoming durable without much democracy (for example, Chile in the 1980s, or China in the 1980s and 90s), and there are examples of lasting depression under authoritarian regimes (for example, Zaire in the 1980s and 90s). And there are plenty of cases of fast growth under democracy, but there are opposite examples too, when growth is sluggish under democracy.

In transition economies it is also a complex issue. So far, in a majority of cases the process of democratization has advanced even faster and further than that of marketization. This is so because the founding of democracy is an easier exercise that the building of a full-fledged market structure. However, even if the bumpy process of democratization in certain countries over certain years did not ease the efforts aimed at economic growth, it does so in the longer run.[7] As for the past, the political turbulence accompanying

---

6. In early 1999, when the price of a barrel of Brent oil was slightly over 10 dollars, that is at the lowest level in real terms since the 1974 oil crisis, *The Economist* was predicting this price to fall further to as low as five dollars. Yet things intervened. In a matter of one year it exceeded 25 dollars. Actually, without such a dramatic turnaround of the oil prices, Russia could not have achieved GDP growth of 1.5 percent in 1999.

7. *The Economist* has proposed an interesting illustration of this. Although it is definitely too early to look for a correlation between the scope of democracy and the level of development in the FSU, a sort of confrontation of the evaluation of 'prosperity' and 'democracy', somehow by rule of thumb, has been done. As a result, in the less prosperous countries—and in this evaluation they are Kyrgyzstan, Moldova, Tajikistan, Turkmenistan, and Uzbekistan—democracy in the latter three is ranked at the lowest possible level. However, the question remains: if there is only a beginning of democracy, is there then also no prosperity—or is it the other way around? Certainly, it is much easier to enjoy democracy with more prosperity, although on the *The Economist* scale in Moldova there is, despite economic misery, a maximum of democracy within the CIS (*Economist* 2000). That can be good hint for future growth.

transition was causing additional difficulties for the implementation of a proper growth-oriented policy. Structural reforms and institution-building, while aiming at the improvement of resources' allocation and the overhauling of the fiscal system, are still more difficult during democratization. Yet without the latter, these changes could be not implemented at all.

In the long run the democracy helps and assists the process of growth, since it may correct the policy excesses. Of course, democracy works better if the market performs well—and the other way around. From such angle it should be foreseen that further progress with democratization, if only supported by growing economy, would pay back in this sense that it will further enhance the growing economy. In the postsocialist countries this positive feedback ought to be one of the main driving forces sustaining fast growth in the very long run.

Fifth, in the recent past severe economic crises and thus output collapse was also due to the lack of responsible macroeconomic policies. The best (that is the worst) examples here are the cases of the failure of fraudulent financial pyramids in Albania in 1997 and the Russian financial crisis of 1998. Yet there were many wrong policies and ill-advised decisions in the course of the 1990s in other transition economies too. It was basically due to weak institutions and underperforming democracy. The more such policies' wrongdoing, the excesses and the mistakes could happen if there is not sufficient professional knowledge how to tackle the issues, and the general political accountability is in short supply.

Nonetheless in the future, due to the increasing maturity of both market and democracy institutions, it is less likely. As a consequence, it is reasonable to expect a wise policy, if not always—then at least more often than during the first decade of transition. Thus the process of learning by doing and further institutional advancement should contribute to relatively higher rate of growth in the future.

Sixth, there were in the past, so for similar reasons there certainly will be in the future ups and downs in economic fluctuations. There will be some external shocks and there will be some policy failures as well. Hence, there will be some periods of acceleration and then a slowing down of economic growth, and then again acceleration and again slowing down, etc. But despite these ups and downs, there will be continuing growth in all of the transition economies. Actually, it will be as it was under centrally planned institutional arrangements, but of a different character.

There are also good arguments in favor of fast growth that are not derived from the lessons of the past and the evolution of the postsocialist system so far, but from other processes taking place concurrently in the global economy and within Europe. Some of these processes are auspicious for the prospects of fast and sustained growth (Fischer, Sahay, Vegh 1997). On this basis, it is rational to expect that the process of catching-up with more developed countries will indeed take place.

The first argument is that the course of catching-up with ongoing technological progress is gaining momentum. The transfer of new technologies from more advanced economies is significantly contributing to a growing competitiveness of all emerging markets, including the postsocialist ones. If only macroeconomic fundamentals are sound and financial stabilization is accomplished, and if only political institutions perform well, than technology transfer will bring a major acceleration of rate of growth. In this precise area the catching-up process is going to be most visible and most fruitful (Cohen 1998). It makes sense to presume that, *ceteris paribus,* at least an additional percentage point of rate of growth can be obtained in the long term due to this factor. Technology transfer is causing faster increase of the skills of labor than it is shifting up the costs of labor compensation. Because of this, the production placed by more developed countries in less developed countries will increase more than average.

Actually, this mechanism of catching-up has been set in motion already; it is difficult, however, to spot it within the complexity of changes influencing the contraction–recovery–growth sequence in transition economies. In another words, without the current phase of global technological revolution and transfer of know-how, the transition recession could be even deeper and last longer in some countries, and in some other countries the recovery would be weaker and growth slower.

Consequently, the positive spillover effect, through spreading out new technologies and know-how, upgrades the qualifications of skilled workers. But there is also a concurrent harmful process of brain drain of skilled labor from transition countries. That, of course, diminishes their ability to compete and expand, and must be counteracted by better compensation for and larger investment in human development. Sound inflow of foreign direct investment (FDI), together with new technologies and managerial know-how, helps to counteract the flight of human capital. In countries leading in transition, and thus also absorbing a bulk of internal FDI, like Hungary or Poland, there is already net inflow of skilled labor. That means that more qualified people are coming into these countries than leaving them. This is good for future growth.

The second argument is related to the process of integration into the global economy. Transition is not only an indispensable part of globalization, but postsocialist economies have a chance to be one of the major beneficiaries of this multi-track process. However, the picture is going to be mixed here. In this case (much more than in any other) the geopolitical position does matter. In the best situation are the EE countries negotiating their access to the European Union. First the Czech Republic, Estonia, Hungary, Poland, and Slovenia, and later Bulgaria, Latvia, Lithuania, Slovakia, and Romania, followed soon by Croatia, will get a strong boost for their growth ability because of this integration.

There are several reasons justifying such a hope. These countries upgrade their institutional arrangements much more quickly than otherwise along the line of the rules observed in the EU. It facilitates the growth ability in the long run. They may also count for a relatively larger inflow of the FDI than other economies. Indeed, expectations for their future membership in the EU have already attracted considerable internal FDI[8] (Table 6). Flow of needed capital will continue, and for that reason this group of countries is going to grow faster than other economies in transition and, most likely, faster than other regions of the world economy. Integration with the EU could accelerate the long-term rate of growth by at least another one percentage point. The net transfer of resources from Western to Eastern Europe will work here as additional catalyst, too.

The third argument is linked to the progress of knowledge of economic and financial matters. Although not appreciated in the same way as technological revolution, it contributes to catching-up also. The macro and microeconomic management is a much more complex challenge now than it used to be (Kozminski 1993). At the same time, our knowledge of how to tackle the issues has advanced outstandingly. The experience suggests that there is certain lag vis-à-vis adopting this knowledge. This is so for both cultural and political reasons. Nonetheless, with respect to these aspects of integration, further progress must be expected. It is already very well on the way, and it seems rational to expect a further acceleration of such learning-by-doing on the international scale. Although impossible to measure, this factor will certainly enhance the rate of growth in transition economies.

And the fourth argument is that lasting transition, particularly the advancement of institution-building, contributes to removing systemic bottlenecks and structural distortions inherited from the past, as well as those created at the early stages of transition. Therefore it enhances labor productivity and overall economic efficiency. Now there is ground to assume that these countries, on average, will grow faster than the global economy and, especially faster than the developed industrial countries. If this is going to be the case, in due time they might catch up with the latter group.

Fulfillment of the catching-up theory—if it proves to be correct—needs support. Various political, cultural, and institutional factors must come into existence, and specific conditions must be met to set the mechanism of catching-up fully in motion. Now, after the first decade of transition, in several countries, though not yet in all of them, these factors and conditions seem to be at least to a certain extent established.

---

8. Out of about 104 billion dollars of internal FDI over the period 1989–99, about 55 percent was located in the group of five EE countries advanced in both transition and their accession negotiations with the EU, i.e., the Czech Republic, Estonia, Hungary, Poland, and Slovenia. The largest of them, Poland, has absorbed about 20 percent of this amount. As for total FDI placed in the EE region, these five countries received about 77 percent of foreign direct capital, while Poland alone received almost 30 percent. It is important to emphasize that the capital flow is actually a net inflow, because external FDI virtually does not exist in these countries. That is, of course, if the capital flight from Russia is disregarded. If it is not, then the net flow of capital to the whole EE and FSU region over the first decade of transition is negative. This implies that more capital has left the region than was invested there—with harmful implications for recovery and growth.

Table 6: Foreign Direct Investment, 1991–99 (in dollars)

	1991	1992	1993	1994	1995	1996	1997	1998	1999	Cumulative FDI Inflow 1991–99	Cumulative FDI per capita 1989–98
Albania	8	32	45	65	89	97	42	45	43	466	132
Bulgaria	56	42	40	105	82	100	497	401	700	2,023	159
Croatia	na	13	77	95	83	529	346	854	750	2,747	444
Czech Republic	511	983	552	749	2,526	1,388	1,275	2,485	3,500	13,969	967
Estonia	na	58	156	212	199	111	130	575	350	1,791	953
FYR Macedonia	na	na	na	24	13	12	18	175	30	272	121
Hungary	1,459	1,471	2,339	1,146	4,453	1,987	1,653	1,453	1,550	17,511	1,627
Latvia	na	43	51	155	244	376	515	220	150	1,604	642
Lithuania	na	na	30	31	72	152	328	921	400	1,934	415
Poland	117	284	580	542	1,134	2,768	3,041	6,600	6,500	21,566	389
Romania	37	73	97	341	417	263	1,224	2,040	1,345	5,837	200
Slovakia	82	100	168	250	202	251	177	508	500	1,738	326
Slovenia	41	113	111	131	170	178	295	154	210	1,403	596
Eastern Europe	2,311	3,212	4,246	3,846	9,684	8,212	9,541	16,431	16,028	72,861	184
Armenia	na	na	na	3	19	22	52	232	150	478	89
Azerbaijan	na	na	20	22	282	661	1,093	1,024	780	3,882	408
Belarus	50	7	18	11	15	73	198	141	188	701	45
Georgia	na	na	na	8	6	54	236	221	96	621	98
Kazakhstan	na	na	473	635	964	1,137	1,320	1,132	800	6,461	372
Kyrgyzstan	na	na	10	45	96	46	83	52	64	396	72
Moldova	na	17	14	18	73	56	64	88	170	500	76
Russia	na	700	400	539	1,710	1,700	3,752	1,200	3,500	13,501	61
Tajikistan	na	8	9	12	20	25	30	34	29	167	22
Turkmenistan	na	11	79	103	233	129	108	110	100	873	157
Ukraine	na	200	200	100	300	526	600	700	600	2,626	52
Uzbekistan	na	9	48	73	-24	90	167	170	226	759	23
CIS	50	952	1,271	1,569	3,694	4,519	7,703	5,104	6,703	30,965	34
Total	2,361	4,164	5,517	5,415	13,378	12,731	17,244	21,535	22,731	103,826	153

Source: EBRD 1997 and 1999.

na—data not available

Chapter Nine

Passive Scenarios and Active Policies for the Twenty-First Century

Against such a background it seems possible to outline some passive scenarios of catching-up in transition economies as well as to provide some policy recommendations for the actions that ought to help realize more positive results among those scenarios.

In a certain sense the transition ought to be seen as a specific historical endeavor shifting part of global economy from one model of growth and development to another. Although their expansion was following the pattern of cycles typical of a centrally planned system, already in the past all these countries were the growing economies. Hence, there was also catching-up with the more developed regions—at least at the earlier stages of a centrally planned episode, before momentum was lost.

From now on—assuming that the Great Transitional Depression is coming to an end in all countries, including those which did not return to the path of growth prior to 2000—there will be growth following the pattern of business cycles typical of a market system. Therefore, under further consideration there is an implicit assumption that long-term growth will evolve around the trend derived from business cycle fluctuations, yet of unknown characteristics.

From such an angle, the postsocialist economies in transition to a market order are going through the long process of changing the substance of their cyclical growth. They do not move from a system where there was no growth to a new system, where the growth will resume and is supposed to be of a 'better character.' The latter must still happen.

For the time being, there are various forecasts for upcoming years. Actually, in the medium term, nobody foresees for any of the transition economies a further decline of output. There are only a couple of cases where a decline in output is expected, and that is only for a single year.[1] Of course,

---

1. For instance, PlanEcon—a leading think tank following the developments in the region for many years—in their prognosis until 2003 for the FSU and 2004 for the EE predicts negative growth in only two cases: for Belarus in 2000, minus 8.1 percent, and for Uzbekistan in 2001, minus 1.0 percent (PlanEcon 1999a).

this outlook presumes that developments go peacefully and that there will not be any severe, unpredictable external shocks. Both misfortunes cannot be ruled out *a priori*, because the things do happen. However, such assumptions seem to be rational at this point. Therefore, in 2003 or 2004, the GDP index, comparing national income in those years with the level of GDP in 1989 and 1999, will look less depressing than it does now, although still more than one would like to see. In 2004, the output will surpass the GDP level of 1989 in only seven (maybe in eight, if Estonia makes it) of twenty-seven countries. At the other end of the list, in another eight countries it will still remain below two-thirds of that standard. And that will be after altogether fifteen years of transition (Table 7).

Table 7. Real GDP Index. Forecast for 2003/4 (1989=100 and 1999=100)

	Index 1999	Rate of Growth					Index 2003(4)*	
	1989=100	2000	2001	2002	2003	2004	1999=100	1989=100
Poland	121.6	4.8	5.1	5.5	5.8	4.9	129.0	156.8
Slovakia	101.5	3.8	4.6	6.4	6.0	6.9	130.9	132.9
Slovenia	107.6	4.0	3.9	4.2	4.1	4.8	122.8	132.2
Albania	92.5	7.0	6.7	8.3	6.9	6.5	140.8	130.2
Hungary	99.2	5.3	5.2	5.4	5.1	5.5	129.5	128.4
Czech Republic	94.7	2.6	3.6	4.8	4.7	4.4	121.8	115.3
Uzbekistan	92.3	3.8	-1.0	2.2	3.8		109.0	100.6
Croatia	77.2	2.6	3.5	4.4	4.8	4.7	121.6	93.9
Romania	73	5.3	5.4	5.3	5.0	4.6	128.4	93.7
Estonia	75.7	5.5	5.5	5.1	4.5		122.2	92.5
FYR Macedonia	72.0	4.8	5.5	5.0	4.5	3.6	125.7	90.5
Bulgaria	66.8	4.1	5.0	5.2	4.7	4.4	125.7	84.0
Lithuania	65.4	5.3	5.3	5.7	5.2		123.3	80.6
Belarus	78.2	-8.1	1.7	3.1	5.7		101.9	79.6
Latvia	60.1	4.9	4.8	5.5	5.3		122.1	73.4
Kazakhstan	60.2	3.3	4.5	5.9	6.1		121.3	73.0
Kyrgyzstan	60.4	4.5	4.1	4.2	4.4		118.3	71.5
Azerbaijan	45.2	7.3	9.1	9.7	9.0		140.0	63.3
Turkmenistan	51.2	5.3	5.1	5.0	6.1		123.3	63.1
Russia	56.1	2.2	2.7	2.0	3.4		110.7	62.1
Armenia	42.5	6.2	6.9	7.1	7.2		130.3	55.4
Tajikistan	44.1	5.0	5.1	5.0	5.9		122.7	54.1
Georgia	33.8	8.0	7.8	7.8	7.5		134.9	45.6
Ukraine	35.7	0.2	3.3	3.9	4.6		112.5	40.2
Moldova	30.5	3.7	4.7	5.6	6.1		121.6	37.1
Bosnia-Herzegovina	na	6.1	4.6	3.8	3.1	3.7	123.2	na
Yugoslavia	na	15.4	13.2	10.9	8.1	5.9	165.8	na

Source: Index 1999 from Table 3. Forecast for 2000–04 from PlanEcon 1999a and 1999b.
na—data not available.
*2003 for the FSU and 2004 for the EE countries

If these scenarios are going, by and large, to come to pass, then the GDP per capita will increase also.[2] In some countries with a low rate of population growth it will be on the par with total output growth.

An interesting phenomenon in the postsocialist emerging markets is, unlike in the EU countries and other advanced market economies, that there is still relatively large gap between the GDP counted at the current, i.e., market exchange rate, and its evaluation on the basis of purchasing power parity (PPP). The trend is that this gap will diminish, as the progress of opening up and integrating transition countries in the world economy continues. In another words, there is going to be a long-lasting process of real appreciation of the currencies of transition economies.[3] Such process is already well under way (Lavigne 1999, Kolodko 2000a). If from time to time the currencies of transition economies do depreciate—and indeed sometimes the devaluation is rather a spectacular event—it is not contrary to the longer tendency.

Owing to the instability of the market exchange rate, the change of the relative value of national currency may even suggest a decline of GDP measured in dollars, or euro, whereas it is now growing.[4] For that reason, it is worthwhile taking a closer look at the evaluation of GDP per capita on a purchasing power parity basis. This indicator ought to be regarded as a point of departure for the catching-up process at the onset of the twenty-first century (Table 8).

These data, if only they are evaluated properly, better reflect the actual level of socioeconomic development and standard of living. Hence, this is also the point where these economies and societies are at the time, and not the GDP per capita measured at current exchange rate. If the latter were taken into account, then Russia, for instance, with GDP per capita according to a market exchange rate at around 1,500 dollars, would stand in 2000 at only thirteen percent of the Slovenian standard. With all the drawbacks, she is not that much far behind even the average EU standard. This gap will decrease along the line of the real appreciation of the ruble that will take place in the future, following the progress vis-à-vis financial stabilization and structural reforms. Additionally, that gap will diminish also

---

2. To be sure, none of the similar scenarios has been fulfilled so far. Thus, considering the experience, it would be indeed unwise to bet that it will be different this time. However, the deviations of these forecasts from the actual developments at this time should be modest.

3. The issue of depreciation, or devaluation, will disappear from the policy agenda when certain countries join the EU and then abandon their national currencies, converting them into the euro. It will be the easiest in countries currently under currency board regime, e.g., Estonia. In such a case it will be done simply by converting from the D-mark (the denomination used under the currency board arrangements as an anchor) to the euro. In the long run, all new EU members from Eastern Europe will join the euro zone as well.

4. It occurred in Poland, for instance, in 1999, when GDP estimated in current dollars dropped by 2.1 percent, whereas in real terms it increased by 3.8 percent.

Table 8. GDP per capita in 1999 and 2003(4), PPP basis*

	1999	2003(4)	Growth (in PPP$)	Growth (in %)
Slovenia	14,267	17,344	3,077	21.6
Estonia	9,096	16,048	6,952	76.4
Czech Republic	9,472	11,442	1,970	20.8
Slovakia	8,395	10,954	2,559	30.5
Hungary	8,063	10,648	2,585	32.1
Croatia	8,284	9,528	1,244	15.0
Poland	7,232	9,255	2,023	28.0
Latvia	6,341	7,877	1,536	24.2
Belarus	5,722	5,737	15	0.3
Russia	4,539	5,087	548	12.1
Bulgaria	3,758	4,796	1,038	27.6
Lithuania	3,680	4,520	840	22.8
Romania	2,962	3,837	875	29.5
Armenia	2,842	3,662	820	28.9
FYR Macedonia	2,897	3,423	526	18.2
Turkmenistan	2,891	3,376	485	16.8
Kazakhstan	2,482	3,028	546	22.0
Yugoslavia	1,828	3,027	1,199	65.6
Uzbekistan	2,612	2,721	109	4.2
Azerbaijan	1,970	2,689	719	36.5
Ukraine	2,348	2,641	293	12.5
Georgia	1,950	2,570	620	31.8
Kyrgyzstan	2,211	2,472	261	11.8
Moldova	1,745	2,104	359	20.6
Albania	1,474	2,025	551	37.4
Tajikistan	748	848	100	13.4

Source: PlanEcon 1999a and 1999b.

*2003 for the FSU and 2004 for the EE countries.

because of a rate of growth in Russia that will most likely be faster than in the most advanced postsocialist countries—if not yet at the onset of the new century, than a little later.

Therefore, we face the question of where all these countries can be in a generation or two. From the perspective of their long-term growth ability, and thus the ability to catch up with advanced industrial countries (or their inability to do so, because none of them *a priori* is bound to succeed), there will be at least four distinct groups of postsocialist economies.

The first group, which may be called 'the gainers', will consist of the economies able to sustain over the very long term the rate of GDP growth at least two times higher than the relevant rate in advanced market economies. As a benchmark in this respect, the recent rate of growth of the EU can be used. Despite the fact that here, too, the future rate of growth is hardly a sure figure, it seems reasonable to assume that it will, by and large, continue around the level accomplished in 1997–2000.[5] Accordingly, it would be about 2.5 percent (IMF 1999).[6] This implies that, for the gainers, the average annual rate of growth will be at least five percent over the coming decades. In reality, if nothing extraordinary occurs, it may oscillate between four and six percent.

The second group—let us call them 'the even-runners'—will be able to maintain the pace of growth along the lines of the EU, or at most to over-come it only slightly. Thus it will oscillate around three percent on average, jumping between two and four percent. As a result, these countries will not be catching up with most advanced part of the European economy, or if doing so, it will happen at a very slow pace. In relative terms the distance between the two groups will change only very modestly. However, given the different bases, the absolute distance will rise still further. Also the de-velopment gap between this group of postsocialist economies and the gain-ers will increase.

The third group—let us call them 'the laggards'—due to their lack of ability to resolve the transition to their advantage, will grow even less over the long term than the EU economies (and hence the even-runners). Their long-term rate of growth will not exceed two percent, or even may stay below this low level. Thus their relative income, compared with those of other groups of transition economies, will lag behind in the future even more than it did at the turn of the millennium. There are many arguments that all postsocialist economies will be growing economies, yet it would be unwise to assume that, owing to the coincidence of unfavorable circum-stances and policies, the worst among them will not be driven from time to time into another recession. Hence, their long-term growth may be very meager.

And there is the fourth group, or at least there is a chance that such group will appear. It can be called 'the frontrunners.' These countries, un-

---

5. Forthcoming growth in the East will cause acceleration of the EU overall rate of growth. Notwithstanding that the new members from Eastern Europe will contribute only a minor part of total European Union GDP, its rate of growth over long term will rise by a fraction of a percentage point. Larger common market participation will also play a positive role with this regard. Therefore, the factual rate of growth could be higher than the current 2.5 percent, possibly being closer to three percent.

6. That is, for the Western European economies. As for the USA, the GDP rate of growth over this period of time was significantly higher—at around four percent. It is believed that that this was due mainly to the so-called new economy, which was fueled by the internet revolution and the far-reaching deregulation of financial markets. Actually, there is one more structural component of this boom. That is globalization itself, since the American economy happens to be the greatest beneficiary of it. Hence, it enjoyed extraordinary growth. Yet this pace of growth, unlike in the EU, does not seem to be sustainable. Aside from the structural features, it seems so dependent on another important factor, the bubble in the stock market. For a certain period of time it may facilitate growth strongly, yet eventually it must burst and come to an end.

der a lucky coincidence of favorable circumstances and good policies, will enjoy an average annual rate of growth around three times higher than that of the current EU zone; that makes 7.5 percent annually. Thus, running between six and nine percent annually, they will gradually approach the EU and OECD development standard,[7] whereas at the same time they will be leaving behind all other postsocialist economies.

These are the general reflections vis-à-vis the alternative pace of growth; it does not mean that each country growing faster will enjoy higher output and, consequently, a better standard of living than a country growing at a lower rate. In the long run, that must eventually happen. However, for several years, it can be just to the contrary, because of the very logic of the catching-up mechanism. It means that countries departing from a lower level of output in 2000, for example, Azerbaijan in the FSU region or Albania in the EE region, although they will report faster growth than, for example, Estonia and Slovenia, will for a number of years still have a relatively lower income.

In Azerbaijan, GDP per capita (at PPP basis) was estimated in 1999 at about 1,970 dollars, while in Estonia at 9,096—almost five times as much. Against this background, it is assumed that, whereas in the former GDP will increase on average between 2000 and 2003 by 7.0 percent, in the latter it will grow only by 4.1 percent per year. However, absolute production will remain much larger.

As for Albania and Slovenia, the relevant GDP per capita on PPP basis is 1,474 and, respectively, 14,267 dollars, which is almost ten times as much, while the expected rates of growth are 7.1 and 4.2 percent. Therefore, while sticking to the categorization given above, during the near future, not surprisingly, Albania and Azerbaijan can be found among the frontrunners, whereas Estonia and Slovenia, which are much better developed, can be found among the gainers, and amongst them—only at the very end of the league (Table 9).

These predictions must be seen as passive scenarios, which are based on both an extrapolation of recent trends and certain assumptions vis-à-vis the policy reforms in forthcoming years. As for the forecast, it is significantly less optimistic than it was only a couple years ago. Such a change of mood results, in part, from the negative external shocks that have influenced not only the real economy, but even more the ways of thinking about it and the expectations. Thus it might happen that this time, contrary to the early 1990s, there is an excessive pessimism.

Nevertheless, it is true that the Russian 'crisis within a crisis' and its 1998 financial climax has affected not only several FSU republics, but also the economies of Slovakia and Estonia, which were previously more rap-

---

7. To OECD belong also the new members, with relatively lower GDP per head, including Mexico. Among them are three transition economies, Hungary, the Czech Republic, and Poland, which have joined the club (in that order) in 1995–96.

Table 9. Average Rate of GDP Growth in 2000–03(4)*

Frontrunners	
Yugoslavia	10.7
Albania	7.1
Azerbaijan	7.0
Georgia	6.2
Gainers	
Slovakia	5.5
Armenia	5.5
Hungary	5.3
Poland	5.2
Romania	5.1
FYR Macedonia	4.7
Bulgaria	4.7
Lithuania	4.3
Turkmenistan	4.3
Bosnia-Herzegovina	4.3
Slovenia	4.2
Tajikistan	4.2
Estonia	4.1
Latvia	4.1
Even-runners	
Czech Republic	4.0
Moldova	4.0
Croatia	4.0
Kazakhstan	4.0
Kyrgyzstan	3.4
Ukraine	2.4
Russia	2.1
Laggards	
Uzbekistan	1.8
Belarus	0.5

Source: Estimated on the basis of the PlanEcon 1999a and 1999b forecast.
*—2003 for the FSU and 2004 for EE economies.

idly growing, owing to their large exposition for trade with Russia. In other rapidly growing countries, such as Poland and Slovenia, deceleration of growth had occurred more as the result of policy mistakes. In Poland in 1998–99 such mistakes had brought down the previous medium-term rate of growth by one to two percentage points (see Figures 2 and 10). As far as the active policies are concerned, they can possibly bring the pace of growth back to nearly 7 percent and sustain it at that level for many years, keeping these economies among the frontrunners. That is possible, and even likely. Consequently, these and other scenarios would soon change in an opposite, more optimistic direction. The forecasts depend mostly upon the policies, not the other way around.

Therefore, four types of long-term growth can be outlined. They correspond with the four types of postsocialist growing economies described above. Accordingly, there will be four paths of long-term growth, respectively, for gainers, even-runners, laggards, and frontrunners. In line with these assumptions, the postsocialist economies will grow along the paths ranging from less than 2 percent per year to as much as 9 percent per year. So, where can a particular country arrive after a journey along certain paths of growth, if it stays the course of a specific pace of growth for a given number of years during the next fifty years? Figure 4 points to some hypothetical answers (Figure 4).

Within these four hypothetical scenarios there are three sub-scenarios, the core scenario A, the minimum scenario B, and the maximum scenario C. The extreme sub-scenarios, the minimum and maximum, are based upon the calculation that, over the entire half-century period of time, the rate of growth is either at the minimum or at the maximum end of the band, the center of which is given by the core scenario. Where would such scenarios lead those countries? (Table 10)

The first scenario presumes an initial medium-term (five years) period of slow growth, due to unstable fundamentals, weak institutions, inadequate policy response, and negative external shocks. Then the growth accelerates for the next five years, due to continuing institution-building and policy reforms, as well as more favorable external factors, for example, an end to the regional conflicts. Later the acceleration gains momentum due to institutional advancement and better policies, because of the experience and knowledge gained from learning by doing. Hence, the growth rate advances these economies to the group of the gainers. That means it bounces within the range of 4 to 6 percent over a full decade. Afterwards, the pace of growth declines for the long-term of three decades, yet only to the pace of the even-runners, that is, 3 percent on average.

Thus, in the span of one generation it lifts national income almost two-fold, and over two generations, that is by 2050, it might increase about five times in real terms. However, considering the range of fluctuations of the rates of growth, in sub-scenarios 1B and 1C, it can be much less or significantly more than in the core scenario 1A (see Figure 4.1).

Such scenarios are likely for the countries that still have weak fundamentals, poor institutions, delayed structural reforms, inconsistent development policies, relatively less favorable geopolitical position, and, in certain cases, might be directly or indirectly affected by local tensions and conflicts, too. For instance, countries like Tajikistan in the FSU, or Romania in the EE region, seem fit to a certain degree in these scenarios. However, the future will bring a lot of mutations that will make the real picture even more colorful. Nevertheless, these countries can accelerate their rate

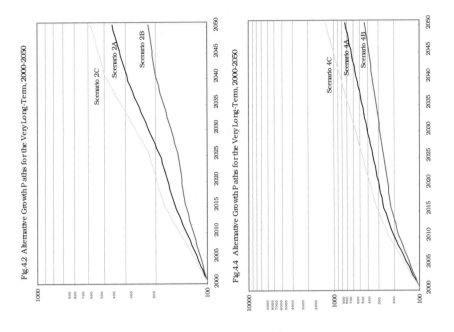

Fig.4.1 Alternative Growth Paths for the Very Long-Term, 2000-2050

Fig.4.2 Alternative Growth Paths for the Very Long-Term, 2000-2050

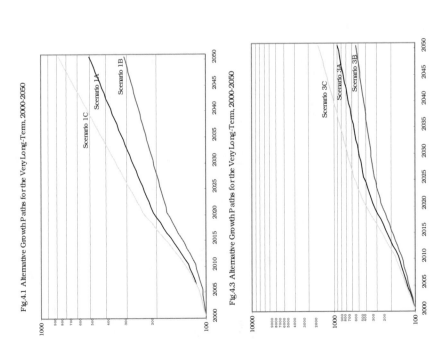

Fig.4.3 Alternative Growth Paths for the Very Long-Term, 2000-2050

Fig.4.4 Alternative Growth Paths for the Very Long-Term, 2000-2050

Table 10. Catching-up in the Transition Economies in the 21st Century

Year	1A	1B	1C	2A	2B	2C	3A	3B	3C	4A	4B	4C
	Laggards-5 Even-runners-5 Gainers-10 Even-runners-30	Min	Max	Even-runners-15 Laggards-10 Even-runners-15 Laggards-10	Min	Max	Gainers-10 Frontrunners-10 Gainers-5 Even-runners-25	Min	Max	Frontrunners-10 Gainers-5 Even-runners-35	Min	Max
2000	100	100	100	100	100	100	100	100	100	100	100	100
2005	110	105	110	116	110	122	128	122	134	144	134	154
2010	128	116	134	134	122	148	163	148	179	206	179	237
2015	163	141	180	156	135	180	234	198	276	263	218	317
2020	208	172	241	172	141	199	336	265	424	305	241	385
2025	242	190	293	192	149	220	428	323	567	354	266	469
2030	280	209	356	222	164	267	497	356	690	410	293	571
2035	325	231	433	258	181	325	576	393	840	475	324	694
2040	377	255	527	296	200	395	668	434	1022	551	357	845
2045	437	282	641	327	210	437	774	479	1243	638	395	1028
2050	506	311	780	361	221	482	897	529	1512	740	436	1250

Source: Author's calculation. See text for assumptions.

of growth later only if they are able, through proper policies, to get rid of various structural and institutional bottlenecks that are still keeping their growth potential in check.

The second scenario is for the countries that will take only limited advantage of the chances the introduction of a market economy is bringing. For this reason they will grow at a rate even lower than they did under the centrally planned system (see Table 1 and 2), yet this growth will surely be accompanied by further increasing inequality (Milanovic 1998, Kolodko 1999c). At the outset, for the first, say, fifteen years, they will grow at about 3 percent annually and then even more slowly, at about only 2 percent. Then, during the period of the second generation, the sequence of the fifteen years as the even-runners and the ten years as the laggards could be repeated.

All these are probable for the countries that at the beginning of the century are still muddling through inconsistent structural reforms and are burdened by the institutional vacuum. Old institutions have been already dismantled, but the new ones are not yet in place. This type of a hybrid system contributes to making the growth more difficult and diverts the opportunity to catch up into an illusion.

If even the geopolitical position helps and the human capital is relatively fine, the weak fundamentals and unstable political situation can discourage domestic capital formation and hinder absorption of the flow of foreign savings, that is the internal FDI. Thus, such a group of countries can be as far behind the average global income in the year 2025 and 2050 as it is in the year 2000, because it will rise only by about 260 percent or so over this long term (see Figure 4.2). What countries can belong to this group, that is, what ought to be left for themselves to decide, since, according to the logic of the way of reasoning presented thus far, none of them is doomed for such a meager growth? Once again, it depends on the policies. In short—the countries do have a choice.

The third scenario reflects a situation when over a span of 10 years or so the average rate of growth sustains about 5 percent, oscillating between 4 and 6. That might be plausible for the gainers with strong institutions and improving fundamentals as well as reasonable policy response and advanced structural reforms. During the succeeding decade the growth might even jump to 7.5 percent and then retreat once more to about 5 percent for the medium term. After a time span of one generation it would slow down to the pace of the even-runners, where it could be maintained for another twenty-five years. That would indeed be an extremely successful path of growth. In such a case the catching-up would be complete, since at the end of the journey along such lines, the income would be on the par with the standard of the developed industrial countries.[8]

---

8. Of course, the income is the flow. As for the standard of living, which is a function of both, the flow and the stocks of assets accumulated in the past, it would be still firmly below the level enjoyed by the most advanced societies.

So, which countries may have a chance, if they meet all necessary criteria, to accomplish such remarkable growth? With luck, perhaps, it may occur with the regard to the best performers amongst the countries aspiring to join the EU, especially those from the first group of applicants. It is hardly imaginable that all of them will take such a path, yet the best among them at least, *ex ante,* seem to have a chance (see Figure 4.3). If so, looking at things realistically, they should fit close to minimum sub-scenario 3B, because the maximum one, i.e. 3A, is rather on the verge of a postsocialist miracle. Of course, a miracle would help; the problem, however, is that the miracles fail to happen not only in East Asia, but in Eastern Europe, too.

The fourth scenario (see Figure 4.4) is also a very optimistic one. An increase of real income over sevenfold during a half-century period has not happened that often in the course of history. Indeed, it has occurred very seldom (Cohen 1995). Nonetheless, under certain circumstances, this can happen in the case of leading transition economies, on the one hand, and in the case of some of them that are quite underdeveloped, on the other. Thus the economies that can aspire to this first group (as in the previous scenario) are those with stronger fundamentals and matured institutions, say, the members of OECD, which are able simultaneously to manage sound policies and firmly take advantage of their integration with the EU, as well as attract a continuously large inflow of FDI.

For instance, for Hungary or Poland among the EE emerging markets, or for Estonia within the FSU region—if they have learned the proper lessons from their own and the other's mistakes—this scenario is not unimaginable. Also important is their very favorable geopolitical position and their good quality of human capital. Yet the policy is going to be decisive, particularly the policy enhancing entrepreneurship. Open product markets, flexible labor markets, and well-developed capital markets make it easier for entrepreneurs to start new firms. This kind of 'venture privatization' and grass-roots entrepreneurship will have a crucial importance for sustaining high-speed growth (Kolodko 2000b). Therefore, over the first decade of the twenty-first century, these types of economies would grow as the frontrunners, having a growth rate at about 7.5 percent on average. It means that, in this case, the GDP would double over ten years, that is two times sooner than under the first scenario. Later, when catching-up will be somehow advanced, the rate of growth would decline to 5 or so percent and then would fall to the level of the EU. By that time all these countries will already be full-fledged members of the union for several years.

But this scenario vis-à-vis the pace of growth and the sequence of its change can match also the characteristics of another type of economies, which is starting from the lowest level of income amongst postsocialist economies. Despite weak institutions and unstable fundamentals, despite lagging behind with structural reforms, and despite often not following the most reasonable policy response, they can take off towards this kind of catching-up, too. That is because of the coincidence of two specific factors, which, at the top of many other features facilitating fast growth, do matter for catching-up. These features are the nascent fruits of transition as such, that is, liberalization and privatization contributing to increasing once again capital accumulation[9] and to the improvement of efficiency. Other factors are the valuable natural resources and very low starting point.

For instance, Azerbaijan fits this category well, as can Tajikistan. Their level of development gives them a better chance to grow fast, since they are starting from a GDP per capita of only 1,970, and about 750 dollars, at PPP basis, respectively (see Table 8). If the other conditions are met—particularly if there is a conclusive end of regional conflicts, and if the policy response gives a chance that the situation is taken toward the advantage of growth—then they can indeed begin their fast growth.

Later, these two very different groups of postsocialist economies, after upgrading their development level remarkably over the next fifteen years or so, will expand at the pace of the even-runners during following thirty-five years. But then, possibly, the first, more advanced group will be closer to the lower limit within the band of 2 to 4 percent annual growth, whereas the less developed counties will be closer to the upper limit, that is to 4 percent. Thus, in this scenario—as in the scenarios two and three—the critical catching-up would occur at the beginning and middle years of the whole period, whereas closer towards its end the rate of growth supposed to be basically on the par with developed countries.

Yet it can happen that the entire process of catching-up will be postponed, if the structural reforms and institution-building are performed profoundly. It can also be delayed if the political situation, both on the domestic as well as on the international and regional scene, turn out to be adverse. It may be deferred, too, if globalization goes off course and instead of streamlining the ongoing process of transition—hampers it.

The true future of postsocialist economies will be much more complicated (as well as interesting and challenging at the same time) than that outlined in these hypothetical scenarios. As in the case of the movies, the best scenarios are inspired by the real occurrences—not the other way around. It is extremely unlikely, if possible at all, that any particular country's course will remain unchanged for the very long run—a time span of a generation or two. The countries may switch from one path of growth to another. And they will do so in both directions, that means up and down, depending on the changing domestic and international conditions and contingent on the changing policies. Some of them will be not able to avoid a threat of recession when hit by external shocks or by their own policies'

---

9. Once again, since the ratio of accumulation (capital formation) over GDP (NMP) under the centrally planned economy usually was quite high and much higher than at the time in the market economies (Bauer 1978, Kolodko 1976 and 1986, Kornai 1986, Lavigne 1999).

excesses. Many of these changes are completely unpredictable at the moment. Many others will be the matter of political decisions that may or may not be taken. That in turn will depend on the institutional aspects of development and the democracy's performance. Of course, the latter is also capricious, especially in the nations with relatively young democratic regimes.

Whereas for some countries the future development game will be about sustaining the path of growth they have been able to take earlier, for some others the struggle will focus on getting to the path of faster progress (Lucas 1999). Or, in certain instances, it might be about making the effort not to lose the momentum and slipping into reversal. Thus, the future of the postsocialist economies depends on their particular path of economic growth and for how long they will be able to remain on that route. If we assume that during the next fifty years each country may take no more than a maximum three of such paths or change the course up and down more than, say, five times, it creates several feasible scenarios of further development. These scenarios are far from uniform. As far as their development levels, and hence the differences between these levels, are concerned, the more time that evolves, the more the former centrally planned economies will grow apart.

In the extreme cases—although it seems almost unlikely—any individual postsocialist economy can expand for the whole period of a half-century as the frontrunner, or it can drag as a laggard for just as long. That probably will not happen, because there are very few arguments that lead us to expect a country running on average at a 7.5 percent rate of growth until 2050, that lead us to be pessimistic enough to think that there will be a country increasing its output by a very low margin, say just one percent per year, if at all.[10]

Rationally, it should be expected that these economies will belong to neither extreme group, but rather to the central one, that is, to the gainers and the even-runners. It implies that time and again they will manage to stay on the course of rate of growth within the range relevant for these two groups, that is between 2 and 6 percent. However, within this still quite wide band one may expect that most often the data on GDP growth for the FSU and EE nascent market economies will fluctuate between 3 and 5 percent.

---

10. However, modern history knows a few examples of similar kinds of expansion and misery. In the case of South Korea, the rate of growth matching a frontrunner pace in this categorization, had lasted for a quarter of a century. The case of China is similar thus far. Moreover, fast growth in South Korea may continue under certain circumstances, if necessary structural reforms and institutional changes in the aftermath of recent crises are properly executed. On the other hand, there is the case of Chad, where over last three decades output has shrunk by a half, and fast sustained growth is hardly around the corner. The same can be said about Myanmar. Unfortunately, these are only a few examples, since there are more similar gloomy examples, especially in Africa.

It depends on several factors that can be read from the way of reasoning thus far. Yet before recapitulating it, it is necessary to distinguish between passive scenarios and active strategies. The path along which travel towards the future (hopefully a better one) will lead depends on many variables. Some of them are given, and hence we can only try to foresee them more or less accurately and clearly. However, the critical mass of the growth process is contingent to chosen policies and the political ability to follow the lead. Again, the geopolitical position, inherited culture, quality of human capital and skilled labor, the number of the population, and thus the scope of products and service markets, the stock of natural resources, the beauty of a country, and its tourist attractiveness—all these given factors do matter for the growth prospect. Some of them are set forever, some can be changed only over a long time and only under the conditions of a growing economy. But what matters most is the policy. Without a sound one, even a comparative advantage given by other factors will not serve the purpose of development well.

Countries with a better geopolitical position, having the advantage of closer proximity to vast markets, as Estonia to Scandinavia, the Czech Republic to Germany, Bulgaria to Turkey, or even Kyrgyzstan to China, are finding themselves in a relatively better situation to grow faster. The countries aiming at integration with the European Union find themselves in an even better position. Countries that with true commitment are taking care of gradual institution-building, as for instance Hungary and Poland, will benefit from this strong foundation in the years to come more than other emerging markets in the region. They do already.

The combination of these two factors—a favorable geopolitical position in Eastern Europe and substantial progress vis-à-vis institution-building— is already boosting growth of the candidates for entrance into the EU. Those countries, especially those realtively more developed, as the Czech Republic, Estonia, or Slovakia, will grow faster than other countries in the region. That entire group can be seen as gainers in the next decade. Some of them, under wrong policies or unfavorable external shocks, might be downgraded to the lower league. Yet before they catch up with Western Europe (or at least with its southern part, relatively less advanced), they should not remain there for too long. It means that even if from time to time they will not succeed in sustaining the rate of growth at about 5 percent annually, they can be back on the path soon after.

As for the countries advancing occasionally to the upper league, they will be coming from two different groups. The first will include the true leaders of transition, who are able to combine sound development strategy with comprehensive structural reforms. These are two different, yet strongly interrelated issues. Healthy institutions brought by structural reforms and improving market culture are not substitutes for good policy and wise development strategy. They are just complementary. In transition economies there is not a straightforward causal relationship between structural re-forms and development. At least there is a clear message from the record of the first decade of transition, that this has not been set in motion thus far. Since this relationship does not work automatically, it must become a can-did concern of the government policy.

So far, there have been only three cases of high-speed growth that de-serve to be counted as the frontrunners. However, it was this way only for a while. Estonia in 1995–97 and Poland, for one year longer, in 1994–97, were growing at average rate of 6.3 percent. So did Croatia for a while. Slovakia was able to follow the suit during the latter period of time with the growth rate of 6.2 percent per year. These three countries, as well as others working out their way toward the EU, have a chance to repeat such accomplishments in the future. It calls for good coordination of fiscal and monetary management, well-designed industrial and trade policies, and sub-ordination of structural reforms to the pro-growth policy.

The problem is that across the region, both the FSU and EE the govern-ments tend to neglect this latter aspect of long-term growth. This is so because they are often advised (and they tend to follow such advice eagerly) that further reforms alone, particularly full liberalization and privatization, will do the job. Later, when the latter unfortunately is not done, the post-ponement of these structural reforms is blamed for 'unexpected' underperformance. And if there is no way to accelerate those reforms still further, owing to the political and social constraints, then the external shocks are used as an excuse for the failures vis-à-vis the growth policy. From this angle, the Russian financial crisis of 1998–99 has come to the rescue of many governments in transition countries, as well as their foreign institu-tional and individual advisors, because it has served the purpose of the scapegoat extremely well.

The second group of economies advancing periodically to the frontrunners is going to surface from the less-developed postsocialist economies, literally catching-up with their more advanced neighbors. If additionally these coun-tries take good advantage of foreign aid, which in some cases, for example, Albania and Bosnia-Herzegovina, is not negligible, they can move forward quickly indeed. It did happen incidentally during the first decade of transi-tion, but it will happen more often over the next decades. Leaving aside Bosnia-Herzegovina with an unusual, soaring rate of growth in 1996–98 (over 40 percent on average)— which was due to the postwar recovery financed entirely from external sources, mainly grants—Albania in 1993–96 had the average rate of growth of 9.2 percent. In Georgia in 1996–97, GDP was increasing by 10.2 percent annually. Similarly, in Azerbaijan, in 1997–98, the average rate of growth was 7.9 percent (see Table 3).

However, all these processes have turned out to be unsustainable in the face of weak fundamentals, poor institutions, inconsistent policies, and negative external shocks. Hopefully, that will change again, this time moving in the right direction. Already, and with good reason, very high rates of growth are predicted for the early 2000s in the three countries mentioned above. All of them—plus Yugoslavia, which is recovering from the devastation of the 1999 war—can turn into frontrunners for some period of time (see Table 9). Yet if that happens, once again, it will not mean that fast growth will be guaranteed for very long. It is necessary that the active policies coordinating proper structural reforms with development strategy will be carried out.

The small differences vis-à-vis rate of growth become large ones in the long term. When considering the next half-century, a difference of only one point between three and the four percent annual rates of growth makes as much as 272 percentage points on a cumulative basis. That is enough to catch up and close quite a big gap. For instance, if a country like Hungary starts from current GDP (on a market exchange basis) of about 5,500 dollars and would be able to sustain, for the next fifty years, a 4 percent rate of growth per year, it would bring GDP up to as much as 39,000 dollars. That is more than today's national per capita income in the United States.

If it grows by only 3 percent over the next five decades, then in 2050 it will make 'only' about 24,000 dollars.[11] This is hardly enough to catch up with the EU average, which is increasing all the time, to the point where it firmly will exceed 50,000 dollars, even if over next fifty years it grows by a mere two percent annually. So, one percentage point does indeed make a difference. And the higher the rates of plausible growth are taken into account, the larger the difference becomes.[12] There are various hypothetical scenarios. Hopefully, some of the optimistic amongst them may become realistic, too, if only the relevant assumptions hold.

What a particular country's GDP per capita will be in the future, depends on its value at the point of departure in 2000 and the pace of growth over the next decades. Assuming that the GDP per capita, on a PPP basis, in the most advanced industrial countries—that is in the EU and USA—is approximately 30,000 dollars, we ask how many times the current level of GDP per capita in transition economies must increase to match the former. The specter of the multiplying factor with this regard is quite vast—from about two times in the case of the most advanced postsocialist economy, that is, in Slovenia, with the GDP per capita at around 14,800 dollars, to about as many as thirty-nine times in the case of the most underdeveloped

---

11. However, it is more rational, for the purpose of catching-up, to consider the GDP measured in terms of purchasing power parity. Therefore, in the example of Hungary, the respective values would be 57,000 and 35,000 dollars.

12. For instance, if the one-point difference is between the annual rates of growth of 1 and 2 percent, the difference after fifty years accumulates to about 170 percentage points. However, if it is between 6 and 7 percent, than the cumulative difference is as large as 1,100 percentage points.

Figure 5: Catching-up with the Developed Countries

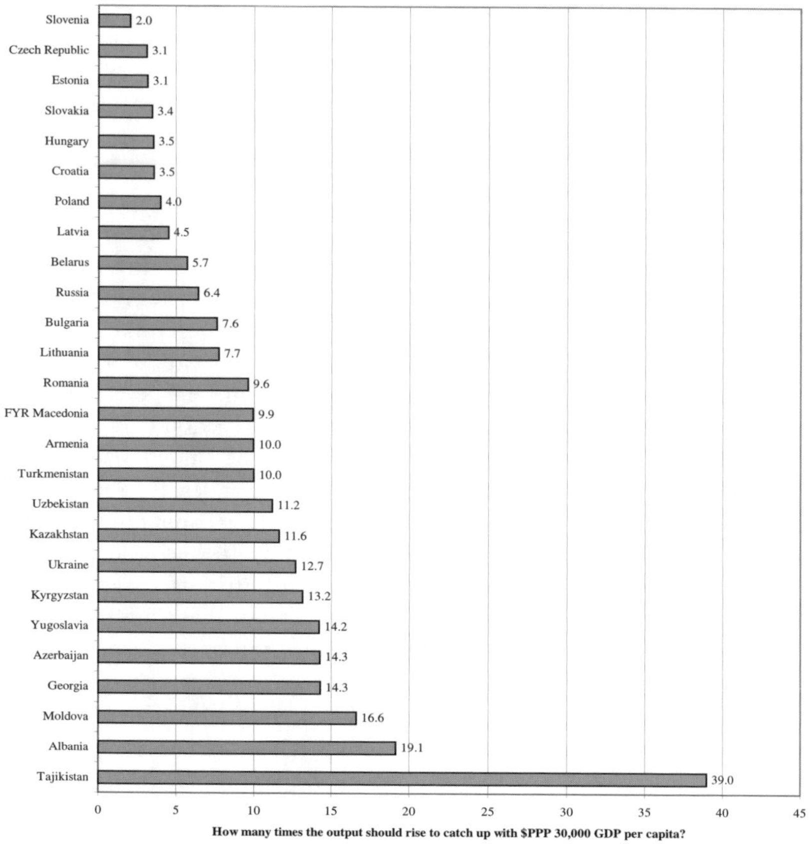

How many times the output should rise to catch up with $PPP 30,000 GDP per capita?

Source: Author's calculation.

country, that is Tajikistan, with the GDP per capita at about 770 dollars. Whereas for only eight countries the ratio is not larger than five to one, in twelve cases it is believed to be no less than ten to one (Figure 5).

Indeed, there are certain methodological concerns about the relevance of the data used for the purpose of this comparison. The evaluation of GDP based on purchasing power parity ought always to be looked at with proper consciousness, and even more, it must be the practice vis-à-vis such proxy for transition economies. It must raise some doubts if the evaluation of GDP per capita (in 1995 PPP dollars) suggests that Estonia is on a par with the Czech Republic, or that Belarus' income is almost twice as much as Ukraine's, or that Macedonia has a GDP per head almost 70 percent larger than Moldova. However, these estimations are based on the same methodological ground and are done along the lines of similar assumptions. So if there is—since certainly there is—some error included in those estimations, it still allows us to rely on these data in a quest for answers to the questions that have been asked in the context of recession, recovery, growth, and catching-up in transition economies.

Moreover, catching-up is about much more than just the closing of a gap between level of income in the most advanced nations and in the ones lagging behind in this respect. On the one hand, even if, in certain cases, after a certain period of time the income gap is closed, the standard of living will still be lower, owing to the accumulated wealth. Liquidation of the difference vis-à-vis the latter will take another number of years of relatively faster growth. That will be also catching-up, though first things must happen first.

On the other hand, many postsocialist countries are not that far behind the countries with the highest GDP per capita as simply the data on GDP might suggest. The GDP is just a flow of current production and does not reflect other aspects of development, otherwise important for the standard of living and the quality of life. In several transition economies—and this time it is a positive legacy from the centrally planned episode—there is relatively long life expectancy, on a par with the OECD, the rate of literacy is very high, secondary school enrollment is similar to that in advanced industrial societies, etc. (UNDP 1999).

This does have a significant implication for the future. It shows that the quality of human capital, and hence the growth potential, which is dormant for the time being, are relatively higher. If the growth in terms of quantity supplied can be considered as a linear process, it is not so with socioeconomic development. The nature of the latter is going to change considerably during the era of globalization and vast expansion of information technology. Altering values of society are contributing to this evolution, too.

In the long run the model of development is going to change. Accordingly, the measures of development will evolve as well. They will take much more into account the quality of human capital, standard of natural environment, access to culture and nature, density of urban areas, and other issues that are omitted in the GDP index. Some of the items that thus far are counted in the GDP, and hence are raising the standard of living, in due time can be considered as an obstacle to this end.[13] Therefore, the catching-

---

13. Actually, the famous mark of economic progress—the car—in the huge cities in emerging markets, including the postsocialist ones, more and more appears as rather an obstacle to the improvement of the quality of life, not a positive contributor to it. The moment to subtract from the composite welfare index the value of time wasted in traffic jams will arrive, as will the moment of including in it the value of space and fresh air. Perhaps it will occur even sooner than the transition economies will be able to catch up with the most developed part of our global village.

up may take a shorter period of time (or sometimes, unfortunately, just to the contrary, it will take longer) than can be seen through the simple prism of catching-up with the quantity of the output flow. Nonetheless, this very output always will be a crucial factor for the nations' standard of living, since this is the true foundation on which one may try to build his or her well-being.

As a consequence of all these circumstances, while regarding the turn of the millennium as the starting point towards catching-up, particular postsocialist countries would catch up with the level of output of the developed world in very different years. Of course, the latter countries are the growing economies, too, so actually this catching-up should be seen as running towards a forward-moving target. Yet here it is assumed that to get only, in due time, to the current level of production of the world leaders would be quite an achievement. Which year it indeed might happen to be— if such a year arrives at all—depends on a path of growth along which the country evolves: is one going to be more like a frontrunner, or rather like just an even-runner? The laggards, of course, do not count (Table 11).

All these paths show how long the distance is to be overcome for the sake of catching-up and closing the development gap, which has risen during the centuries and, unfortunately, deepened even more during just one decade of the last century, when the postsocialist transition had just gained momentum. It might happen that in certain cases not a half-century, but several centuries will be needed to liquidate it completely, if at all, because the catching-up of transition economies does not mean that it is an imperative. It is only an option or a chance, which can be made use of, or can be lost—as it has happened so many times in the course of the mankind's history.

It would be more reasonable for the purpose of catching-up—and that means, too, for upgrading people's living standard—to sustain a stable, yet relatively high rate of growth for a very long period of time, than to attempt its maximization over a certain time, which comes to its limits sooner than expected. In such a case, owing to the risks involved and the likeliness that the economy may get out of balance and consequently slow down, even if for only a couple of years, the final result might be less impressive. In another words, it is a better strategy to be the gainer all the time than to be the frontrunner for a while, but at the price that later one becomes an even-runner only, if not a laggard.

Thus in the medium term, say for the next decade or two, several postsocialist countries should try to find the path of growth that will enable them to advance in the catching-up process only as much as feasible. This will make unquestionable sense of the whole transition and can even make it a final success. Such success is contingent on patience, good policies, and years of hard work.

Table 11. The Year of Catching-up with the Developed Countries

	GDP per capita in 2000 (in 1995 $PPP)	The Year of Catching-up with the GDP per capita of 30,000 $PPP		
		Frontrunner	Gainer	Even-runner
Albania	1,569	2041	2060	2100
Armenia	3,009	2032	2047	2078
Azerbaijan	2,101	2037	2055	2090
Belarus	5,238	2024	2036	2059
Bulgaria	3,930	2028	2042	2069
Croatia	8,484	2017	2026	2042
Czech Republic	9,699	2016	2023	2038
Estonia	9,606	2016	2023	2038
FYR Macedonia	3,017	2032	2047	2077
Georgia	2,099	2037	2055	2090
Hungary	8,525	2017	2026	2042
Kazakhstan	2,576	2034	2050	2083
Kyrgyzstan	2,279	2036	2053	2087
Latvia	6,681	2021	2031	2051
Lithuania	3,872	2028	2042	2069
Moldova	1,805	2039	2058	2095
Poland	7,575	2019	2028	2047
Romania	3,124	2031	2046	2076
Russia	4,654	2026	2038	2063
Slovakia	8,707	2017	2025	2041
Slovenia	14,802	2010	2014	2024
Tajikistan	770	2051	2075	2124
Turkmenistan	3,004	2032	2047	2078
Ukraine	2,357	2035	2052	2086
Uzbekistan	2,681	2034	2048	2082
Yugoslavia	2,108	2037	2055	2090

Source: The 2000 GDP per capita from PlanEcon 1999a and 1999b.

Forecasts—author's own calculation.

Chapter Ten

Policy Conclusions

Having said that much, it is now time to ask one more essential question: are all these analyses and conclusions correct, and especially are the forecasts reasonable, if they happen to have been wrong so many times in the recent postsocialist past? The answer consists of three parts. First, there were many warnings and predictions that accurately were pointing to the risks and to the future unpleasant occurrences, yet they had not been taken sufficiently into account by the policymakers, including international organizations. Second, theoretical assumptions that the transition countries can become fast-growing economies have been correct, nonetheless the conditions for such a take-off were not fulfilled at the time, due, among other things, to policy failures. And third, now is a time to presume rationally that such conditions can be met, so that growth can accelerate as well. However, there are differences and there are also risks.

One difference between then and now is that now we suppose we know much better than earlier what works in postsocialist economies, and why, and what does not work, and why. Although, there has been the false assumption that unleashed market forces will themselves do the development job. They will not. For this reason, the governments' sound development strategies and wise involvement of the international community, including official and non-government organizations, must support the market forces. Hence, the first risk is that such involvement can be insufficient or guided by wrong economic theory.

A second difference between then and now is that at the onset of new century all these transition economies are already growing. So the question is not any more how to stop recession and depression, but how to accelerate the rate of growth and sustain it at the highest possible level for the longest possible period. All the time there is a challenge how to do it within the framework of specific institutional and political environments of nascent postsocialist market and democracy. A negligence of this enduring specificity creates the second risk.

Policies exercised during the first decade of transition have, to a large extent, been derived from the so-called Washington consensus, although this set of structural reforms was designed for another challenge (Williamson 1990 and 1997). Yet while applied towards postsocialist economies, these policies have greatly influenced the direction of systemic reforms and the course of change (Stiglitz 1998a). However, the transition has also had a significant counter-impact. The policies have not generated the anticipated results, and this has led to a search for alternative measures (Kolodko and Nuti 1997). As the postsocialist markets have emerged, so have fresh issues, problems, and concerns. The reactions to these have differed, and new approaches have evolved. Following the conclusions and policy options formulated so far, another ten major policy conclusions must be put forward here (Kolodko 1999a).

First, institutional arrangements are the most important factor in the achievement of fast and durable growth. They should be established through a process directed by government (by design) rather than spontaneously (by chance). In those nations in which government has been committed to this approach, recovery has come sooner, growth has been more robust, and there are more prospects for sustainable development. Those countries in which government has relied on the spontaneous appearance of new institutions have not been able to manage this complex process adequately and are lagging behind both vis-à-vis systemic transition and the growth of the real economy. Institution-building must be a gradual process. The effects of specific inputs in this process must be constantly monitored, and policies must be regularly adjusted and corrected. One should not depend on the experiences in distorted market economies, but should understand the special features of the emerging postsocialist markets. This is especially true in privatization and the development of capital markets.

Second, the size of government is less important than the quality of government policies and the manner in which the changes are implemented (Tanzi 1997). In transition economies a profound restructuring of the public finance system is more important than is the downsizing of government. Fiscal transfers should be redirected from non-competitive sectors towards institution-building (including behavioral and cultural changes) and investments in human capital and hard infrastructure. Attempts to downsize government through expenditure cuts can do more harm than good in terms of recovery from transitional recession and the achievement of sustained and fast growth. Even if one believes that small government is better than big government (what usually is true), to downsize may lead to economic contraction and deterioration in standards of living. Expenditures should not be cut for the sake of the illusion of fiscal prudence, but should be restructured.

Third, if institutional arrangements are neglected and left to spontaneous processes and liberalized market forces, then there will be a systemic vacuum, and 'informal institutionalization' will occur. Spreading corruption and organized crime are extreme examples of informal institutionalization. These are the two principal diseases in countries in which liberalization and privatization have taken place under weak government. Governments may sometimes be too weak because they are too big, but in transition economies they are often too weak because they have been downsized too soon, before the emerging market and the NGOs were able to take over relevant functions of the state. Even if the aim of the downsizing is to reduce the scope of fiscal redistribution so as to encourage capital formation, and hence investment and growth, one must not overlook the fact that the struggle against informal institutions is costly in fiscal terms, too. A prematurely or too thoroughly downsized government may not be strong enough to lead in this struggle, and the market may quickly expand within the informal sector, while the difficulties are mounting in the official economy. Thus, profits accrue to the informal sector, while revenues drop in the official sector. Profits are thereby 'privatized', while loses are 'socialized' in a politically unsustainable process full of negative consequences for the budget and for social policy.

Fourth, in transition economies policies must aim at transforming and streamlining the legal system so that it can serve the market economy. The establishment and development of new laws—trade and tax codes, capital market regulations, the protection of property rights, antitrust regulations, banking supervision, consumer protection, environmental protection—are extremely important and ought to be addressed before state assets are fully privatized. The establishment of a legal framework that is appropriate for the market economy should be much higher on the agenda of international financial organizations. It must be a more urgent and important issue than trade liberalization and assets privatization, since these latter can contribute to sound growth only if the former has been assured.

Fifth, a shift in functions from the central government to local governments is necessary for deregulation in the postsocialist economy. This means that some decentralization must be undertaken in the public finance system and that local governments must be given more fiscal autonomy. The process of taking functions away from the central government must be matched by reinforcing local governments. Both levels of government must be seen as two parts of a single entity, which is essential for gradual institution-building. If local governments are not strengthened as the central government is reduced, then healthy market forces cannot be supported by new institutional arrangements, and liberalization and privatization are less likely to improve capital allocation and raise efficiency.

Sixth, the development of non-governmental organizations must be accelerated. More significant international technical and financial assistance must be channeled into the effort to empower non-governmental organizations. Along with the private sector and the state, these organizations are an indispensable third pillar of the contemporary market economy and civic society. A wide range of non-governmental organizations active in various areas of public life is needed to ease the constant tension between the state and society. The expanding private sector alone cannot adequately fill this gap. Certain areas of public life can rely neither on the state, nor on the business-oriented private sector. Without the institutional infrastructure provided by non-governmental organizations, successful systemic change and high-quality growth become more problematic, the infant market economy and democracy in postsocialist nations cannot evolve properly, and the transition will remain incomplete.

Seventh, income policy and equitable growth are very important for the growth sustainability and thus the ultimate success of the transition (Tanzi, Chu, and Gupta 1999). Because increasing inequity is unavoidable during the initial years of transition, the state, through fiscal and social policies, must play an active role in managing income dispersion. Beyond a certain limit, income disparities inhibit the expansion of economic activity, delay recovery, and slow down economic growth. Substantial inequities hamper crucial institutional and structural reform.

Eighth, the postsocialist transition to a market economy is taking place in a context of globalization. Hence integration with the world economy is an indispensable part of the process. This must be managed carefully. Special attention must be paid to short-term capital liberalization, which must be monitored and controlled by fiscal and monetary authorities and supported by international financial institutions. It is better to liberalize capital markets later rather than sooner. Institution-building must first be sufficiently advanced, and stabilization ought to be already consolidated into stability. Only then should financial markets be liberalized in a gradual manner. Otherwise the populations in the young and emerging democracies will not back the introduction of market mechanisms or integration with the world economy and may even become hostile to these steps.[1]

Ninth, international organizations not only should support globalization, but ought to encourage regional integration and cooperation. Fast and durable growth requires export expansion, which depends on strong regional linkages. In turn, this calls for institutional support through import-export banks, commodity exchanges, credit insurance agencies, and

---

1. Actually, the rampant demonstrations during the summit of the World Trade Organization in Seattle in September 1999, during the World Economic Forum in Davos in January 2000, and at the time of the UNCTAD meeting in Bangkok in February 2000, as well as in certain other places where the international organizations gather for their meetings, are clearly corresponding with such a diagnosis. However, these demonstrations were organized vis-à-vis a wider scope of issues linked (or only believed to be so) to certain by-effects of globalization in developing countries. It must be remembered that from this angle the postsocialist economies have taken many of the features of such economies. Hence, it may happen that the anti-globalization sentiments will rise as transition and its globalization aspect will evolve still further. It should be the opposite, yet in the foreseeable future, this may happen in several countries. In this odd way, globalization is turning against itself.

so on. This should be the main focus of the institution-building effort of the EBRD through its direct lending and technical assistance. This sort of market infrastructure is now underdeveloped in transition economies, and regional trade and direct cross-country investment are lagging behind in the process of changes. What should be a driving force behind sustainable growth is actually now a major obstacle.

Tenth, the Bretton Woods institutions should reconsider their policy approach towards transition economies. While the IMF should emphasize financial liquidity, currency convertibility, and fiscal and monetary stabilization, the World Bank should focus mainly on supporting equitable growth and sustainable development. These two areas of economic policy are frequently at odds. There is a tendency to confuse the means and the ends of policy, to favor short-term stabilization over long-term growth and development. Decisionmakers should not rely only on stabilization policies, but should seek a proper balance between stabilization policies and medium- and long-term development strategies. Fiscal and monetary policies must be subordinated to development policy—not the other way around. The World Bank performance criteria for socioeconomic development are needed as much as are the IMF fiscal and monetary criteria. There should always be an eye on the impact of financial policies in terms of growth, capital allocation, income distribution, and the social safety net.

As conditions change and challenges appear, policies must be revised in the future as well. Consequently, the quest for a comprehensive and achievable policy consensus, which facilitates sustained and fast growth, must be ongoing, especially since there is the occasion to catch up. Such chance should not be lost.

Statistical Appendix:

From Growth Cycles under a Centrally Planned Economy to Business Cycles under a Market Economy, 1950–2004

Fig. 6 Economic Growth Cycles in Bulgaria
(1953-2004)

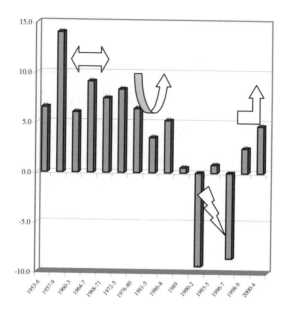

Fig. 7 Economic Growth Cycles in Czechoslovakia
(1950-92) and the Czech Republic (1993-2004)

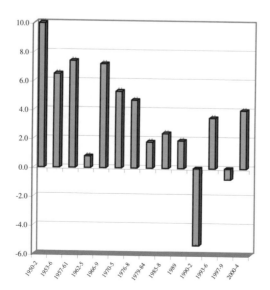

Fig.8 Economic Growth Cycles in Czechoslovakia
(1950-92) and Slovakia (1993-2004)

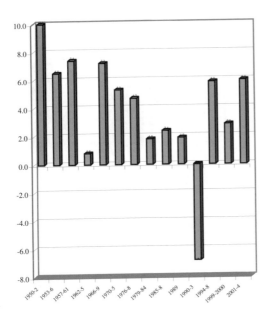

Fig. 9 Economic Growth Cycles in Hungary
(1951-2004)

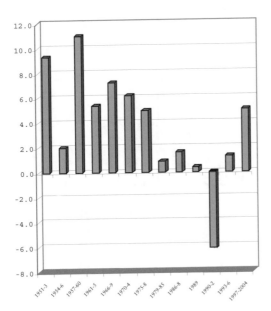

Fig. 10 Economic Growth Cycles in Poland
(1950-2004)

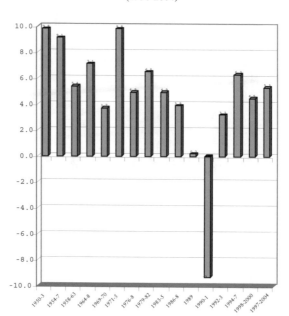

Fig. 11 Economic Growth Cycles in Romania
(1951-2004)

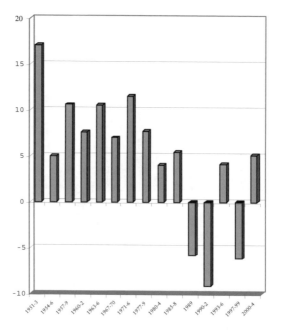

Fig. 12 Economic Growth Cycles in the Soviet Union (1950-88) and Armenia (1989-2003)

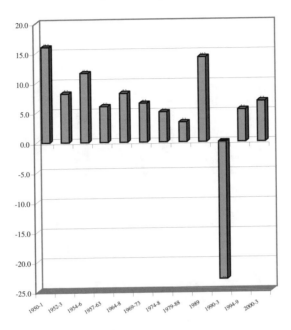

Fig. 13 Economic Growth Cycles in the Soviet Union (1950-88) and Estonia (1989-2003)

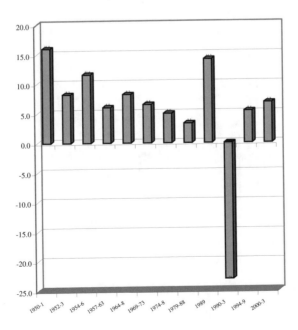

Fig. 14 Economic Growth Cycles in the Soviet Union (1950-88) and Moldova (1989-2003)

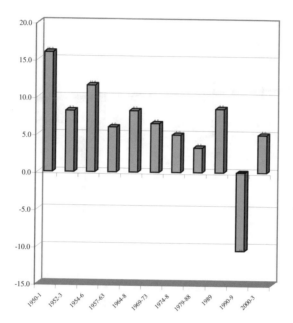

Fig. 15 Economic Growth Cycles in the Soviet Union (1950-88) and Russia (1989-2003)

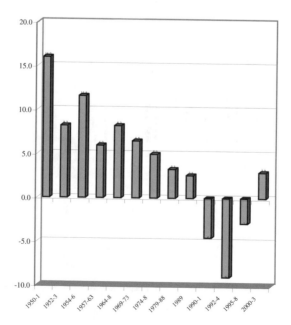

Fig. 16 Economic Growth Cycles in the Soviet Union (1950-88) and Ukraine (1989-2003)

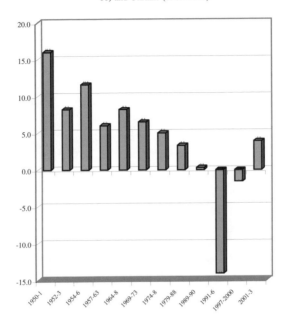

Fig. 17 Economic Growth Cycles in the Soviet Union (1950-88) and Uzbekistan (1989-2003)

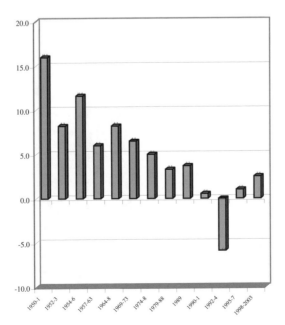

References

Alesina, Alberto. 1997. "The Political Economy of High and Low Growth." In *Annual Bank Conference on Development Economics 1996*, edited by Boris Pleskovic and Joseph E. Stiglitz, 217–37. Washington, D.C.: World Bank.

———. 1998. "Too Large and Too Small Governments." In *Economic Policy and Equity*, edited by Vito Tanzi, Ke-young Chu, and Sanjeev Gupta. Washington, D.C.: International Monetary Fund.

Bauer, Tamas. 1978. "Investment Cycles in Planned Economies." *Acta Economica* 21, March, 243–60.

Berg, Andrew, and Jeffrey Sachs. 1992. "Structural Adjustment and International Trade in Eastern Europe: The Case of Poland." *Economic Policy* No. 14, 117–73.

Blejer, Mario I., and Marko Skreb, eds. Forthcoming. *Transition: The First Decade*. Boston: MIT Press.

Borensztein, Eduardo, and Peter J. Montiel. 1991. "Savings, Investment, and Growth in Eastern Europe." In *Central and Eastern Europe Roads to Growth*, edited by Georg H. Winckler, 153–87. Washington, D.C.: International Monetary Fund and Austrian National Bank.

Cohen, Daniel (1995). *The Misfortunes of Prosperity: An Introduction to Modern Political Economy*. Cambridge, Mass.: Massachussets Institute of Technology.

———. 1998. *The Wealth of the World and the Poverty of Nations*. Cambridge, Mass.: Massachussets Institute of Technology.

Commander, S., H. Davoodi, and V. Lee. 1996. "The Causes and Consequences of Government for Growth and Well-Being." Washington, D.C.: World Bank.

Czyzewski, Adam B., Witold M. Orlowski, and Leszek Zienkowski. 1996. "Country Study for Poland: A Comparative Study of Causes of Output Decline in Transition Economies." Paper presented at 'Third Workshop on Output Decline in Eastern Europe,' Prague, 12–13 April.

DeBroeck, Mark, and Vincent Koen. 2000. "The 'Soaring Eagle': Anatomy of the Polish Take-Off in the 1990s. Washington, D.C.: *IMF Working Paper* (January).

Development News. 1998. *After Russian Bailout, IMF Turns Attention to Ukrainian Ills*. Washington, D.C.: World Bank, 23 July.

EBRD. 1997. *Transition Report 1997: Enterprise Performance and Growth*. London: European Bank for Reconstruction and Development.

———. 1999. *Transition Report 1999: Ten Years of Transition.* London: European Bank for Reconstruction and Development.

Economist. 1997. "The Future of the State: A Survey of the World Economy," 20 September.

"Ex-Soviet Union: A Ghost Lurks." 2000. *The Economist,* 29 January, p. 60.

Fischer, Stanley, Ratna Sahay, and Carlos A. Vegh. 1997. "From Transition to Market: Evidence and Growth Prospects." In *Lessons from the Economic Transition. Central and Eastern Europe in the 1990s,* edited by Salvatore Zechinni, 79–102. Dordrecht: Kluwer Academic Publishers.

"The Future of the State: A Survey of the World Economy." 1997. *Economist,* 20 September.

Gomulka, Stanislaw. 1990. "Stabilizacja i wzrost: Polska 1989–2000" ["Stabilization and Growth: Poland 1989–2000"]. In *Polityka finansowa–nierownowaga–stabilizacja (II)* [*Financial Policy–Disequilibrium–Stabilization (II)*], edited by Grzegorz W. Kolodko, 303–21. Warsaw: Research Institute of Finance.

———. 2000. "Budzet i prognozy" ["Budget and forecasts"]. *Prawo i Gospodarka,* 17 January, p. 20.

IMF. 1991. "World Economic Outlook." Washington, D.C.: International Monetary Fund, May.

———. 1992. "World Economic Outlook." Washington, D.C.: International Monetary Fund, October.

———. 1998. "World Economic Outlook: Financial Crises, Causes, and Indicators." Washington, D.C.: International Monetary Fund, May.

———. 1999. "World Economic Outlook." Washington, D.C.: International Monetary Fund, October.

Kaufmann, Daniel, and Daniel Kaliberda. 1996. "Integrating the Unofficial Economy into the Dynamic of Postsocialist Economies: A Fframework of Analysis and Evidence." In *Economic Transition in Russia and the New States of Eurasia,* edited by Bart Kaminski. Armonk, N.Y.: M. E. Sharpe.

Kolodko, Grzegorz W. 1976. "Economic Growth Cycles in the Centrally Planned Economy: The Case of Poland." *Working Papers.* Warsaw: Institute for Economic Development, Warsaw School of Economics (SGPiS).

———. 1986. "Economic Growth Cycles in the Centrally Planned Economies: A Hypothesis of the 'Long Cycle.'" *Faculty Working Papers,* 1,280 (September). Champaign-Urbana, IL: College of Commerce and Business Administration, Bureau of Economic and Business Research, University of Illinois.

———. 1991. "Inflation Stabilization in Poland: A Year After." *Rivista di Politica Economica* 6 (June): 289–330.

———. 1992a. "Economics of Transition: From Shortageflation to Stagflation, the Case of Poland." In *Preventing a New East-West Divide: The Economic and Social Imperatives of the Future Europe,* edited by Armand Clesse and Rudolf Tökes, 172–81. Baden-Baden: Nomos Verlagsgesellschaft.

———. 1992b. "From Output Collapse to Sustainable Growth in Transition Economies: The Fiscal Implications." Washington, D.C.: International Monetary Fund (December).

———. 1998. "Economic Neoliberalism Became Almost Irrelevant. . . ." *Transition* 9, 3 (June): 1–6.

———. 1999a. "Ten Years of Postsocialist Transition: Lessons for Policy Reform." *Policy Research Working Paper,* 2095 (April). Washington, D.C.: The World Bank.

———. 1999b. "Fiscal Policy and Capital Formation in Transition Economies." Washington, D.C.: International Monetary Fund, Fiscal Affairs Department (April).

———. 1999c. "Equity Issues in Policymaking in Transition Economies." In *Economic Policy and Equity,* edited by Vito Tanzi, Ke-young Chu, and Sanjeev Gupta, 150–88. Washington, D.C.: International Monetary Fund.

———. 1999d. "Transition to a Market Economy and Sustained Growth: Implications for the Post-Washington Consensus." *Communist and Post-Communist Studies* 32, No. 3 (September): 233–61.

———. 2000a. *From Shock to Therapy: The Political Economy of Postsocialist Transformation.* Oxford: Oxford University Press.

———. 2000b. "Transition to a Market and Entrepreneurship: The Systemic Factors and Policy Options," *Communist and Post-Communist Studies* 33, No. 2 (June): 271–93.

———. 2000c. *Post-Communist Transition: The Thorny Road.* Rochester, N.Y.: University of Rochester Press.

———, and Walter W. McMahon. 1987. "Stagflation and Shortageflation: A Comparative Approach." *Kyklos* 40, 2: 176–97.

———, and Domenico M. Nuti. 1997. "The Polish Alternative: Old Myths, Hard Facts, and New Strategies in the Successful Transformation of the Polish Economy." Research for Action 33. Helsinki: UNU/WIDER.

Kornai, Janos (1986). "The Hungarian Reform Process: Visions, Hopes, and Reality." *Journal of Economic Literature* 24, 4, 1: 687–737.

Kozminski Andrzej K. 1993. *Catching Up? Organizational and Management Change in The Ex-Socialist Block.* Albany, N.Y.: State University of New York Press.

Lavigne, Marie. 1999. *The Economics of Transition: From Socialist Economy to Market Economy.* 2nd edition. Chatham, Kent: Macmillan.

Lucas, Robert E. 1999. "Some Macroeconomics for the 21st Century." Chicago: The University of Chicago (September), mimeograph.

Milanovic, Branko. 1998. *Income, Inequality, and Poverty during the Transition from Planned to Market Economy.* Washington, D.C.: World Bank.

Montes, Manuel, and Vladimir Popov. 1999. *The Asian Crisis Turns Global*. Singapore: Institute of Southeast Asian Studies.

Mundell, Robert A. 1997. "The Great Contractions in Transition Economies." In *Macroeconomic Stabilization in Transition Economies,* edited by Mario I. Blejer and Marko Skreb, 73–99. London: Cambridge University Press.

Nafziger, E. Wayne. 1998. "Root of Human Suffering." *Financial Times,* 21 January.

North, Douglass C. 1997. "The Contribution of the New Institutional Economics to an Understanding of the Transition Problem." WIDER Annual Lectures 1. Helsinki: UNU/WIDER (March).

Nuti, Domenico M. 1992. "Lessons from Stabilization and Reform in Central Eastern Europe." CEC Working Papers, 92. Brussels: Council of the European Community (May).

PlanEcon. 1999a "Review and Outlook for the Former Soviet Republics." Washington, D.C.: PlanEcon, Inc., (October).

———. 1999b. "Review and Outlook for the Eastern Europe." Washington, D.C.: PlanEcon, Inc., (December).

Poznanski, Kazimierz. 1996. *Poland's Protracted Transition: Institutional Change and Economic Growth*. Cambridge: Cambridge University Press.

———. 1997. "Comparative Transition Theory: Recession and Recovery in Post-Communist Economies." Conference paper presented at "Transition Strategies, Alternatives, and Outcomes," Helsinki, 15–17 May.

Ravallion, Martin. 1997. "Good and Bad Growth: The Human Development Reports." *World Development,* 25, 5: 631–38.

Sachs, Jeffrey. 1993. "Poland's Jump to the Market Economy." Cambridge, Mass.: MIT Press.

Stern, Nicholas, and Joseph E. Stiglitz. 1997. "A Framework for a Development Strategy in a Market Economy: Objectives, Scope, Institutions, and Instruments." *EBRD Working Papers,* 20 (April).

Stiglitz, Joseph E. 1998a. "More Instruments and Broader Goals: Moving towards the Post-Washington Consensus." *WIDER Annual Lectures,* 2, Helsinki: UNU/WIDER (January).

———. 1998b. "Economic Science, Economic Policy, and Economic Advice." Conference paper presented at 'Knowledge for Development,' Washington, D.C.: World Bank (20–21 April).

Summers, Lawrence. 1992. "The Next Decade in Central and Eastern Europe." In *The Emergence of Market Economies in Eastern Europe,* edited by Christopher Clague and Gordon C. Rausser, 25–34. Cambridge, Mass. and Oxford: Blackwell.

Tanzi, Vito. 1991. "Tax Reform and the Move to a Market Economy: Overview of the Issues." In *The Role of Tax Reform in Central and Eastern European Economies,* 19–34. Paris: Organization for Economic Cooperation and Development.

———. 1997. "Reconsidering the Fiscal Role of Government: The International Perspective." *American Economic Review,* 87, No. 2 (May): 164–68.

———, Ke-young Chu, and Sanjeev Gupta, eds. 1999. *Economic Policy and Equity.* Washington, D.C.: International Monetary Fund.

———, and Ludger Schuknecht. 1995. "The Growth of Government and the Reform of the State in Industrial Countries." *IMF Working Papers,* WP/95/130.

UNDP (1992). "Human Development Report 1992." New York: Oxford University Press.

———. 1997. "Human Development Report 1997." New York: Oxford University Press.

Williamson, John. 1990. "What Washington Means by Policy Reform." In *Latin American Adjustment: How Much Has Happened?*, edited by John Williamson. Washington, D.C.: Institute for International Economics.

———. 1997. "The Washington Consensus Revisited." In *Economic and Social Development into the XXI Century,* edited by Louis Emmerij. Washington, D.C.: Inter-American Development Bank.

World Bank. 1995. "World Development Report 1995." New York: Oxford University Press.

———. 1997a. "World Development Indicators." Washington, D.C.: World Bank.

———. 1997b. "World Development Report 1997: The State in a Changing World." New York: Oxford University Press.

———. 1997c. "Global Economic Prospects and the Developing Countries." Washington, D.C.: World Bank.

Yergin, Daniel, and Joseph Stanislaw. 1998. "The Commanding Heights: The Battle between Government and the Marketplace That is Remaking the Modern World." New York: Simon and Schuster.

Index

Abstract

The transitional recession in Eastern Europe and the former Soviet Union has been more severe and has lasted much longer than expected. It has been the result of both the legacy of the past and of contemporary policy mistakes. Due to structural reforms and gradual institution-building, the postsocialist economies have started to recover, and some leading countries have been able to build up a certain amount of momentum towards fast growth. There is a possibility that, within the wider context of globalization, several of these emerging market economies will be able, in a matter of one or two generations, to catch up with the more advanced industrial countries. Yet the final outcome of the whole transition process will depend on the quality of growth policy and the coordination between development strategy and the vast effort at structural reform. Transition and globalization both represent a challenge and an opportunity for these countries to catch up with the developed economies.

JEL Classification Numbers: E37; F43; N10; O47; P24; P27

Keywords: globalization, transition, institution-building, recession, growth

Author's e-mail address: kolodko@tiger.edu.pl